Buddhism
BETRAYED?

A Monograph of the
World Institute for Development
Economics Research (WIDER)
of the
United Nations University

Buddhism BETRAYED?

Religion, Politics, and Violence in Sri Lanka

Stanley Jeyaraja Tambiah

The University of Chicago Press
Chicago and London

The University of Chicago Press, Chicago 60637
The University of Chicago Press, Ltd., London
© 1992 by The University of Chicago
All rights reserved. Published 1992
Printed in the United States of America

01 00 99 98 97 96 95 94   5 4 3 2

ISBN (cloth): 0-226-78949-7
ISBN (paper): 0-226-78950-0

Library of Congress Cataloging-in-Publication Data

Tambiah, Stanley Jeyaraja, 1929–
    Buddhism betrayed? : religion, politics, and violence in Sri Lanka
/ Stanley Jeyaraja Tambiah.
        p.   cm. — (A Monograph of the World Institute for Development
Economics Research (WIDER) of the United Nations University)
    Includes bibliographical references and index.
    1. Buddhism and politics—Sri Lanka.   2. Buddhism—Social aspects—
Sri Lanka.   I. Title.   II. Series.
BQ359.T36   1992
294.3'377'095493—dc20   91-38944

World Institute for Development Economics
Research (WIDER) of the United Nations
University (UNU)

WIDER was established in 1984 in Helsinki,
Finland, as a UNU research and training institute.
The principal purpose of WIDER is to help
identify and meet the need for policy-oriented
socioeconomic research on pressing global and
development problems, as well as common
domestic problems and their interrelationships.

Contents

Foreword

When the acronym WIDER was chosen to describe the World Institute for Development Economics Research of the United Nations University, the decision was not accidental. WIDER's mandate was not merely to study development economics from the standpoint of economists but to enlist the skills of such other social scientists as anthropologists, sociologists, and political scientists, to throw light on issues which may not be comprehended by the narrow expertise of economists alone. The ways in which economic development is affected by and in turn affects social conflicts stemming from ethnic and religious differences raise issues on which economists alone are not competent to pronounce, and it was natural for WIDER to analyze the problem in the context of the experience of particular countries.

My own country Sri Lanka provides almost a laboratory example of a problem that threatens to loom large in much of the developing world and indeed in Eastern Europe and the Soviet Union. Over the period since independence in 1948, Sri Lanka has been identified as a leading exponent of what is described as a basic needs-oriented development strategy. More recent descriptions are in terms of a "support-led" development strategy,[1] or a strategy premised on "human development,"[2] in both cases involving extensive public intervention. Sri Lanka's achievements in this regard are encapsulated both in the Physical Quality of Life Index (PQLI), devised by the U.S. Overseas Development Council, and the Human Development Index, introduced by the United Nations Development Program. The simpler PQLI combines measures of life expectancy, infant mortality, and literacy into a single index with a maximum value of 100, and in the study that intro-

---

1. See Jean Dreze and Amartya Sen, *Hunger and Public Action* (Oxford, 1990).
2. See UNDP, *Human Development Report, 1989.*

duces the PQLI concept[3] Sri Lanka's PQLI stood at 82 on a per capita income, in the 1970s, of US$179. The study observed, "If countries having per capita incomes of more than US$179 and a PQLI less than 82, could duplicate Sri Lanka's experience, 1.6 billion people could be affected." The clear implication was that other countries should follow Sri Lanka's example.

Yet the record, both before and after the 1970s, shows that Sri Lanka's basic needs achievements coexisted with periodic outbursts of ethnic and religious tension which have now become more or less endemic during the 1980s. The country has experienced twin insurgencies, with Tamil militants seeking a separate state encompassing the north and the east of the island and a Sinhalese militant group, the Janatha Vimukthi Peramuna (JVP), drawing sustenance from the slogan of Sinhala Buddhism and anti-Indian sentiment. The end result is that the development process has virtually ground to a halt.

To an economist, the underlying problem appears straightforward. The flip-side of the coin of a basic needs-oriented development strategy, with its diversion of substantial public resources to subsidize health, education, and food, was a relatively low rate of investment and, hence, economic growth which in the 1970s averaged under 3 percent and in the 1980s, 5 percent. Low growth, in turn, makes for high unemployment, in Sri Lanka's case reaching 20 percent of the labor force today. It is easy to show that if unemployment is to be reduced to a socially and politically manageable level of 4 to 5 percent of the labor force within a five-year period, the Sri Lanka economy will have to grow at around 7 percent per annum. If the country's political fabric could afford the luxury of a ten-year time horizon to reduce unemployment to these levels, then Sri Lanka could get by with an average annual growth rate of 5.5 percent. But while these rates have been exceeded in particular years as the ad hoc by-product of economic reform, what is required is a *continuing* process of achieving high average rates of growth, which has proved elusive so far. Although growth rates of the kind needed in Sri Lanka are a commonplace in other parts of Southeast Asia, as long as the current condition of civil unrest resulting from ethnic and religious differences persists, such a growth process appears unlikely, and in the absence of rapid growth, the continuation of high levels of unemployment—which to an economist contributes to this unrest—will further reinforce it.

3. Morris David Morris, *Measuring the Condition of the World's Poor* (New York: Pergamon Press, 1979), p. 64.

If, for whatever reason, the high-growth strategy cannot be implemented within the political time frame needed to reduce unemployment to manageable levels, there is an alternative transitional strategy available. Pioneered by China, this has been described as a strategy of "walking on two legs." In this design, the high-growth "modern" sector coexists for a transitional period with a low-growth "traditional" or "informal" sector characterized by labor-intensive production techniques which provide viable livelihoods to the unemployed through small-scale self-employment, trading, and construction activities. The modern sector is also enabled in this design to subcontract some part of its production to the traditional sector. This indeed seems to be the prevailing model in much of the developing world whether by accident or design, and Sri Lanka's variant is to be found in its Janasaviya Program for poverty alleviation through self-employment in the "traditional" sector. But "walking on two legs" in this fashion may not always succeed in reducing unemployment to manageable levels in the relevant political time frame. The problem becomes especially acute if the white-collar employment aspirations of literate youth generated by a basic-needs strategy cannot be met in time, provoking widespread youth unrest and often insurrection.

It is at this point that the economist runs out of steam. He has to look to the skills of other social scientists to explain how Sri Lanka's ethnic and religious conflict reached its present pass of being able completely to frustrate the development process. The reasons are embedded in history, the political process, and the ideology of religion and nationalism, and I was especially fortunate in being able to enlist the cooperation of Professor Stanley J. Tambiah, chairman of the Department of Anthropology of Harvard University from 1984 to 1987 to lead an inquiry into them in the company of several other scholars. The present study is Professor Tambiah's own contribution to this WIDER research project. The principal task he has set himself is that of probing "the extent to which, and the manner in which, Buddhism, as a 'religion' espoused by Sri Lankans of the late nineteenth and the twentieth centuries, has contributed to the current ethnic conflict and collective violence in Sri Lanka. If it has contributed," he asks, "were there changes in the nature of that contribution over time? And if there have been changes, how are we to describe the changing or changed shape of Buddhism itself as a lived reality?"

The argument he develops is that Buddhism became the vehicle for the assertion of Sinhalese nationalism by newer rural social groups seeking political power who were excluded from the largely urban, westernized power elite that inherited and first administered independent Sri Lanka in 1948. What eventually emerged broadly was a two-party system whereby the monopoly of the political party that inherited independence, the United National party (UNP), was broken in 1956 for a brief period and subsequently for much of the decade of the 1970s by a coalition of forces espousing Sinhala Buddhist nationalism led by the Sri Lanka Freedom party (SLFP). The inevitable outcome of electoral democratic politics, Professor Tambiah argues, was for the UNP itself to don the mantle of Sinhala Buddhist nationalism so that, in effect, a bipartisan political consensus centered around this ideology emerged from which the Tamil community was effectively excluded. In this process, there was also a harking back to an idealized village community of peasant owners, assumed to characterize ancient Ceylon, as constituting a valid model for Sri Lanka's modern development. The underlying formula of Sinhala cultural identity comprised the *vava* (irrigation tank), *dagoba* (temple), and *yaya* (paddy field) and it is significant that in inaugurating Sri Lanka's largest modern river development project, the Mahavali development scheme in 1983, the UNP minister concerned revived these same symbolic associations. "The soul of the new Mahavali society will be the cherished values of the ancient society which was inspired and nourished by the tank, the temple, and the paddy field." The values, of course, were those of Buddhism, but the effect of the bipartisan consensus that emerged was a limitation on "the capacity of Sinhala Buddhist nationalism to grant equal democratic rights to those outside its fold." Professor Tambiah indeed argues that this "ideology is so hegemonic that it has led to the inferiorization of a minority in Sri Lanka and to the generation of a resistant attitude among many Buddhist nationalists toward any suggestion of devolutionary authority, let alone the division and dismemberment of the island."

Professor Tambiah poses the question "whether the framework of current Buddhist nationalism can in the future stretch and incorporate a greater amount of pluralist tolerance in the name of Buddhist conceptions of righteous rule" and sees "no reason to foreclose on this possibility, for there are precedents that can be positively employed to urge a new view."

It is, however, in the remedy that is proposed for moving toward this pluralism that the economist and the anthropologist join hands. As Professor Tambiah argues the measures of the "welfare" state and its promise of wider social mobility have produced more frustration than relief. As we have seen, the system of "free education" in the local languages created a vast literate and semiliterate pool of youth of the lower levels of rural society who, having invested so much hope in education, became the rebels of the JVP as well as of the Tamil insurgency. In the meantime, the old elite, and the new elite who have joined them, reproduced their educational and social advantages by enabling their children to acquire a knowledge of English, either locally or by sending their children abroad to Britain, the United States, and elsewhere, and the technical knowledge that will secure for them the most rewarding and prestigious positions in Sri Lanka.

In so far as Sinhala Buddhist nationalism is a gospel for excluding Tamils from competition, it is fuelled by these frustrations of unemployment and poor employment, and of Lebensraum in a crowded island.

The problems of this crowded island are compounded by its narrow industrial base. Its dependence on agriculture, and its dedication to an entrenched pattern of agricultural expansion through the medium of newly opened settlements on a peasant basis directly feeds, as we have underscored, the ethnic conflict. And the ethnic conflict in turn has slowed down economic development, derailed a growing tourism, and made foreign investors nervous.

The common ground between the economist and the anthropologist suggested by these observations is indeed that more rapid and diversified economic growth provides the only basis for expanding the effective Lebensraum of a crowded island in a manner which would permit coexistence between the two major communities. In the absence of rapid growth, the ideology of Sinhala Buddhist nationalism serves merely to ration out the available Lebensraum for the Sinhalese, at the cost of excluding the Tamils and provoking thereby a separatist and no less extremist Tamil nationalism by way of response.

The challenge before Sri Lanka, as indicated by Professor Tambiah, is whether Sinhala Buddhist nationalism can in the future stretch and incorporate a greater amount of pluralist tolerance in the name of Buddhist conceptions of righteous rule. But such a widening of Sinhala Buddhist nationalism will have to be associated with an expansion of economic opportunities substantial enough for both communities to coexist in harmony, which, as mentioned, presupposes significantly more rapid economic growth. It is this goal of rapid growth that will require the abandonment by today's bipartisan Sinhala elite of a prevailing ideology which proves to be the key obstacle to growth and industrialization today. This ideology is described by Professor Tambiah:

> What is of interest to us at the level of ideology, which structures perceptions and frames political actions, is that many of the elite—planners as well as many persons at all levels of society, especially the rural peasantry—focused on the tank, the temple, and the rice field as the most desirable form of a Sinhala Buddhist national existence. The elite, living a different style of life and reproducing a different pattern of privileged domination in their role as planners and rulers, wish upon the vast majority of the people an indefinitely expanding network of peasant "villages" as the answer to the island's demographic and employment problems. And the ideologies of the society, the activist "scholar-monks," the populist "literary" circles, the vote-seeking politicians, and the creators of rituals of national development and television dramas unite to image and propagate this vision of a (utopian) past that could be a prospective (utopian) future. These are the parameters of a national perspective that at present hinder the envisioning of a more realistic and workable regime of Buddhist democracy and righteous rule that can accommodate minorities.

Rapid growth and the abandonment of ideologies that hamper it are of course no more than necessary conditions for the restoration of communal harmony. What is open to question is to what degree these ingredients are also sufficient conditions, for the rift between the two communities has, in all probability, now widened to the point where questions of political power assume overriding importance. In other words, today's militant Tamil leadership may have reached the point of being reluctant, if not unwilling, to compromise its separatist demands. In that event, there would be little prospect of a political settlement, even if Sinhala Buddhist nationalism were to accommodate itself to Tamil concerns by providing a greater measure of pluralist tolerance along the lines advocated by Professor Tambiah. The situation today may well be one of intransigence begetting further intransigence, and the question then is what kind of political initiative needs to be taken.

It is, in this context, a matter for serious consideration whether there exists a political solution that falls short of the creation of two separate states. What requires now to be explored is whether the present structure of provincial councils in Sri Lanka has exhausted the limits to devolution that can be reached within the framework of a unitary state. In other words, what requires definition is the degree of *further* devolution that can meet the political aspirations of both communities and establish the climate of ethnic peace needed for rapid economic growth to deliver the expansion of economic opportunities that can alone consolidate ethnic harmony on a durable basis by providing the necessary economic Lebensraum.

It is important to appreciate that the problem is by no means peculiar to Sri Lanka and that several other countries are engaged in confronting similar, if not identical, issues. The Soviet Union and the countries of Eastern Europe, for example, are experimenting with every kind of institutional innovation in the attempt simultaneously to accommodate the requirements of political pluralism, the shift to a market economy, and the resolution of the numerous ethnic tensions that have surfaced with the erosion of the central authority previously exercised by a single-party state administering a command economy. In particular, President Gorbachev appears ready to alter the political structure of the Soviet Union in the direction of conceding whatever degree of devolution is necessary to accommodate its ethnic diversities so as to enable the union itself to survive as a viable entity. For Sri Lankans to seek to learn from this experience may not be entirely out of place and Professor Tambiah's book constitutes, in my view, the obvious starting point for anyone embarking on this task.

Helsinki
March 1990   Lal Jayawardena

Acknowledgments

I thank WIDER, and in particular its director, Dr. Lal Jayawardena, for sponsoring this study and writing the foreword. I am indebted to the following persons for providing me with valuable information, especially on recent developments and current events in Sri Lanka: Kumari Jayawardena, Sarath Amunugama, Steven Kemper, H. L. Seneviratne, and C. R. de Silva. I thank John Rogers for his informed suggestions for improving the text. None of these persons is responsible for the views expressed in this study. Sriyantha Walpola has kindly provided me with the photographs, which lend a visual charge to the text. Finally, I thank Rebecca Grow and Karen Ciacera for typing and preparing the manuscript, always a taxing task.

Stanley J. Tambiah

xvii

Abbreviations

ACBC	All Ceylon Buddhist Congress
CNC	Ceylon National Congress
CP	Communist party
DJV	Deshapremi Janatha Vijayaparaya
EBP	Eksath Bhikkhu Peramuna
JVP	Janatha Vimukthi Peramuna
LEBM	Lanka Eksath Bhikkhu Mandalaya
LSSP	Lanka Sama Samaja party
LTTE	Liberation Tigers of Tamil Eelam
MEP	Mahajana Eksath Peramuna
MSV	Mavibima Surakime Vyaparaya
SMS	Sinhala Maha Sabha
SLFP	Sri Lanka Freedom party
TULF	Tamil United Liberation Front
UNP	United National party

1 Introduction: The Question

Frequently during my travels in the United States colleagues, friends, and acquaintances ask me the discomfiting question, "If Buddhism preaches nonviolence, why is there so much political violence in Sri Lanka today?"

I could reply that although Christianity preaches brotherly love, Catholics and Protestants are killing each other in Northern Ireland, or that despite Gandhi's advocacy of *ahimsa* (nonviolence) and *satyagraha* (renunciation of coercion), there is much religious and ethnic violence in India. This is not a helpful reply, but one that temporarily puts the questioner on the defensive. Furthermore, it carries the cynical implication that religion is merely an epiphenomenon and has little impact on realpolitik.

I could take a different path and explore the question by reference to the classical past, with its exemplary cases. There is the great story of the agonizing remorse Emperor Asoka showed after the Kalinga war, when he allegedly changed from Asoka the fierce to Asoka the righteous. Then there is the career of Dutthagamani, the hero-king of Sri Lanka's famous chronicle, the *Mahavamsa,* whose moral dilemma and remorse surrounding the slaughter of Damilas (Tamils) during his war to unify the island was posed and answered in a less charitable way. The king was comforted by eight *arahants* (enlightened saints) with the words that he had slain only one and a half human beings: one had embraced the three refuges of the Buddha, the *dhamma* (doctrine) and the *sangha* (order of monks), and the other had taken the five precepts; the rest were "unbelievers and men of evil life" (*Mahavamsa,* chap. 25, verses 101–11). Both these exemplary cases have been probed by many scholars.[1] I have myself elsewhere discussed the issue

---

1. See Stanley J. Tambiah, *World Conqueror and World Renouncer* (Cambridge: Cambridge University Press, 1976), and *The Buddhist Conception of Universal King and Its Manifestations in South and Southeast Asia* (Kuala Lumpur: University of Ma-

of how Buddhist kings in Southeast Asia have through time sought to implement the conceptions of *cakkavatti* (wheel-rolling universal king) and *dharmaraja* (righteous king) in their political practices and to reconcile their use of violence and engagement in warfare with those ideals.[2] Finally, Bruce Kapferer has sought to demonstrate how a powerful "cosmology" of hierarchy, inclusion, and expulsion embedded not only in the Sinhalese chronicle tradition but also in their current exorcism ritual powerfully shapes and directs Sinhalese nationalism in the recent ethnic conflict.[3] Kapferer's imaginative thesis is that Sinhalese Buddhist notions of destructive violence are encapsulated in the idea of the "demonic." The demonic signifies the divisive and fragmenting processes that ordered Buddhist society as hierarchy seeks to encompass and integrate. The Sinhalese see the Tamil movement for a separate state as an instance of demonic fragmentation and the violence of the riots as an act of "powerful rehierarchization."[4] Kapferer's thesis, which implies a deep-seated powerful cosmology at work, will be considered in the final chapter. The above-mentioned perspectives and contributions have no doubt illuminated and continue to illuminate aspects of the linkage among Buddhism, politics, and violence.

Leaving aside the question of the legacy from the deep past, I begin this essay with the recent past, and with the events generated subsequently. The main question I shall probe is the extent to which, and the manner in which, Buddhism, as a "religion" espoused by Sri Lankans of the late nineteenth and the twentieth centuries, has contributed to the current ethnic conflict and collective violence in Sri Lanka. If it has contributed, were there changes in the nature of that contribution over time? And if there have been changes, how are we to describe the changing or changed shape of Buddhism itself as a lived reality?

---

laya, 1987); see also John Strong, *The Legend of King Asoka: A Study and Translation of the Asokavadana* (Princeton: Princeton University Press, 1983); Gananath Obeyesekere, *A Meditation on Conscience,* Social Scientists' Association of Sri Lanka, Occasional Papers (Colombo: Navamaga, 1988); R. A. L. H. Gunawardena, "The People of the Lion: Sinhala Consciousness in History and Historiography," in *Ethnicity and Social Change in Sri Lanka,* Social Scientists' Association (Colombo: Navamaga, 1985).

2. Stanley J. Tambiah, *The Buddhist Conception of Universal King.*

3. Bruce Kapferer, *Legends of People, Myths of State* (Washington, D.C.: Smithsonian Institution Press, 1988).

4. Bruce Kapferer, "Nationalist Ideology and Comparative Anthropology" (unpublished essay).

The investigation must, it seems to me, begin with what has come to be called "Buddhist revivalism," which began in the latter part of the nineteenth century, because it is a significant transforming development and a distinct shift in the island's history. What I propose to do is cover a whole century, say from the 1880s to the 1980s, focusing on the main landmarks and watersheds that figure in the story of how Buddhism as a collective and public religion was interwoven with the changing politics of the island and how that meshing contributed to ethnic conflicts, especially to various violent episodes such as civilian riots and insurrections.

For the most part, this essay is written not for Sri Lankan specialists, but for general readers, both inside and outside of academia, who have a certain standard conception of Buddhism as a philosophy and "religion" dedicated to nonviolence and liberation from "suffering" and are puzzled by the present-day violence in Sri Lanka in which many Buddhists seem to be participating. It addresses this issue in terms the general reader can understand. The epilogue, however, should be of interest to the specialist as well.

A major aspect of this task is the manner and extent to which issues defined as "Buddhist" issues, and the actors, both monks and laity, who have espoused "Buddhist" causes, have contributed to the outbreaks of collective violence in the form of ethnic riots.

All too often a certain type of scholarship, especially that purveyed by what I dub the Pali text puritans, has essentialized Buddhism in terms of its "pristine" teachings and has viewed all subsequent historical developments, especially those of a political kind, as deviations and distortions from the canonical form. I have taken the approach that in order to understand Buddhists, I must look not at something reified as Buddhism, but at the universe, so far as possible, through the eyes and practices of Buddhist actors situated in history and in their local contexts.

In pursuit of this objective, I have adopted these authorial strategies. I have tried to present in narrative form the unfolding of events over a period of about one hundred years. I have tried to locate the primary Buddhist actors, state their "causes," and describe their political interventions. Obviously the narrative is no natural chain of one fact mechanically following another; I have periodized and thematized it in terms of the patterns and processes I saw as emerging from the perspective I had chosen. So while on the one hand the main thread of the story is diachronic, at various points I have interjected comments that look backward as well as forward. In the last three chapters I review the scope and limits of current Buddhist political thought and I address the issue of Sinhala historical consciousness as a composite exercise. In short, I have adopted diachronic and synchronic frames, cast retrospective looks and signalled prospective views, and marked continuities, ruptures, and changes.

2 The Period of Buddhist Revivalism, 1860–1915

The most vivid and consequential formulation of Sinhala Buddhist revivalism with nationalist overtones is to be witnessed in the anti-Christian movement begun by monks like Migettuwatte Gunananda and Hikkaduwe Sumangala in the mid-nineteenth century, then given an institutional and propagandist basis by the Theosophists, notably by Colonel Olcott as their leader in the 1880s, and taken to its ideological limits by the charismatic Anagarika Dharmapala (1864–1933). Fortunately, this period of Buddhist revivalism during the latter phase of the British raj has been thickly documented, and in this essay I need only sketch in the main points.[1]

There is no doubt that Sinhala Buddhist revivalism and nationalism, in the form we can recognize today, had its origin in the late nineteenth and early twentieth centuries. It is in this earlier period that we see most clearly the contours and impulsions of a movement that acted as a major shaper of a Sinhala consciousness and a sense of national identity and purpose.

Kumari Jayawardena correctly insists that the religious revival of the 1880s had salient political and economic dimensions. "The new revival, taking place during a period when local capitalism was expanding, was linked to the nationalist stirrings of Buddhist sections of

1. The following are some selected examples: Kitsiri Malalgoda, *Buddhism in Sinhalese Society, 1750–1900: A Study of Religious Revival and Change* (Berkeley: University of California Press, 1976); Sarath Amunugama, "Anagarika Dharmapala (1864–1933) and the Transformation of Sinhala Buddhist Organization in a Colonial Setting," *Social Science Information* 24, no. 4 (1985): 697–730; Ananda Guruge, ed., *Return to Righteousness: A Collection of Speeches, Essays, and Letters of the Anagarika Dharmapala* (Colombo: Government Press, 1965); George Bond, *The Buddhist Revival in Sri Lanka: The Religious Tradition, Reinterpretation and Response* (Columbia: University of South Carolina Press, 1988); Richard Gombrich and Gananath Obeyesekere, *Buddhism Transformed: Religious Change in Sri Lanka* (Princeton: Princeton University Press, 1988).

the emergent bourgeoisie and was also associated with certain dissident trends in Britain such as anti-Christian rationalism."[2]

Even before Colonel Olcott arrived on the island, certain prominent monks had begun to launch a Buddhist revival with a political thrust. The dominant leader of the revival movement was Migettuwatte Gunananda, "an aggressive and dynamic bhikkhu who was the first to start mass agitation on Buddhist grievances among the urban and rural masses. In contrast to other learned bhikkhus of the period, he was a fiery orator, pamphleteer and a fighter who led the challenge to Christianity and the missionaries" (Jayawardena, "Bhikkus," p. 13). Gunananda was the acclaimed orator in the famous debate between Christians and Buddhists staged in 1873. And together with several wealthy Sinhala traders, arrack renters, and coconut planters, Gunananda became a member of the Theosophical Society. Although in the following years the most prominent Sri Lankan actors in the Buddhist revivalist *cum* nationalist movement would be laymen such as Dharmapala, it is important to remember that some prominent monks (such as Hikkaduwe Sri Sumangala, Valane Siddharta, Weligama Sri Sumangala, and Ratmalane Sri Dharmaloka) were involved with the causes promoted by the revivalist and nationalist upsurge, such as the establishment of Buddhist schools and the temperance movements of 1904 and 1912 (ibid., p. 14).

The most significant activity of the Buddhist revivalism stimulated and sponsored by Colonel Olcott and the Buddhist Theosophical Society founded in 1880 was the establishment of Buddhist schools to counter the near-monopoly that the Protestant missions (and to a lesser extent the Catholic Church) had over the educational system. Looking ahead, we shall see that this issue will surface again in the 1940s and 1950s.

Dharmapala first found his vocation and acquired his propagandist skills in association with the Theosophists, but later broke away to propagate Buddhist causes as he envisaged them. His revivalism has been dubbed "Protestant Buddhism," a useful label if not overly credited with being a world transforming this "worldly asceticism."

The major features of Dharmapala's Buddhist revivalism are a selective retrieval of norms from canonical Buddhism; a denigration of

2. "Bhikkus in Revolt," part 2: "Revival, Revolt, and Race," *Lanka Guardian*, June 15, 1979, p. 13.

alleged non-Buddhist ritual practices and magical manipulations (an attitude probably influenced by Christian missionary denunciation of "heathen" beliefs and practices); enunciation of a code for lay conduct, suited for the emergent Sinhalese urban middle-class and business interests, which emphasized a puritanical sexual morality and etiquette in family life; and, most important of all, an appeal to the past glories of Buddhism and Sinhalese civilization celebrated in the *Mahavamsa* and other chronicles as a way of infusing the Sinhalese with a new nationalist identity and self-respect in the face of humiliation and restrictions suffered under British rule and Christian missionary influence.

For our purposes it is most relevant to note that Dharmapala's brand of Sinhala Buddhist revivalism and nationalism was supported by and served the interests of a rising Sinhala Buddhist middle class and a circle of businessmen and that some of these latter were implicated in the anti-Muslim riots of 1915 directed against their competitors— Muslim shopkeepers and businessmen, who were branded as exploiters of the Sinhalese consumer public at large.[3]

The ethnic overtones of the Buddhist-nationalist journalism of the time has been amply documented.[4] The newspaper *Sinhala Jatiya*, edited by the novelist Piyadasa Sirisena, not only invoked a Sinhalese "national awakening" but also in tandem carried anti-Moor stories in its columns shortly before the riots. In 1909 Sirisena urged the Sinhalese to "refrain from . . . transactions with the Coast Moors, the Cochins, and the foreigner." In 1915, when the hostility had reached a higher intensity, the *Lakmina*, a Sinhala daily, writing of the Coast Moors, said, "A suitable plan should be adopted to send this damnable lot out of the country," and the *Dinamina*, another newspaper, condemned "our inveterate enemies, the Moors."

Dharmapala was an uncharitable propagandist in the same vein. In a 1910 issue of the *Mahabodhi Journal*, which he published, he de-

3. The anti-Muslim riots of 1915 are well documented. For example, see *Journal of Asian Studies* 24, no. 2 (1970): 219–66, in which there are three essays under the rubric "The 1915 Riots in Ceylon: A Symposium," with an introduction by Robert Kearney; Ameer Ali "The 1915 Racial Riots in Ceylon (Sri Lanka): A Reappraisal of Its Causes," *South Asia*, n.s., 4, no. 2 (1981): 1–20; A. P. Kannangara, "The Riots of 1915 in Sri Lanka: A Study in the Roots of Communal Violence," *Past and Present*, no. 102 (1983): 130–65.

4. See especially Kumari Jayawardena, *Ethnic and Class Conflicts in Sri Lanka* (Colombo: Navamaga Printers, 1986).

nounced the "merchants from Bombay and peddlers from South India" who trade in Ceylon while the "sons of the soil" abandon agriculture and "work like galley slaves" in urban clerical jobs.[5] *Sinhala Bauddhaya*, also run by Dharmapala, was most vociferous in its attacks; in 1912 this journal complained, "From the day the foreign white man stepped in this country, the industries, habits, and customs of the Sinhalese began to disappear and now the Sinhalese are obliged to fall at the feet of the Coast Moors and Tamils." In this same paper Dharmapala later printed verses describing how the Sinhalese were exploited by aliens together with a cartoon that showed the helpless Sinhala in the grip of alien traders, money lenders, and land grabbers. It should come as no surprise, therefore, that the *Sinhala Bauddhaya*, together with the *Sinhala Jatiya*, was prosecuted and banned in 1915 for carrying inflammatory statements that helped fuel the riots.

Dharmapala's letter to the secretary of state for the colonies, which he wrote from Calcutta on June 15, 1915, demanding a royal commission to investigate the causes of the riots and denouncing the Muslims gives some idea of the anger that fueled this reformer's romantic search for and reinstitution of a lost pristine Buddhism and an ancient robust, just, and noble Sinhala civilization.[6] His condemnations of the alien influences that had spoiled his people and religion were vigorous, even coarse:

> The Muhammadans, an alien people who in the early part of the nineteenth century were common traders, by Shylockian methods became prosperous like the Jews. The Sinhalese, sons of the soil, whose ancestors for 2,358 years had shed rivers of blood to keep the country from alien invaders, . . . today . . . are in the eyes of the British only vagabonds. . . . The alien South Indian Muhammadan comes to Ceylon, sees the neglected, illiterate villagers, without any experience in trade, without any knowledge of any kind of technical industry, and isolated from the whole of Asia on account of his language, religion, and race, and the result is that the Muhammadan thrives and the sons of the soil go to the wall.[7]

Dharmapala was duly interned in Calcutta in 1915 for his political efforts and his previous activities in Ceylon.

5. *Mahabodhi Journal*, Oct. 1909.
6. This letter is reproduced in Guruge, ed., *Return to Righteousness*.
7. Ibid., p. 540.

3 Politics and Constitutional Progress, 1915–1946

The twilight of the British raj was a time of gestation for a number of developments, both contradictory and complementary. They foreshadowed things to come.

A remarkable feature of the Buddhist revivalist and Sinhala nationalist movement spearheaded by Anagarika Dharmapala is that after the British raj's show of armed strength and suppression of the 1915 riots, its incarceration of the temperance leaders (which included F. R. and D. S. Senanayake) and Dharmapala's prolonged absences in India, where he concentrated on the recovery of Buddha Gaya for Buddhism, the movement itself seemed to lose prominence and surrendered the limelight to a different cast of Sinhalese and Tamil politicians, who were to initiate a phase of collaboration rather than confrontation in their dealings with the British.

It seems as if the trauma of the riots, during which British officials, the police, and volunteers took punitive and disgracing actions against many Sri Lankan leaders, persons of education and high social standing, energized these leaders first to protest,[1] and then, in a mood of collaborative dialogue, to form political associations in order to negotiate with authorities.

These leaders were educated in English, were in distinct ways Westernized in "dress" and style of life, and dedicated to a policy of gradualism in seeking more political rights for the Ceylonese through constitutional means. The Ceylon Reform League was formed in 1916 and was subsequently transformed into the Ceylon National Congress (CNC) in 1919, which through a series of respectful "memorials" to the governor and the Colonial Office sought an increased representation for its elite supporters in the administration of the colony.

---

1. See P. Ramanathan, *Riots and Martial Law in Ceylon, 1915* (London: St. Martin's Press, 1915).

In fact the older nationalist thrust, focused on religious and cultural revivalism, identity and "uplift" through a rejection of Christian privilege and a Western lifestyle, seemed to be upstaged by the newer movement led by the Ceylon National Congress, which was committed to a gradualist program of winning political independence through concessions relating to representative government.[2]

The politicians of the Ceylon National Congress, in their deliberations with the raj, did gain political concessions. The two most important of these gains, stemming from the Donoughmore Constitution, were the universal franchise achieved in 1931 (against the wishes of most members of the Congress, who advocated property and literacy qualifications for the voters) and a large measure of internal autonomy for a state council consisting of 61 members, the majority of whom (50) were to be elected through universal suffrage from territorial constituencies.

But a decade before the beginning of the Donoughmore era, a troubling dissension and divergence had already taken place among leaders, especially Tamil and Sinhalese, who had hitherto stood together in advocating political reform. I refer to a well-known event, namely, the departure from the Ceylon National Congress of the Ceylon Tamil politicians (led earlier by the brothers Arunachalam and Ramanathan) who with every expansion in territorial representation increasingly felt the inevitable domination of the Sinhalese majority in the island's politics. The Tamils boycotted the 1931 elections of the State Council under the Donoughmore Constitution, and the Sinhalese obtained for the first time an absolute legislative majority over the representatives of all other ethnic groups combined. The epoch of the Donoughmore Constitution established forcefully the reality of Sinhalese majoritarian rule and the Sinhalese monopoly, especially from 1936 to 1942, on the office of ministers of the executive committees, which, except for finance, defense, and external affairs ran the business of

2. As R. Kearney (*Communalism and Language in the Politics of Ceylon* [Durham, N.C.: Duke University Press, 1967], pp. 47–48) put it: "Although originating in the same social and ideological discontents and sharing hostility toward colonial rule, the two streams of sentiment developed markedly different characteristics. The Congress was led by men who, although occasionally displaying a sentimental attachment to the Sinhalese past and idealized village life, used the English language for the home and the public platform and adopted Western dress, manner of living, and mode of thought. Whereas the Sinhalese traditionalists defined their social and cultural goals by reference to the Sinhalese past, the congressmen tended to seek their goals in a closer emulation of modern Britain."

the country. In 1943, D. S. Senanayake saw to it that a Tamil, A. Mahadeva, Arunachalam's son, was made head of the Ministry of Home Affairs. The Tamils did subsequently participate in the elections to the State Council. As for the tenor of the politics between the 1920s and independence, although the Dharmapala brand of Buddhist nationalist thrust seemed to become muted, or even pushed off the stage, the Ceylonese elitist politicians in fact conducted throughout a revealingly two-sided discourse, simultaneously "communalist" and parochial and "constitutionalist" and secular. Right through the period of the Donoughmore Constitution (1931–47), although the "Buddhist" rhetoric was muted, there was a lively manifestation of communal sensitivities and ethnic politics among the Sinhalese, Tamils, and Muslims, behind which lay the demographics of a huge Sinhalese majority ranged against minorities, who at best did not form more than a quarter of the population.

As Jane Russell has convincingly documented for this period, communal politics and the arithmetic of communal representation informed many of the debates that took place in the two state councils that covered this span of time.[3] As representative government on a territorial basis was extended and made more participatory with the granting of universal franchise in 1931, the Sinhalese, Tamils, and other minorities bickered over two issues that would continue to be salient for many decades to come. First was the issue of the rights of the majority community to dominate the State Council (and subsequent elected parliaments) versus the minorities' demand that special provisions be made for their representation in order to protect their interests. Second was the issue of the criteria for recruitment to public service, and on this matter the two parties reversed their positions. The Sinhalese politicians frequently accused the Tamils in terms of "race" and in relation to their number in the population of being overrepresented in public service, while the Tamils argued for open recruitment on the basis of technical qualifications and competence. Against the Tamil defense of meritocratic principles, the Sinhalese offered objections of unfair educational advantage and even communal networking.

Given the integral role of these bread-and-butter communal (or ethnic) issues in twentieth-century Sri Lankan politics, one may ask what

3. Jane Russell, *Communal Politics under the Donoughmore Constitution* (Colombo: Tisara Press, 1982).

the role of Buddhist revivalism was in these political and economic issues, which were at the heart of the struggles of the Donoughmore era and afterwards. As we shall see, once Sinhala "nationalism" gained momentum, its very conceptualization, phenomenological basis, and practical realization were inseparable from the identity and historical pride provided by the Buddhist legacy, the cultural capital that Buddhist projects generated, and the languages in which Buddhist literature were couched and transmitted. Moreover, the demands for correcting past and present injustices committed against the Buddhist religion—and its primary carriers, the monks, and its lay adherents— did become translated and substantialized in terms of concrete measures that were political, economic, educational, occupational, and administrative in character. This is the surge that we must track.

There is, however, the need to sketch in here a second discourse between the local politicians and their colonial rulers. Throughout this same era of ethnic bickering, the CNC politicians could and did phrase many of their submissions for progress toward self-government in a secular constitutionalist language. The era that produced the leading politicians of the CNC, like Ponnambalam Arunachalam, James Pieris, E. W. Perera, D. B. Jayatileke, F. R. and D. S. Senanayake, can without distortion be labelled as also one of "collaborationist politics." Just as the Donoughmore commissioners had insisted, so did the Soulbury commissioners insist, true to their "liberal" ideals, that Sri Lankans should transcend ethnic claims and the need to seek special provisions for the protection of minorities. D. S. Senanayake and his followers played this game and employed the right rhetoric when occasion demanded and achieved the ultimate reward in the form of independence in 1948, accompanied by a constitution committed to representative democracy.

There were certain important developments, even fissures and breakthroughs, that took place during this period of constitutional progress, which would create some turbulence in the postindependence era. One of them was the formation of radical left-wing parties; another was the emergence of radical, politically committed monks.

Although the CNC was the umbrella organization of the constitutionalist politicians, their dominance would be questioned and complicated by the formation of a Marxist party in 1935. This was the Lanka Sama Samaja party (LSSP), from which a section split to form the Communist party (CP) in 1943. (In an earlier time, in the twenties, there had arisen the left-oriented Labour party, which had begun the trade union movement, but it had a checkered career).[4] Though appealing to only narrow segments of the constituency, such as the wage workers in Colombo and on the tea plantations, the LSSP and CP would be powerful critics of, and irritants to, the breed of State Council politicians who formed the United National party (UNP) at the time of the transfer of power.

These leftist parties (whose leaders were similar in their social origins to the CNC politicians) were also in their earlier phase not only secular and antireligious but also noncommunal; championing the uplift of urban workers and plantation labor, they advocated socialist reforms.

Between the years 1928 and 1936 were also launched a number of Sinhala Buddhist societies that would propagate the "opposite interests," as compared with the leftist parties, along ethnic, religious, and linguistic lines. The most important of these were the All Ceylon Buddhist Congress (ACBC), an umbrella organization for local Buddhist societies, and the Sinhala Maha Sabha (SMS), founded in 1935 by S. W. R. D. Bandaranaike. The chief ideologues of the SMS, such as Piyadasa Sirisena and Cumaratunga, advocated the creation of Sinhalese vernacular literature and supported the view of the vernacular teachers' associations, that teaching in schools should be done in the vernacular languages.

By the late thirties, however, Sirisena and Cumaratunga had severed their involvement with the SMS, which now developed into a loose but ideologically noteworthy political organization under the leadership of Bandaranaike. "In the State Council it was nominally the largest political grouping in 1939, and it had a very substantial following among the electors in the Sinhalese provinces."[5] The SMS would make its political presence felt more than a decade and a half later, in 1956.

We now turn to another thrust, this time from within the *sangha*,

---

4. Visakha Kumari Jayawardena, *The Rise of the Labor Movement in Ceylon* (Durham, N.C.: Duke University Press, 1972).

5. Russell, *Communal Politics*, p. 143. But see James Manor, *The Expedient Utopian: Bandaranaike and Ceylon* (Cambridge: Cambridge University Press, 1989), chaps. 4–6, whose evaluation of the organizational structure and political effectiveness of the SMS is much more skeptical and qualified. K. M. de Silva (*A History of Sri Lanka* [London: Hurst & Co., 1981], pp. 445–48) states that many influential congressmen had links with the SMS, and although the SMS brand of "religio-linguistic nationalism" was at odds with Congress policy, neither was strong enough to impose its will on the other.

which would spawn a coterie of radical monks, who would combine leftist socialist themes with Sinhala Buddhist causes, thereby trying to fuse the two developments, which I have discussed before as being oppositional and contradictory.

4 Radical Monks and the Legitimation of Monks' Participation in Politics

What is intriguing for us is that before and during the very first general election of 1947 a group of radical, able, left-oriented Buddhist monks labeled the Vidyalankara group exploded on the political scene in support of the leftist parties, especially the LSSP, which were explicitly dedicated to secular politics and to the devaluation of religion in human affairs. How did this come about?

It would be inaccurate to think that these radical monks of the 1940s centered in Vidyalankara Pirivena, a premier monastic college situated in Kelaniya, just outside Colombo, had no predecessors. Both lay and monk Buddhist enthusiasts had in earlier decades not only been involved in the temperance movements but had also lent support to various labor strikes because to them working-class agitation was a facet of the anticolonial struggle as well as a component of the Sinhala Buddhist awakening.[1] When A. E. Goonesinha, as a progressive trade union leader,[2] led several labor strikes in the twenties (including the general strike of 1923, the harbor strike of 1927, and the tramway strike of 1929), he had the support of some *bhikkhus* who spoke at strike meetings and wrote for the political journal *Swaraj*, which he edited.[3]

1. For example, Dharmapala and Walisinha Harischandra, prominent Buddhist advocates, supported the labor movement and had some influence on A. E. Goonesinha and even on leftist leaders like Dr. S. A. Wickremasinghe. Dharmapala applauded the actions of the railway workers when they struck in 1912 as giving "unmistakeable proof of the national spirit among the Sinhalese" and donated money to their strike fund. See Jayawardena, *Rise of the Labor Movement in Ceylon* (Durham, N.C.: Duke University Press, 1982), p. 154.

2. Goonesinha's labor movement would succumb to "racial" and "ethnic" (communal) prejudices and slogans during the economic depression of the early thirties. In general Sinhala revivalism and anticolonial nationalism would also progressively turn into chauvinism invoking an Aryan racial inheritance.

3. Kumari Jayawardena, "Bhikkus in Revolt," part 3: "Buddhist Radicals and the Labor Movement," *Lanka Guardian*, July 1, 1979. The author identifies Boose

15

It seems that when the left-oriented LSSP was formed in 1935, there were several *bhikkhus* who spoke in its favor and saw nothing incompatible between following Buddhism and espousing Marxist socialism.

> These included Balangoda Ananda Maitreya, who approved of the anti-imperialist stand of the party and its attack on class privilege, Naravila Dhammaratana, who expressed radical ideas in articles regularly written for the *Silumina,* and Dumbara Palitha, an LSSP member who worked among the peasantry. However the most outstanding monk of the period was Udakandawela Siri Saranankara. Born in 1902, Saranankara went to India as an acolyte of Dharmapala in 1921 and joined Santiniketan, where he came into contact with Tagore and the Bengali renaissance movement; he was also associated with the Indian national movement which was particularly militant in Bengal and with Bengali communists.[4]

In 1931 Saranankara joined the Calcutta City College and became a leader of the student union. He was jailed by the police in Calcutta for subversive anti-British activities, and while in prison he met Subhas Chandra Bose as well as members of the communist movement. Around 1936 Saranankara returned to Sri Lanka and joined the newly formed LSSP.

> He soon became active in many battles against conservative politicians, using the temple sermon as a method of propagating socialist ideas. He wrote a book entitled *Why Sri Lanka Needs Sama Samajism.* . . . When the LSSP split in 1940, Saranankara joined the communist group— and presided over the first meeting of the communist-led Ceylon Trade Union Federation in 1940. He was jailed for the second time from 1942 to 1944, being sentenced to two years' imprisonment for a seditious speech. . . . In later years he became the vice-president of the Communist party, was active in the postwar peace movement, and received the prestigious Lenin peace prize. (Jayawardena, part 3, p. 11)

Dhammarakhita and Udakandawela Siri Saranankara as radical monks who wrote for the journal *Swaraj.*

4. Once again I am citing from Jayawardena's "Bhikkus in Revolt," part 3, p. 11. See this essay for more details about the career of Saranankara.

In view of this preceding tradition of politically active monks, some of them leftist radicals, it would be a mistake to think that it was only in the 1940s that a new breed of political monks burst on the scene. But it is important to realize that this radicalism involved only a small number within a large and differentiated *sangha* (order of monks), the majority of whom were inactive.

In earlier elections individual *bhikkhus* may have supported certain political candidates who as *dayakas* (lay patrons) may have sought their blessings and legitimation. Such participation in politics by the main body of monks was limited and informal. Whenever a Christian candidate had to be overcome, the slogan of Buddhism and the informal support of monks could be effective.

But it was in the mid-forties that a sufficient number of highly educated and vocal monks, whose leaders were labeled the Vidyalankara group by virtue of their association with the monastic college bearing that name, began to set several precedents which would influence the public posture of large numbers of contemporary and later monks. One was the unclouded and self-conscious pronouncement of the right and responsibility of monks to participate in politics, in matters to do with the public weal, and in the nationalist movement and decolonization process. The second was their banding together in significant numbers as a pressure group engaging in political activism. They delivered the politically engaged monk in full-fledged form, and he was no longer an eccentric.

"The election of 1947," writes Phadnis, "marked the emergence of a group of young, highly articulate Bhikkhus supporting the left parties like the LSSP and the CP. They mostly belonged to the pirivenas [monastic colleges] in Colombo or in adjacent areas and both students and teachers participated in the campaign. . . . These left-inclined monks had certain points in common; virtually all of them had been to India; they had been influenced by the nationalist movement and were closely associated with some of its eminent socialist leaders."[5] Many

---

5. Urimila Phadnis, *Religion and Politics in Sri Lanka* (London: C. Hurst & Co., 1976), p. 163. Some of the prominent monks in the so-called Vidyalankara group were Rev. Naravila Dharmaratna, Rev. Udakandawela Saranankara, Rev. Walpola Rahula (all three had studied in Calcutta), Rev. Bambarenda Siriseevali and Kotahena Pannakitti (who had studied in Varanasi), and Rev. Kallalelle Anandasagara. Some of the younger monks at Vidyalankara Pirivena were also influenced by radical Indian *bhikkhus*—such as Ananda Kausalyana and Rahul Sanskrityana, later a member of the Indian Communist party—who were at this monastic college in the 1940s.

of these militant monks had studied in India, especially in Calcutta and Varanasi, and had been stimulated and influenced by the swirl of movements bearing on cultural renaissance, Indian nationalism, and left-wing politics (Jayawardena, part 3, p. 11).

The years 1946 and 1947 proved to be a landmark because they witnessed the trenchant articulation of the debate: should monks participate in politics? Out of this polemic emerged the self-conscious "political monk" in Sri Lanka. Though tested, rebuked, and even reviled by certain conservative establishment monks within the *Sangha* and by many members of the laity, both pious Buddhists and iconoclastic "leftists," the political monk established his niche and his right to participate in politics within certain limits. (We shall investigate as we proceed to what extent such political monks and their ideologies and activities actually fanned the fires of ethnic and religious violence in subsequent times, especially in 1956 and 1958).

Two scholar-monks in particular propounded radical ideas at this time. Walpola Rahula, who later wrote scholarly books on Buddhism[6] and became increasingly conservative and chauvinistic, wrote a book in 1946 called *Bhiksuvage Urumaya* (*The Heritage of the Bhikkhu*), in which he sought to establish that monks had from earliest times played a significant political and social role in Ceylon. I shall deal with this text in the next chapter. The second was K. Pannasara, principal of Vidyalankara Pirivena. In "Bhikkhus and Politics" (1946), a response to the charge by UNP politicians (including D. S. Senanayake and his nephew, R. G. Senanayake) that monks should avoid political campaigning, he declared that politics included all aspects of public welfare, and it was the vocation of monks to direct efforts in that area.[7] Pannasara's reply contained this famous declaration: "We believe that politics today embraces all fields of human activity directed towards the public weal. . . . It is nothing but fitting for bhikkhus to identify themselves with activities conducive to the welfare of our people—whether these be labelled politics or not. . . . we believe that it is incumbent on the bhikkhus not only to further the efforts directed towards the welfare of the country, but also oppose such measures as are detrimental to the common good" (Jayawardena, part 4, p. 7).

6. Walpola Rahula authored these two standard works in English: *History of Buddhism in Ceylon* (Colombo: Gunasena, 1956); *What the Buddha Taught* (Bedford: Gordon Fraser, 1959).

7. See Phadnis, *Religion and Politics,* pp. 163–65; see also Kumari Jayawardena, "Bhikkus in Revolt," part 4: "Yellow-robed Comrades or Pararthacharya?" in *Lanka Guardian,* July 15, 1979.

The radical monks stepped up their criticism and increased their following when various sections of the clergy and laity—such as the chief priests of the Malwatte chapter and Ramanna Nikaya, the Maha Bodhi Society (founded in 1891 by Dharmapala)—and the press sought to censure them. Even the All Ceylon Buddhist Congress (ACBC), composed of lay Buddhists committed to the restoration of Buddhism, felt obliged to declare that no monk should seek or exercise the rights of a voter and no monk should seek election to a political office at a local or national level.

The radical monks at a meeting held in June 1946 determined to form the Lanka Eksath Bhikkhu Mandalaya (LEBM, the Ceylon Union of Bhikkhus). This body, now with a larger reach attracting many oppositional monks, declared its intention to protect the civil and political rights of the *sangha,* affirmed that monks should take part in politics, and aired its aim to overthrow the current UNP capitalist government. The radical political mood of the LEBM can be gauged from these resolutions adopted in a meeting held in the following year (March 1947): the rejection of the Soulbury Constitution as falling short of Ceylon's desire to be a free and independent sovereign state; the support for a socialist program for the nationalization of transport, mines, and estates; the necessity to control foreign investments; and the support for a scheme of free education.

During the general strike of 1946 staged by the left-wing parties, many monks openly supported the strikers, and, at a mass meeting in Colombo in October 1946, some two hundred "political *bhikkhus*" were reported as taking part. One of them was Bhikkhu Rahula, who vehemently criticized the Board of Ministers. The same support was given by these monks to the general strike of 1947.

There was lively political canvassing during the national election of 1947. All major parties, including the UNP, had monks on their platforms as speakers and legitimators, and the left-wing parties had many radical monks actively campaigning for them.[8]

The LEBM and the radical monks both proved to be ahead of their time but paved the way for things to come. Once the election of 1947 was over and the UNP won, they soon became defunct. Being politically radical, the LEBM platform had little to differentiate it from

---

8. Jayawardena (part 4, p. 8) reports Walpola Rahula, Nattandiye Pannakara, Kallalelle Anandasagara, Kotahena Pannakitti, and Naravila Dharmaratna as being in demand at left-wing rallies and meetings. Rahula and Anandasagara explicitly campaigned against the prospective prime minister D. S. Senanayake in his constituency (Mirigama).

those of the leftist parties like the LSSP and CP, who found it difficult
to withstand the charge that Buddhism should be saved "from the
flame of Marxism." The LEBM was tarred with the same brush. And
many monks who had actively participated in the strikes and the election were demoralized by, and chagrined at, the verbal, even physical,
attacks they had suffered. Moreover, in the following years, the cause
of Buddhist restoration would become entwined with issues of national language and Sinhalese majoritarian interests vis-à-vis the
Tamil minority, and monk-activists would find a more congenial and
less controversial role as supporters of a different political coalition.
The voice of the radical monks and the formation of the LEBM
marked historic moments of various kinds.[9]

First of all, the LEBM was primarily a movement among monks
drawn from Colombo and its suburban and satellite regions; it was distinctly urban-based and reflected the ferment in the island's principal
city. It was therefore also concentrated in the low country, especially
in the southwest coastal regions.

Second, it was a movement that reflected the animus and aspirations
of young monks, most of them placed in the more poorly endowed
temples. They were opposed to the elderly monks, in particular the
incumbents of rich temples, especially those of the Siyam Nikaya in
the Kandyan provinces. The LEBM monks were educated, many of
them were teacher-monks in the *pirivenas* and monastic schools, but
they were not from the traditional land-endowed temples or the families that were closely connected with their control.

The real significance of the LEBM was that it was the forerunner of
forceful and effective participation by monks in the elections to come,
most important that of 1956, in their capacity as voice for the powerful
claims of Sinhala Buddhist nationalism. In time this form of Buddhist
nationalism championed by the political *bhikkhus* progressively shed
its socialist (Marxist) aspects and took on the mantle of populist
chauvinism. This is part of our story: that whatever Marxist and socialist working-class trade unions and political parties emerged in Sri
Lanka, they had their birth and their canonical expression in the thirties and forties, rather than afterwards, when they made a succession
of compromises and weakened to the point of irrelevance. At the same
time, whatever revivalist and conduct-reforming ingredients Buddhist

---

9. In composing this summing up, I am indebted to the discussion of Phadnis, *Religion and Politics*, chap. 4.

nationalism had in the time of Dharmapala, they too would be progressively leached out and would provide the space for the fomentation of a political Buddhism that would in the name of Buddhist identity and privilege practice discrimination and majoritarian domination and thereby contribute to ethnic strife. Sri Lankan politics would take an increasingly narrow path limited to a range of issues framed within the confines of a Sinhala Buddhist nationalism, and the major Sinhala parties would in time by and large reach a consensus.

5 The Betrayal and Restoration of Buddhism: Accusations and Remedies

What did the Sinhala Buddhist leaders, the activists and protestors both lay and clerical, mean by such slogans as "the restoration of Buddhism to its rightful place" and "the betrayal of Buddhism" during colonial rule, especially under the British raj?

The enumeration of wrongs committed and the restoration of due rights, as described and interpreted in detail by Buddhist activists, are our best entry into understanding what the revival and restoration of Buddhism meant to them in substantive terms. This is one way to see how the cause of Buddhism entered, informed, and directed Sri Lankan politics, that is, the relationship between Buddhism and politics.

If we take this investigative and interpretive strategy, we must examine three texts produced in the mid-forties and fifties in Sri Lanka that could be said to act as ideological charters of the Buddhist activists: First is Walpola Rahula, *Bhiksuvage Urumaya* (Colombo: Svatsika Press, 1946). Second is *The Betrayal of Buddhism* (1956), a report published by the Buddhist Committee of Inquiry, which was set up in 1954 by virtue of a resolution passed by the All Ceylon Buddhist Congress at its thirty-third annual conference held in December 1953. The committee's brief was "to inquire into the present state of Buddhism in Ceylon and to report on the conditions necessary to improve and strengthen the position of Buddhism, and the means whereby those conditions may be fulfilled." And third is D. C. Vijayawardhana, *Dharma-Vijaya, or The Revolt in the Temple* (Colombo: Sinha Publications, 1953), composed to commemorate 2,500 years of the land, the race, and the faith. These texts are important as ideological statements because they focus on three objectives: the positive construction and defense of the monk as a political actor from early times; a critique of British colonial rule as injurious to Buddhism, the *sangha*, and lay Buddhists; a program for the restoration of Buddhism and the *sangha* to their rightful place.

From among the ranks of the *bhikkhus* perhaps the most important tract that emerged was that composed by Bhikkhu Walpola Rahula. It was published in Sinhalese in 1946 under the title *Bhiksuvage Urumaya*. This work was revised and translated into English and published under the title *The Heritage of the Bhikkhu*.[1] Walpola Rahula had written many works in Sinhalese before he became an internationally famous scholar-monk with the publication of authoritative texts such as *What the Buddha Taught* (1959) and *History of Buddhism in Ceylon* (1956),[2] published in the year of Buddha Jayanthi. In the mid-forties he was a member of the vocal Vidyalankara group that championed the monks' right and obligation to participate actively in the shaping of a better society. Before examining *The Heritage of the Bhikkhu*, it is instructive to review some features of Rahula's biography as illustrative of one kind of Buddhist ideologue who emerged at this time.[3]

Walpola Rahula was born in 1907 in a village in the Galle district of the Southern Province of Sri Lanka. After attending the village school for a while, he was ordained as a novice in the village Buddhist temple and participated in the monastic system of education, mastering Pali, and Buddhist doctrine and history. Then in 1936 he made history as the first Buddhist monk to enter as an undergraduate the Ceylon University College, which was at that time affiliated to the University of London. His initiative and breaking of tradition were not appreciated by some conservative elements.

It is remarkable that it was after completing his monastic education at the age of about twenty-two that Rahula began to study English, in which task he was assisted and encouraged by an eminent and well-known teacher of English literature at the local university and a mem-

1. Walpola Rahula, *The Heritage of the Bhikkhu: A Short History of the Bhikkhu in the Educational, Cultural, Social, and Political Life* (New York: Grove Press, 1974).

2. Walpola Rahula, *What the Buddha Taught* (Bedford: Gordon Fraser, 1959), and *History of Buddhism in Ceylon* (Colombo: M. D. Gunasena, 1956). These books, the first a manual setting out Buddhism's central concepts and doctrines and the second giving a historical sketch of Buddhism in Ceylon in the Anuradhapura period, are widely used internationally. Rahula studied in Paris in the late fifties and was associated with Paul Demiéville. He later returned to Sri Lanka and served as vice-chancellor of Vidyodaya University for a while, before returning to private life.

3. This biographical sketch is based primarily on two essays contained in Somaratna Balasooriya, André Bareau, et al., *Buddhist Studies in Honour of Walpola Rahula* (London: Gordon Fraser, 1980), Udaya Mallawarachchi's "Walpola Rahula: A Brief Biographical Sketch" and E. F. C. Ludowyk's "Thinking of Rahula."

ber of the "English-speaking elite," Dr. E. F. C. Ludowyk, a "Dutch burgher" by origin, with socialist leanings.

During the early 1930s, before entering the university, Rahula had already acquired a reputation as a preacher and a pamphleteer who criticized some popular Buddhist practices.

Ludowyk remarks that it was Rahula's "very difference from the world and horizons of the English-speaking elite" and his intellectual curiosity and liveliness of mind that convinced him that Rahula would succeed at the university and be different from the majority of those "put through the mill of higher education in a colony" (Ludowyk, p. 133). "As a student, Rahula identified himself with everything in which he, as a *bhikkhu,* could share. I remember his contesting student elections and organizing student meetings. He wanted equally keenly to know about various things from which as a *bhikkhu* he had been excluded" (ibid.). Rahula not only read Chaucer and Shakespeare with zest, he was also smuggled into dress rehearsals of the University Dramatic Society. (His public appearance in a theatrical performance would constitute the breaking of a rule of monastic discipline and would have shocked orthodox Buddhists). In 1934–35, when the country was ravaged by a serious epidemic of malaria, Rahula joined other university students in relief work (and did not on occasion allow the rule of not eating a meal after noontime to take priority over his relief work). (Many years later in the 1950s, when he conducted his research in Paris in association with Professor Demiéville, he devised a distinctive clothing of trousers and cap to withstand the cold and sometimes relaxed the rule regarding meals, thereby again demonstrating that he would not allow conventional rules to obstruct the pursuit of more worthwhile and serious goals.) Rahula left the university with an honors degree in Indo-Aryan studies and as an accredited master of Pali literature.

I would highlight two aspects of the career of Rahula as monk: on the one side as a masterly scholar in Buddhist studies and on the other as a propagandist and activist on behalf of a Buddhist society and state. Both orientations and activities were interwoven no doubt, but they also probably caused discontinuities and changes of course in his career and prevented a consistent progress toward a commanding summit.

In 1943, Rahula proceeded to the University of Calcutta on a Ceylon government scholarship for postgraduate research, and there worked under the direction of two renowned scholars, S. N. Das Gupta, a great Sanskritist, and B. M. Barua, both of whom he considered his gurus and regarded with the greatest veneration and affection. His sojourn in Calcutta was crucial for Rahula's intellectual and political development. Calcutta seemed to have the same kind of stimulating effect on Rahula that it had previously on Anagarika Dharmapala. Rahula returned to Sri Lanka in 1945. On the one hand his academic career prospered. He was appointed a senior teacher at Vidyalankara Pirivena, one of the two leading monastic colleges, and also to the posts of academic secretary of the College and secretary general of the Governing Body. He worked on his doctoral thesis for the University of Ceylon, and it was later published in 1956 as *The History of Buddhism in Ceylon*. This book treated the grand theme of the relationship between the *sangha* and the Sinhalese kingdom and foregrounded the focal role of the *bhikkhu* in the public affairs of ancient Ceylon, a theme he propagandized in his 1946 tract.

But he was also thoroughly involved in politics:

> he actively supported the working-class movement and workers' strikes and found himself in the remand jail in Colombo, confined there for three days . . . [in 1947]. He encouraged Buddhist monks, allegedly in keeping with their ancient historical tradition, to leave their secluded life of leisure in monasteries and to devote their energies for "the good of the many, for the happiness of the many." It was during this period that, in reply to his critics as well as a manifesto for his movement, Rahula published *Bhiksuvage Urumaya* (1946), which became a manual not only for young monks but also for young social workers and politicians. (Mallawarachchi, p. viii)

Rahula campaigned actively on behalf of the strikers in 1946 and 1947 and the leftist candidates in the general election of 1947, and he was critical of the independence the colonial rulers had bequeathed to a wealthy and Westernized elite. Ludowyk writes: "I remember him on public platforms, dilating scornfully on independence of this kind. He and the other *bhikkhus* associated with him were intemperately abused as being 'political bhikkhus.' Four hundred years of colonial rule had abstracted the *bhikkhu* in the popular imagination from the world of his time and transformed him into the counterpart of the Trappist monk" (pp. 136–37). Rahula enjoyed the challenge of debate and political controversy, and it was in the midst of holding mass meetings that he hurriedly wrote the *Bhiksuvage Urumaya*.

Rahula left for Paris in 1950 to take up a scholarship at the Sorbonne offered him by Professor Demiéville. He immersed himself in studies and worked with Demiéville on the Tibetan and Chinese versions of the philosophy of Asanga. But he returned to Ceylon in 1966 to take up the vice-chancellorship of Vidyodaya University. But resisting and objecting to bureaucratic encroachment of political authorities on academic appointments and competence, he resigned his vice-chancellorship in 1969 and returned to Europe. Thereafter he would make much appreciated academic visits to the United States and hold a professorship at Northwestern University. He is now living in virtual retirement in London and continuing his scholarly work.

In the introduction of the second Sinhala edition of this tract Rahula recounts the circumstances under which he composed it.

> In early January 1946, the Hon. D. S. Senanayake, the first Prime Minister of Ceylon, and some others voiced the opinion that Buddhist monks should not participate in public affairs. . . . On January 26, 1946, at a public meeting held in Prince College, Kotahena, by way of an open public reply, I explained the fallacy of the view of Mr. Senanayake and his followers. The English as well as Sinhala-language newspapers carried a large number of letters and editorials for and against it. Some of the chief monks supported the position of the wealthy and the powerful and even went to the extent of issuing ecclesiastical injunctions through the media prohibiting the participation of *bhikkhus* in political activities.
>
> The difference of opinion in the country was so great that the Vidyalankara Pirivena . . . deemed it necessary to make a declaration on the subject. Thus, on February 13, 1946, the famous Vidyalankara declaration entitled "Bhikkhus and Politics" was issued. It stated that it was nothing but fitting for *bhikkhus* to identify themselves with activities conducive to the welfare of the people—whether these activities be labeled politics or not—as long as the activity did not impede the religious life of a *bhikkhu*. (Pp. xix–xx)

A few days later, a public meeting of *bhikkhus* held at the Buddhist Theosophical Society headquarters in Colombo resolved that *bhikkhus* alone should determine their course of action and that it was improper for laymen to interfere.

After this, public debate became more intense. *Bhikkhus* and laymen, Rahula said, divided into two camps, "progressive" and "reactionary." "There was hardly an issue on which so many letters and articles were written in the newspapers or so many public meetings held in this country" (p. xx). Then on March 9, 1946, at a public meeting at Kandy, Rahula "gave a detailed academic exposition of the issue in a long speech," which became the basis for the tract published in 1946 under the title *Bhiksuvage Urumaya*.

Rahula asserted that "the great reawakening of the *bhikkhus* and laymen regarding current religious, social, economic, and political problems" was in large part made possible by the Eksath Bhiksu Mandalaya (United Bhikkhu Council), which was instituted in May 1946 for that purpose, and of which Rahula himself became the first secretary general as the prime mover and founder. He illuminatingly remarks that "As a result of this movement two important expressions with deep meaning and historical significance—'*Bhikkhu* Politics' and 'Political *Bhikkhu*'—found their way into current Buddhist literature" (p. xxii). He ends with the flourish that *bhikkhus*, who are the "sons of the Buddha," altruistic, bold, upright, and honest, who work for the benefit of the common man, should hereafter be regarded as "political bhikkhus."

In the first part of *The Heritage of the Bhikkhu*, Rahula shows his virtuosity as a scholar to support with references from the Pali canonical *suttas* and from commentaries his assertion that "the Buddha and the *bhikkhus* taught important ideas pertaining to health, sanitation, earning wealth, mutual relationships, well-being of society, and righteous government—all for the good of the people" (p. 6). The references are well known to Buddhist scholars and they are marshalled to argue the point that Buddhism carries the message of social service to others.

Regarding the evolution of the discipline of the *bhikkhus*, the holding of the first three councils to clarify sectarian differences which were themselves evidence of the wide spread of Buddhism, Rahula locates the endpoint of this trajectory in Ceylon as the time when Buddhism became "the national religion of the Sinhala people" so that it is not possible anymore to separate "nationalism" and "natural culture" from "religion" itself—hence his use of expressions such as "religio-nationalism," "religio-patriotism," and the like. The burden of Rahula's exposition of Sri Lankan history as evidenced in chronicles, such as the *Mahavamsa, Dipavamsa,* and the later chronicles, and commentaries, is to give numerous examples of the great contribution made by Buddhist monks to the development of Sinhala civilization, culture, art, and literature during the early and medieval times until the arrival of the Western powers. All of a piece with this panegyric is Rahula's highlighting of the shift among monks toward the vocation of learning and scholarship (*gantha-dhura*) in preference to the vocation of meditation (*vipassana-dhura*). Even more important, Rahula marshalls examples to establish that time and again monks participated in the politics of the country—settling court and succession disputes, sometimes actively selecting a candidate and conferring kingship on him, and even marching to war as in the time of Dutthagamani. "Custodians of freedom" on every occasion of danger to both nation and religion, the monks came forward to save and protect them. This comment by Rahula will resonate well into the latter part of the twentieth century: "The religio-patriotism at that time assumed such overpowering proportions that both *bhikkhus* and laymen considered that even killing people in order to liberate the religion and the country was not a heinous crime" (p. 21).

It is the last third of the book that is both innovative and compelling, polemical and controversial dialogue-provoking as an original distinctive understanding of the enervating and castrating effect of foreign, especially British, rule upon the *sangha* and the vocation and public position of the monk in society. Under British subjugation monks headed the rebellions of 1818, 1834, and 1848. What the British soon became aware of was that a close identification and solidarity existed between the laity and the *sangha* and that *this unity between them had to be severed* if they were to gain control and rule peacefully. So Rahula proposes a conspiracy theory of divide and rule and illustrates the strategies used by successive governors—Maitland, Torrington, Brownrigg—dedicated to the aim of Christianizing the country and weakening the hold of Buddhism. He claims that they set out to cultivate their own "quisling" monks, dispense acts of appointment to high office to monks on pain of loyalty to the raj, and deliberately weaken the institutional structure of the *sangha* by withdrawing protection of temple properties. The innovative part of these charges is that while on the one hand the Christian missionaries displaced and appropriated the educational, social, and welfare activities of the monks, they also indoctrinated the children of the elite Sinhala families to look down upon and despise Sinhala culture, language, and literature. These attitudes took root *not only among the Christian converts but also among the high-status Sinhala Buddhist families.*

Thus, as the position of the *bhikkhus* deteriorated—a deterioration quickened by the monks' inability to participate in and adapt to the new changes and to new knowledge—"they were rendered useless to society. . . . They had no plan of action. Their word was no more respected. Laymen had nothing to learn from them. Therefore, laymen—particularly those of the upper class—dissociated themselves from *bhikkhus* and the bond between the laity and the clergy declined" (p. 91).

"Thus the *bhikkhu*, circumscribed both with regard to personality and education, was by force of circumstance driven to limit his activities to the recitation of the *Suttas* (*Pirit* chanting), preaching a sermon, attendance at funeral rites and alms-giving in memory of the departed, and to an idle cloistered life in the temple" (p. 91).

It was thus that "the wealthy Sinhalese of the upper classes" who were associated with "the western Christian environment . . . neither understand *bhikkhus* nor do they realize the national services performed or performable by these *bhikkhus*. Brought up according to the teachings of missionaries, they believe that *bhikkhus* should keep out of national activities and limit themselves only to receiving alms, chanting *pirit*, performing funeral rites and preaching sermons. They believe that *bhikkhus* should live a life limited to the four walls of their temples. They do not realize that the nation and the religion have to move together" (p. 95).

In his introduction to Rahula's tract, Edmund F. Perry highlights what I take to be Rahula's most innovative and arguable thesis that served as a potent irritant and as an inspiring charter to monks dedicated to restoring the *sangha* to its alleged former relevance.

> The image of the Buddhist monk as a public leader engaging in social and political activities has been obscured, deliberately so, by Western colonialists and their accompanying Christian missionaries. By imposing a particular type of Christian monasticism upon Buddhist clergy, restricting the clergy's activity to individual purification and temple ministries, the colonial administrators dispossessed the *bhikkhus* of their influence on the public life of their people, and actually succeeded in instituting a tradition of Buddhist recluses, to the near exclusion of other types of clergy. (P. xii)

6 The Betrayal of Buddhism: Report of the Committee of Inquiry

The professional and vocational backgrounds of the members of the Committee of Inquiry who wrote *The Betrayal of Buddhism* are instructive. The committee had seven Buddhist monks, six of whom could be identified as "scholar-monks," most of them active as vice-principals or senior teachers at *pirivenas* (monastic colleges). The country's most famous *pirivenas,* such as Vidyodaya, Vidyalankara, and Balagalla, and the major sects, Siyam, Amarapura, and Ramanna Nikayas, were represented.[1]

1. Here are some details about the bhikkhu members of the committee:
    1. Ambanvalle Siddharta, deputy chief priest (*anunayaka*) of Malvatta chapter, Kandy, a conservative monk of the Siyam Nikaya, was chosen for diplomatic reasons to represent one wing of the establishment.
    2. Saliyale Sumanatissa was deputy chief priest of Asgiriya chapter, of the Siyam Nikaya, Kandy, a scholar-monk, and principal of Asgiriya Pirivena. In his later career, he was a staunch supporter of the Sri Lanka Freedom party, and a proponent of the thesis that monks should adapt themselves to changing circumstances. He, too, was chosen for diplomatic reasons to represent the other wing of the establishment.
    3. Palannoruve Vimaladhamma, vice-principal of the Vidyodaya Pirivena (later became principal) and a scholar-monk of the Siyam Nikaya, subsequently became a supporter of the United National party.
    4. Balangoda Ananda Maitreya, scholar-monk of the Amarapura sect, was at this time a supporter of the Sri Lanka Freedom party. He may have been associated with Mrs. Bandaranaike's family as lay patrons in Balangoda; later he became the first chief priest (*mahanayake*) of the federated Amarapura sect (a consolidation of five subsects).
    5. Pandita Sri Hisselle Nanaloka, vice-principal of the Balagalla Sarasvati Pirivena, belonged to the Ramanna sect and later became a SLFP supporter.
    6. Kotahena Pannakitti, vice-principal of the Vidyalankara Pirivena, Siyam Nikaya affiliation, and a scholar-monk, was sympathetic to views of the Vidyalankara activist monks. He went to Benares University to further Sanskrit and Pali studies. He held left-wing views and was editor of *Kalaya,* the organ of activist monks; as a polemicist he was equal in importance to Walpola Rahula.

30

The lay members of the committee numbered seven, and three of them were well-known educators. They were G. P. Malalasekera, professor of Pali and Buddhist civilization, dean of the Faculty of Oriental Studies at Peradeniya University, who served at the height of his career as president of the All Ceylon Buddhist Congress and, later, as president of the World Buddhist Congress; P. de S. Kularatne, at one time principal of Ananda College, the most famous of the Buddhist schools in the island, and later manager of the Buddhist Theosophical Society schools; and L. H. Mettananda, a strong critic of the Catholic Church and its activities and also an important educator associated with BTS schools: he served as principal of Dharmaraja College in Kandy before becoming the head of the premier Ananda College.[2]

The Betrayal of Buddhism, composed by this Committee of Inquiry which explicitly pleaded a cause, must be seen as reflecting the views of some of the island's foremost Buddhist scholars and educators, both clerical and lay. It should come as no surprise that their cause concerned the system of education in the country, especially in the nineteenth and twentieth centuries, and the consequences of that system for Sinhala Buddhists as the majority category in the population.

The most eminent of these educators with an international reputa-

---

7. Madihe Pannasiha, after serving on the committee, became chief priest (*mahanayake*) of the Amarapura sect (rotational position), a federation of five subsects. He had strong Buddhist nationalist and anti-Catholic views and was head of an Amarapura sect linked to Durava caste interests.

I am indebted to H. L. Seneviratne and Sarath Amunugama for this information.

2. Malalasekera inaugurated the World Fellowship of Buddhists in Colombo in 1950. The remaining lay members of the Committee of Inquiry were:

1. D. C. Wijewardena (Vijayawardhana), author of *Dharma-Vijaya, or The Revolt in the Temple,* was conservative. His family was associated with the Lake House Press and had connections as lay patrons of the Kelaniya Temple (Siyam Nikaya). His wife, Vimala, served for a while as minister of health in the 1956 SLFP government. The chief priest of Kelaniya Temple at this time was Buddharakhita, who would become a leading member of the Eksath Bhikkhu Peramuna. Buddharakhita was later incriminated in the assassination of Prime Minister Bandaranaike.

2. T. Vimalananda was lecturer in history at the University of Ceylon, Peradeniya, in 1950. Later he became professor of archaeology at Vidyalankara University. He was a disciple and protégé of Anagarika Dharmapala, pro-Kandyan vis-à-vis the low country Sinhalese.

3. C. de S. Siriwardhane, a lawyer and lecturer at the Law College, has written on Buddhist temporalities.

4. T. B. Ellepola was a retired government officer, of Kandyan aristocratic status; he resigned before the report was written.

tion was Malalasekera, whose social origins, educational history, and professional career are noteworthy by comparison with Bhikkhu Walpola Rahula's. Whereas Rahula started his journey from small-scale landed peasantry and village origins, then traversed the monastic educational system, and used it to the fullest before making the leap into the secular university networks and international cosmopolitan scholarship, Malalasekera's upward mobility starts from a better-positioned traditional Sinhala urban background associated with the rising "middle class" of the western coastal region and the heart of Buddhist revivalism since the 1860s. His father was a successful ayurvedic physician in the town of Panadura, south of Colombo.

A laudatory obituary notice says that Malalasekera was in his formative years "greatly influenced by his father who was a storehouse of traditional learning and culture" and who "was conversant with Sanskrit, Pali, Sinhala, and Buddhism." The father imparted this knowledge "to his intelligent son, while he drove him to school in his ox-drawn cart and back." Moreover, the young scholar accompanied his father when the latter visited learned monks, who "no doubt kindled in him the spark of patriotism."[3]

At the same time the father and son seem to have realized which educational opportunities to seize in a colonial society. Malalasekera had his secondary education in that town in English and Sinhalese in a Protestant school called St. John's College. He came to the university following his father's wishes in order to study medicine but found his true interests in oriental studies (especially Pali language and literature) under the guidance of I. B. Horner. He changed his name from George Perera to Gunapala Piyasena. After a spell of teaching at Ananda College in 1923, he proceeded to London for his doctoral studies at the School of Oriental and African Studies and became an eminent Pali scholar. On his return to Ceylon—and this is noteworthy— Malalasekera became involved with the English-teaching Buddhist schools established by the Buddhist Theosophical Society: he served as the principal of Nalanda College before he was recruited to the faculty of University College in 1939, and when the University of Ceylon was created in 1942, he was appointed professor of Pali and Buddhist civilization and dean of the Faculty of Oriental Studies. Malalasekera,

3. N. A. Jayawickrama and W. G. Weeraratne, *The World Fellowship of Buddhists and Its Founder President G. P. Malalasekera* (Colombo: World Fellowship of Buddhists, 1982).

while an advocate of Buddhist and Sinhala nationalist causes, was politically not a radical; he was no supporter of the activist "political *bhikkhu*"; his form of liberalism could consort comfortably with the liberal wings of the SLFP and the UNP and his life illustrates a selective assimilation of Western influences and ideas and a rejection of those that subordinated Buddhism.

Malalasekera was actively involved with the All Ceylon Buddhist Congress and served as its president for 19 consecutive years, from 1939 to 1957. The very year that Bandaranaike came to power in 1956, Malalasekera was appointed ambassador to the Soviet Union. This was the beginning of a diplomatic career that removed him from active involvement in local politics and lasted until 1967, when he returned to Sri Lanka. He was conspicuous at international conferences on Buddhism where his oratorical skills were impressively displayed. It might be said that Malalasekera's most important contributions to the cause of Sinhala Buddhist nationalism were made before his diplomatic career began, for example, as a member of the Commission on Higher Education in Swabasha (1954) and the Official Languages Commission (1956) and as spokesman for the All Ceylon Buddhist Congress.

The Report

The report *The Betrayal of Buddhism* begins with a tragic sketch and beleaguered view of Sinhala Buddhist history. This historical sense of being in constant danger, even of being overrun by hostile external forces, whether Tamil invaders from South India or, later, Western colonial powers, is a world view that reveals the Sinhalese people by and large to be a majority with a minority complex. Buddhism, the special treasure of the island, has always been endangered and has been in steady decline since the glorious time of "the three great kings," Devanampiya Tissa, who received Buddhism from Emperor Asoka, Dutthagamani, who defeated Elara the Tamil king and united the island (Anuradhapura period), and Parakrama Bahu I, who unified the island and was the hero of the Polonnaruwa period. After them the island's history has been one of decline with the successive inroads made by the Portuguese, then the Dutch, and finally the British. It is because of this steady decline in religion, culture, and political autonomy that there is the need for a "restoration" in the period of independence.

The Betrayal of Buddhism in essence made two major comparisons between the status of the Christian missions and of the Buddhist *sangha* in Sri Lanka, especially during the British period (1796–1948) and in the first years of independence.

One comparison portrays the missions as having an effective organizational structure as corporations and enjoying special immunities and privileges from the raj in order to pursue their activities; the Buddhist *sangha* on the other hand was fragmented and suffered in addition from certain limitations which restricted their activities. The second comparison, closely related to the first, focuses on the successful educational (and proselytizing) activities of the Protestant missions, which had highly favorable relations with the colonial government throughout, and the Roman Catholic Church in more recent times. By comparison, the educational activities of the Buddhist *sangha* enjoyed little support from the British, and Buddhist Sinhalese schools were minuscule in number compared with the Christian schools on the one hand and the Buddhist Sinhala majority population on the other. The report's conclusion and exhortation was as follows: "Education in Ceylon today should be oriented towards the bringing forth of a generation with an intimate awareness of its national language, history and culture and capable of enriching that national heritage" (p. 92).

The report submitted two basic remedies for the two major disabilities suffered by Buddhism by comparison with Christianity. One remedy was that the government should pass a Buddha Sasana Act by which it "would create an incorporated Buddha Sasana Council to which may be entrusted all the prerogatives of the Buddhist kings as regards the Buddhist religion." (The Buddhist kings of the past in collaboration with the *sangha* regulated the religion and periodically purified it [*sasanavisodhana*]). The proposed council, composed of elected and appointed representatives of the *sangha* and the laity, would act as "a centralized authority" to prevent the disintegration of Buddhism in the face of competition from hostile Christian missions. Because of past colonial confiscations of *sangha* properties, temple lands, and income, a yearly sum of money should be given to the council as compensation in order to conduct educational activities on behalf of the *sangha*. Furthermore, the government should appoint a minister for religious affairs who would act "to rehabilitate the religions which had suffered under Colonial rule."

The second major remedy proposed had as its purpose the withdrawal of grants in aid to Christian mission schools (and other "assisted schools") and the subsequent takeover of all assisted schools by the state. In due course the control and administration of schools should be transferred to central and local government agencies. The same policy of state takeover should be applied to all teacher-training colleges. The logic of the approval of state takeover of all schools and teacher-training colleges was that the monopoly of English education enjoyed by Christian mission schools, and the advantage over other religions enjoyed by Christian teachers' colleges, would be taken away. The Buddhist activists did not mind at all the government takeover of Buddhist schools, because they were advocates of religious education to be imparted in state schools and were confident that government policy would favor the transmission of Buddhist values, Sinhalese language and literature, and "traditional culture."

The Buddhist activists did not balk at arguing for special affirmative action on behalf of Buddhism and the *sangha* in future state action, thereby opening themselves to criticism from the religious bodies that were excluded from favored treatment.

One thing was clear about the tenor and the emphasis, to the point of obsession, of the report: its anger, condemnation, and deep hostility toward the Christian missions, mainly for the control they had over the island's educational system. It seems to me that the Sri Lankan Buddhist concern for control of education probably surpasses the attitudes Hindus have expressed in India and may be traced partly to the fact that in Sri Lanka (as in Burma, another Theravada Buddhist country) the *sangha* was always implicated in the education not only of monks and novices but also of lay children and had in its ranks the literati who composed famous commentaries and chronicles, in fact the main body of literature in Pali and Sinhalese. Both countries, with their tradition of temple schools for lay children and *pirivenas* for monks, have had in precolonial times higher literacy rates than most regions of India.

British colonial law created two classes of religious bodies: The Christians with their missions and school boards, enjoyed a "fully autonomous status" not available to them even in their home countries, whereas Buddhist, Hindu, and Muslim bodies were kept in a subordinate status. The report alleged that "all Christian religious bodies are incorporated and that they have the fullest powers as regards property. . . . These bodies may engage in trade, agriculture and industry, run schools, orphanages, undertake colonization schemes and acquire wealth without limit; and in fact they do all these things" (pp. 19–20). In contrast to such unsupervised autonomy and freedom given the Christian bodies, each Buddhist temple was separately administered, and the public trustee supervised the expenditure of its income, and forbade the use of revenue "for political purposes." Moreover, the acquisition of property by Buddhist institutions was subject to the rules of mortmain (a license had to be obtained before a bequest or gift of land could be obtained and placed in charitable trust), but the Christian bodies were exempted from these rules and could acquire property at will.

In the sphere of education, the immunities, grants, and patronage heaped on the Protestant missions were highlighted by the report. The arrival dates of the main sects were Baptists in 1812, Wesleyans in 1814, the American Mission in 1816, and Anglicans in 1818. In the 1820s was formed the Ecclesiastical Department, whose members were missionaries headed by the colonial chaplain who was also the principal of schools. In the late twenties and thirties education in Ceylon was developed in close relationship with this department. "In 1827, 96 Government schools were controlled by Christian ministers"; while mission schools proliferated, the government, the report alleges, showed no interest in the Buddhist temple schools.

When, in the 1830s, there was a change in educational policy following recommendations by the Colebrooke Commission and emphasis was placed on the founding of English schools in order to produce a supply of minor administrators and clerks, the School Commission, set up to implement the policy, was entrusted to the archdeacon of Colombo as the president and to ministers from various Christian missions. The Central School Commission, which took its place in 1842, was packed with Christian ministers but no Buddhist, Hindu, or Muslim was included. (The number of English schools rose from 38 in 1841 to 60 in 1848).

The most powerful accusations made by the report can be reduced to two. On the one hand the management of schools founded as state schools throughout the nineteenth century, especially the English schools, were placed in the hands of Christian ministers, who drew government salaries, which in turn added to the funds of the missions.

Moreover, all schools established as private schools were eligible on the basis of results to receive grants-in-aid as "assisted schools," and the vast majority of those schools considered eligible were Christian mission schools. For example, until 1879 every grant-in-aid school was a Christian school, and in 1899 out of a total of 1172 grant-in-aid schools, fewer than a hundred were Buddhist institutions.

The implications of this situation, as viewed by the Buddhist educators who wrote *The Betrayal of Buddhism* in 1956, were intolerable: the school system, both state and private, was managed and run by Christians, who contributed the majority of teachers in schools, and shaped the educational policy and the content of education; these schools admitted a large number of Christian students, who were represented disproportionately among those being educated; the largest number in the school-going population, the Buddhists, had both lesser access and were, if admitted, exposed to Christian proselytization and left without adequate instruction in their own language.

The Buddhists began to correct such imbalances with energy and some success only after 1880 with the arrival of Olcott in the island to found the Buddhist Theosophical Society, whose main purpose was to set up Buddhist schools and publish texts and teaching materials. The success of the Buddhist revival movement, though notable and important, was gradual. The Board of Education Council set up in 1891 had only one Buddhist member; and in 1900 the strength of Christian control of schools can be gauged by the fact that 1,117 of 1,328 grant-in-aid schools were Christian controlled. At that time there existed only 500 government schools.

It was only "after the 1931 reforms [of the Donoughmore Constitution], when a majority of Buddhist members were in the State Council, that the number of State schools rapidly increased" (p. 60). According to the Buddhist activists, it was The Free Education Act of 1947 that constituted the first successful action on the part of government "to free education from the stronghold of the missionaries." By this act the state undertook the payment of teachers and forbade the levying of fees in state or state-aided schools.

But the report concluded that there was still much left to be done, for from their point of view "the only educational system which would be equitable to all religious sects would be for the State to take over all schools" (p. 83). As we shall see that step would take another decade.

The Views of a Sinhala Buddhist Lay Activist

The book *Dharma-Vijaya, or The Revolt in the Temple*[4] ends with the statement that it was composed by D. C. Vijayawardhana "to commemorate 2,500 years of Buddhism, of civilization in Lanka, and of the Sinhalese Nation that came into being with the Buddha's blessing" (p. 676).

---

4. *Dharma-Vijaya, or The Revolt in the Temple:* Composed to Commemorate 2500 years of the Land, the Race, and the Faith (Colombo: Sinha Publications, 1953).

Don Charles Vijayawardhana (Wijewardena) was one of seven sons born to Muhandiram Don Philip Wijayawardena, who made his fortune in the latter part of the nineteenth century as a merchant of timber, bricks, and river sand for the construction of buildings in Colombo and the breakwater in the port of Colombo. D. C. Wijayawardena's mother, Helena, was the daughter of Arnolis Dep, a prosperous arrack renter of the late nineteenth century. The liquor trade laid the foundation for later Buddhist piety. She contributed liberally to the restoration of the historic temple at Kelaniya, Raja Maha Vihara, the site of important religious and political activity in our time. D. C.'s brother, Don Richard, became Ceylon's most important newspaper magnate, and his Lake House published, among others, the *Daily News* in English and the *Dinamina* in Sinhalese.[5] D. C. did not become a public figure of similar stature, but he continued, together with another brother Don Walter, the parental interest in the Kelaniya temple and in Buddhist affairs.

D. C. Wijayawardena served as a member of the Buddhist Committee of Inquiry, which published *The Betrayal of Buddhism* in 1956. Therefore, *The Revolt in the Temple* reflects some themes and assertions to be found in *The Betrayal*. On the one hand, D. C. asserts a strongly nationalist position—that the island was primordially destined as a land that united Buddhism with the Sinhalese nation; and on the other hand, he generously peppers his eclectic text with morsels of Western philosophy, history, poetry, and other intellectual tidbits he had collected in the course of a colonial style "public school" education in English followed by studies in England. The book's insistent denunciation of Marxism and the left as inimical to the island's religious and spiritual welfare stems from this legacy.

His nationalist thesis is contained in this synoptic historical sketch:

> Throughout their history, the stimulus to action, for the Sinhalese, was the ideology that they were a nation brought into being for the definite purpose of carrying, "for full five thousand years", the torch lit by the "Guide of the World" twenty-five centuries ago; and the structure of Sinhalese society has been shaped in pursuance of this ideology. Buddhism was the State Religion. The chosen king was always a Buddhist, and the people supported

---

5. See H. A. J. Hulugalle, *The Life and Times of D. R. Wijewardena* (Colombo: Lake House, 1960), p. 60.

him with wholehearted loyalty, because he, as the chief
citizen of the country, was the leader in shaping and sus-
taining their ideology, and the protector of the national
faith. *The temple became the centre from which radiated
learning, arts, and culture. The Sangha were the guides of
the king's conscience and the mentors of the people,
whose joys they shared and whose sorrows they assuaged.*
(P. 513; emphasis added)

The theme of the supremacy of Buddhism as state religion, maintained and guaranteed by kingship (a "royalist" thesis), is the premise
which legitimated the Buddhist nationalist "historical" assertion that
the religion that went into decline under foreign colonial rule must be
restored to its former position.

A second theme in the book is italicized in the above quotation, and
it provides the key to the book's curious title. *Dharma-Vijaya* means
"triumph of righteousness"; it does not mean literally "the revolt in the
temple." The phrase "the revolt in the temple" does not refer to sectarian struggles within the *sangha* or to popular rebellions sponsored
by the *sangha* but to the theme that the *sangha* and its monks had always played throughout the island's history a *political* role in order to
ensure the peace, prosperity, and welfare of the country. This theme of
the rightful participation of the monks in politics was, as I have stated
before, already proposed by the Vidyalankara monks. Thus the author
of the foreword to *The Revolt in the Temple*, Rev. Pahamune Sri
Sumangala, cites many references in the *Mahavamsa* (the fifth-
century A.D. chronicle composed by the monks of the orthodox Mahavihara fraternity) confirming the *sangha*'s participation in politics:
some examples are the monks' causing the reconciliation between
King Dutthagamani and his estranged brother Tissa, and between
Parakrama Bahu and his cousin Gajabahu in the twelfth century; the
election of certain kings "with the consent of the Sangha"; the be-
stowal of kingship on certain kings by the Sangha composed of the
eight chief *viharas;* and so forth. Sumangala thus concludes: "our national chronicles have recorded for posterity the manner in which the
Sangha of old not only wielded influence in the election, coronation,
and conduct of kings and sub-kings, but also, whenever the occasion
arose, directed and actively participated in the work of the emancipa-
tion of the country and its people."

Wijayawardena, making the same claim, asserts: "The discharge of
this dual responsibility, that of acting as the religious as well as social

guides of the Sinhalese, is, in terms of the last words of the Master on his deathbed, a service which devolves even today on the 'Sangha of Lanka' " (p. 17). "The claim of the Sangha today to be heard in relation to social, political and economic problems and to guide the people is . . . but a reassertion of a right universally exercised and equally widely acknowledged, up to the British occupation of the country" (p. 19). *The Revolt in the Temple* is relevant not because of its originality but because its reiterates themes already enunciated by Walpola Rahula and other activist monks. Wijayawardena is an example of the wealthy educated Buddhist layman who championed the cause of Buddhist restoration.

The Accuracy of the Charges

The reader may want to know how "objective" the main charges made by the Buddhist Committee of Inquiry were and whether they can be sustained by testing them against other kinds of evidence. In the appendix I comment on the "factuality" of the charges made with regard to two main issues: first, the policies of the British raj with regard to grant-in-aid schools that acted to favor the already established schools of the Christian missions and to hinder the founding of Buddhist schools; and second the restrictions that were placed on the maximal use of profits and incomes deriving from Buddhist temple properties.

As documented in the appendix, the first charge of favoring the entrenched Christian mission schools is largely true. But the second charge is largely misplaced, because what emerges is that the Buddhist temporalities placed in the hands of Sinhala Buddhist trustees, both monk-incumbents and lay officials, were mostly inefficiently managed or subject to corrupt practices. Poor maintenance of temples and monasteries was also in evidence. Moreover, efforts by the colonial government to "rationalize" their management were largely obstructed by these trustees and incumbents. In the postindependence era, as we shall see, those branches of the *sangha,* which have land endowments, have strictly resisted the management of Buddhist temporalities by a single national *sasana* council. So this aspect of the Buddhist Committee of Inquiry's program for reform would be stifled. However, it is the committee's call for action against the advantages enjoyed by Christian mission schools and for the government's sponsorship of Buddhist education that will be honored in time. Both the success and failure of the committee's proposals have much to teach us about the contradictions and differential interests that are at play within the clerical and lay institutions and constituencies of Sri Lankan Buddhism.

7 The Social Revolution of 1956 and Its Aftermath

The year 1956 was historic, because it saw the political success of Sinhala Buddhist nationalism, which had remained latent for some time and began to gain momentum in the early fifties. There was a confluence of many concerns and aspirations which had a cumulative effect upon the elections held at this date. These concerns were the rehabilitation and restoration of Buddhism to its precolonial status; the shift from the English language as medium of administration (official language) and education to indigenous mother tongues, especially Sinhalese; and the fostering by the Sinhalese of their national identity and their national culture.

More immediately, the year 1956 was one of great expectations because it would be the time for staging the celebration of Buddha Jayanthi (as marking 2500 years since the death of the Buddha, and the landing of Vijaya the first Sinhalese, together with his band of followers, in Sri Lanka). The UNP government had appointed a body called the Lanka Bauddha Mandalaya to plan the celebrations and to initiate projects for the compilation and translation of religious texts. There was much "politics" surrounding the nomination of members to this body.

In the preceding years certain recommendations had been made by the All Ceylon Buddhist Congress (ACBC). One was that the government should protect and maintain Buddhism and Buddhist institutions. Proposals were also made for the creation of a Buddha Sasana department and for the appointment of a Buddhist commission to inquire into the state of Buddhism.

The ACBC, shunning government sponsorship, appointed its own Buddhist Committee of Inquiry which produced on the eve of the 1956 elections the explosive report called *The Betrayal of Buddhism*. Finally on the question of official language(s), there was adverse commentary on the UNP's vacillation regarding the declaration of Sinhalese as the *only* official language.

All those issues led to the defeat of the UNP in the fateful elections of 1956, when that party's monopoly of power since independence came to a traumatic end.

The developments that I particularly want to highlight which ultimately contributed to the overthrow of the UNP and the success of the MEP (headed by S. W. R. D. Bandaranaike, leader of the SLFP) are organizational and mobilizational at the grass-roots level, involving both Buddhist monks and laity.

Noteworthy are the efforts of a civil servant, N. Q. Dias, who first launched a Buddhist movement among the government administrative officers. He—together with a monk, Gnanasiha Thero—launched in Sabaragamuwa Province what came to be called Buddha Sasana Samiti, which were societies formed to look after the *bhikkhus'* needs, to manage *dhamma* schools, etc. These societies then caught on and spread all over the country (3,500 in the mid-fifties). Thereafter Dias, operating from Colombo, in collaboration with L. H. Mettananda, principal of Ananda College, established associations of monks called sangha sabhas in many electorates (72 by 1954). The importance of these efforts is that central government officials and local government servants used their positions and their networks to organize associations of monks at the local level. The 72 *sabhas* formed the Sri Lanka Maha Sangha Sabha (SLMSS), a national Colombo-based aggregation.

The even more dramatic development that raised intensity just before the 1956 election was the formation of the Eksath Bhikkhu Peramuna (United Front of the Monks). This front was a potent combination of two monk organizations, namely, the SLMSS and the Samastha Lanka Bhikkhu Sammalanaya (SLBS) (All Ceylon Congress of Buddhists) whose members mostly belonged to the LEBM, the movement of "progressive monks" of the forties, which I described earlier.

We may note the geographical and sectarian representation of the EBP. Its leading lights were Colombo-based. The leaders and the majority of the membership came from the Amarapura and Ramanna Nikaya, the so-called reform sects which in the nineteenth century began in the southwest urban coastal areas. By contrast the establishment Siyam Nikaya, whose main chapters (Malvatta and Asgiriya) were located up country in Kandy, was largely unrepresented. However, its low-country chapter located in Kotte just outside Colombo and the monks of the historic and wealthy temple of Kelaniya, just outside Colombo, also belonging to the Siyam Nikaya, joined ranks with the EBP. Indeed the forceful politician-monk, Mapitigama Buddharakkhita, the head (*viharadhipati*) of the Kelaniya temple, would be in the forefront of the election campaign. (It was he too who would a few years later gain notoriety for being implicated in the assassination of Premier Bandaranaike.)

The EBP, fiercely anti-UNP, listed ten points that Buddhists should take into account in their voting: these included the willingness to implement the proposals in *The Betrayal of Buddhism*, to make Sinhala the only official language, and to support the implementation of democratic socialism. The EBP was anti-West, anti-Catholic, and anti-UNP. One of its slogans was "A vote for the UNP is a vote for the Catholics; a vote for the MEP is a vote for the Buddhists."

The EBP staged demonstrations to defer elections ("No elections before Jayanthi"). A fast by 250 monks at the doors of Parliament was a dramatic act that would be repeated later. The monks popularized and exploited the connotations of a famous episode called "Mara Yuddha," Mara's attack on Buddha at the point of his reaching enlightenment. They transposed its symbolism to modern times and painted the UNP, especially Prime Minister Kotelawela, as the enemy of Buddhists' interests. (This powerful symbol was immortalized in a famous cartoon-poster which held Kotelawela up to ridicule and poured contempt on him).[1]

The EBP monks, working through the network of local *sangha sabhas*, proved to be formidable and untiring election campaigners—making personal house-to-house visits and distributing pamphlets. It is said that between three thousand and four thousand monks—about a fourth of the national total—participated as campaign workers. Although the UNP did enlist on its side some establishment monks, even the leaders of first-rank *pirivenas*, who tried to prevent the monk-activists from electioneering, by and large their support was not effective. Thus, it is no exaggeration to claim that the 1956 election, which swept Bandaranaike and the MEP to power, was the climactic and sin-

1. The poster showed Sir John Kotelawela riding an elephant (the symbol of the UNP), pointing a spear at the seated Buddha (statue) under a Bo tree; at the back were persons in Western garb drinking and dancing; in the foreground was a calf killed and ready to be barbecued.

gular moment in twentieth-century political life, when a significant number of monks temporarily organized to win an election. Never again in the ensuing decades would the *sangha* show this much purpose and action. As Phadnis put it, the EBP's decisive contribution lay in "its role in the support mobilization of the Buddhists and in providing a country-wide Bhikkhu cadre to a party [the MEP] with very little organization and projecting its image as the party of the common man."[2] At the same time, we should be careful not to credit the EBP with a strong organizational structure that would provide the basis for systematic and long-term action.

The Turbulent Years 1956–58

In recent times, since independence, there have been many occurrences of mass violence and civilian riots. The majority of them have been in today's jargon labelled as ethnic conflicts of the kind where segments of the Sinhalese population have unleashed collective violence against the Tamils. The most destructive of these took place in 1958, 1977, 1981, and 1983.

There have been other kinds of civilian violence not directed at the Tamils as such. The most important of these was the insurrection in 1971 of Sinhalese youth, labeling their movement Janatha Vimukthi Peramuna (JVP), against the Sinhalese majority government at that time led by Premier Sirimavo Bandaranaike. It was fueled by the dissatisfactions felt by Sinhala youth mainly of rural origins against a Sinhala government for its failure to fulfill their aspirations. The same youth movement surfaced again in recent years and is dedicated to destabilizing the present UNP government. To its earlier dissatisfaction with the economic progress of the country and its espousal of radical populist, socialist goals, the movement has recently added two other causes, namely, the rejection of the presence of the Indian army in Sri Lanka and the refusal to concede any devolutionary concessions to the Tamils. Thus the JVP insurrectionists are now also implicated in the larger ethnic conflict between the Sinhalese and Tamils.

Recently, with the signing of the Indo–Sri Lanka Peace Accord in July 1987 and the presence of the Indian army in the northern and eastern provinces, demonstrations and rallies have been mounted in Colombo objecting to the presence of the alien enemy who the Sinhalese fear have imperial ambitions. In 1987 on the eve of the arrival of Rajiv

---

2. Urmila Phadnis, *Religion and Politics in Sri Lanka* (London: C. Hurst & Co., 1976), p. 187.

Gandhi in Colombo to sign the accord, civilian riots took place in Colombo as a protest.[3] These events will be covered in greater detail as my narration unfolds.

The Riots of 1956 and 1958

In the years immediately following the 1956 elections and the ushering in of an alleged "social revolution" dedicated to the restoration of Buddhism and the achievement by the Sinhalese of their due rights as a nation, there occurred two riots. To what extent can we say that revivalist Buddhism and the Buddhist component of Sinhalese nationalism, and within them the political activism of Buddhist monks, contributed to these violent outbursts?

The first piece of legislation submitted by the Bandaranaike government was to establish Sinhalese as the sole official language. The issue of contention was what role was to be assigned the Tamil language in the public affairs of the country. Certain concessions to the Tamils were considered, for example, allowing the opportunity for persons trained in English or Tamil to take examinations in those languages for entry into the public service, letting local bodies decide for themselves the language of their business, and giving persons the right to communicate with the government in their own language.

Wriggins describes the turmoil over the issue thus: "Such explicit legislative guarantees would have gone a long way to reassure the bulk of Tamils, but the reactions of extremists among the Tamils and the Sinhalese were decidedly unfavorable. A group of Buddhist *bhikkhus* connected with the Eksath Bhikkhu Peramuna protested against the inclusion of a clause permitting individuals who had been educated in English or Tamil to take public examinations in that language until 1967 and urged the government to press ahead more rapidly with language changes. Their rally on the steps of the house of representatives culminated in a fast by a prominent university lecturer."[4] The latter

---

3. In this listing of riots and insurrections I am leaving out of my account the impulsions and motivations behind the insurrection and the civil war begun and continued unabated since the 1970s by the Tamil militant youth, with a good measure of Tamil civilian support, against the Sri Lankan army (virtually Sinhalese in composition) and, after the Indo–Sri Lanka Peace Accord, against the Indian army. I am excluding the Tamil insurrection and its ideological components from consideration in this essay because I am primarily concerned with the nature of the involvement of Buddhism in recent politics and in the occurrence of civilian violence.

4. W. Howard Wriggins, *Dilemmas of a New Nation* (Princeton, N.J.: Princeton University Press, 1960), p. 260.

also opposed giving local bodies the right to decide the language of their business. "Antagonism became so great that a Tamil sit-down demonstration, near the house of representatives, called by the Federalist leader the day the controversial legislation was submitted to parliament, led to bitter riots in which over 100 people were injured. In a few days they spread to Eastern Province, where Tamils and Sinhalese lived intermingled; in Batticaloa and the Gal Oya Valley there was such violence that between 20 and 200 persons were killed, depending on which side was doing the tallying" (Wriggins, 1960, p. 261).

While about two hundred Tamil protesters, including leading politicians, staged a *satyagraha* on Galle Face Green to protest the Sinhala only bill, small bands of Sinhalese roamed through the city looting some shops and destroying a few vehicles. The next morning, more serious looting was perpetrated in the Pettah shopping zone. The official estimates of damage done during two days was 87 injuries to persons and 43 lootings of shops. Some 113 persons were arrested.

A few days later the riots spread to the eastern provinces where Tamils and Sinhalese lived intermingled. Violence and arson broke out in the town of Batticaloa, where a mass demonstration by about ten thousand Tamils was met with police firing resulting in at least two deaths.

But it was in the Gal Oya Valley, the site of the country's largest multipurpose development scheme including peasant resettlement, that violence broke out on a scale hitherto unknown and set the precedent for even more destructive violence two years later. James Manor writes, "Sinhalese toughs—inspired as always by fantastic rumors—seized government cars, bulldozers and high explosives and for a few days terrorized the Tamil minority in the colony. Scores of Tamils, certainly well over one hundred, were massacred and hundreds more were driven into hiding. The army was sent to quell disturbances."[5]

If one wonders what could be the relationship between the official language controversy and the ethnic violence taking place at this time in the eastern province, the answer is that around this time the language issue was also becoming interwoven with the government's policy of peasant resettlement in the less populous parts of the island. Just as the first issue had implications for the educational and employment prospects of the Tamils, so would the second be construed as causing

---

5. James Manor, *The Expedient Utopian: Bandaranaike and Ceylon* (Cambridge: Cambridge University Press, 1989), p. 262.

demographic changes in Sinhalese and Tamil (and Muslim) ethnic ratios in the eastern province and therefore as bearing on the politics of territorial control and of "homelands."

The 1956 riots did not delay the passing of the official language legislation (the Sinhala only bill): among all members present, the two main Sinhala parties, the MEP and the UNP voted for it, and the Tamil and leftist parties voted against it.

The 1958 riots were much more serious than those that had occurred two years previously. The slide to more acrimonious confrontation between the Tamils and Sinhalese was quick. While the government proceeded to translate the Sinhala only policy into action—such as reserving a leading teachers' training college for training Sinhalese teachers only, creating scholarships and distributing them on a quota basis six to one in favor of the Sinhalese—the Federal party in turn in June 1956 proclaimed its objective of establishing an "autonomous Tamil linguistic state within a Federal Union of Ceylon" in order to protect the cultural freedom and identity of the Tamil-speaking people. The Federal party, however, committed itself to nonviolent direct action (*satyagraha*) to achieve its goal of a federal union.

For a while it seemed as if Bandaranaike and the Tamil leaders would reach an understanding on two fronts: the reasonable use of Tamil, as the language of a minority, especially in the administration of the northern and eastern provinces; and the creation of regional councils to correct the overcentralization of the administration and to enable Tamils to exercise some measure of control over local affairs through devolution of powers. This was the substance of the famous Bandaranaike-Chelvanayagam pact, which might have settled the ethnic conflict. But it was precisely at this time that the Buddhist monk pressure groups, such as the Eksath Bhikkhu Peramuna and the Sri Lanka Sangha Sabha, in conjunction with their lay sponsors and allies, stepped up their protest against a surrender to Tamil demands and themselves threatened to conduct a *satyagraha* campaign unless the prime minister repudiated the agreement. A Kandyan organization called the Tri Sinhala Peramuna and the UNP, now in opposition, also protested against any concession to the Tamils.

The about-face by the UNP, especially under the influence of J. R. Jayawardene (who would some decades later lead the country and rue this maneuver), is noteworthy for marking "the first cycle in a pattern which has recurred as a central and poisonous feature of the political process at critical junctures. The party in power strives to foster communal accommodation. The major party in opposition manipulates Sinhalese parochialism to wreck that attempt" (Manor, 1989, p. 269).

This bipolar oscillation in the politics of the Sinhalese majority, of which I shall have more to say later, would also hereafter find its support among groupings of a divided *sangha*.

So now the UNP in new-found righteousness joined hands with Sinhalese extremists, both monks and laity, and stoked the fires of ethnic resentment. J. R. Jayawardene led the chorus of protests against the projected pact and called it a "betrayal of the Sinhalese," and the UNP's propaganda sheets reeked of racism. And in October 1957, J. R. Jayawardene and other UNP leaders staged a march from Colombo to the Temple of the Tooth in Kandy as a pilgrimage to worship and to protest at that shrine, where the relic that served as the palladium of the earlier Sinhalese kingdoms, and by extension, of the modern polity resided. The procession included a group of chanting monks. It was stopped in its progress by supporters of the SLFP and of Philip Gunawardena, and the police were forced to ban it.

Four days later, however, "UNP opponents of the pact with the Tamils rallied and worshipped before the Temple of the Tooth. . . . The *Mahanayakes* (high priests) of the great Asgiriya and Malwatte chapters presided and invocations were offered at the four *devales* (shrines) beside the temple to persuade the gods to destroy the pact. All this was attended by noisy counter-demonstrations which were met by repeated baton charges from the police" (ibid., pp. 272–73).

The next episode in the mounting crisis was highly provocative from the Sinhalese point of view. Toward the end of March 1958, the National Transport Board sent a fleet of new buses to the north with Sinhalese letters on the license plates, and the Federalists defaced them and substituted Tamil letters. Wriggins relates the sequel as follows: "Over one hundred and fifty Tamils were arrested. In retaliation in the south, Sinhalese gangs smeared tar over Tamil lettering on stores run by Tamils. The police were slow to restore order" (Wriggins, p. 267).

Manor continues the story thus: "Within twenty-four hours, things in the capital had got out of hand. Two large groups of defacers, one of them led by *bhikkhus*, systematically combed the city, and even managed to obliterate the Tamil section of a sign in three languages on Bandaranaike's official Cadillac which read 'left hand drive.' " Police were instructed to show restraint and, while guarding Tamil and Indian shops in central Colombo from attack, were lenient about other actions, such as the stopping of vehicles with Tamil lettering and the assault of Tamil truck drivers in Sinhalese majority areas. As a result "some Sinhalese lawbreakers assumed from the restrained posture of the police that 'our government' did not object to such doings" (Manor, 1989, p. 285).

There were other sporadic incidents at the time when Bandaranaike and Chelvanayagam met on April 4 to discuss the implementation of their pact. Apparently thinking that the talks went well, Chelvanayagam went to Jaffna four days later to seek a formal end to the anti-Sri campaign. But the enemies of the pact among the Sinhalese began to air their protests, and at a rally in Bandaranaike's own constituency a *bhikkhu* announced that the pact would "lead to the total annihilation of the Sinhalese race" (quoted in Manor, p. 286). Thereafter the story belongs to the *bhikkhus* as the final wreckers of the pact.

Several dozen *bhikkhus* staged a sitdown near the prime minister's home in Rosmead Place and refused to move until the pact was rescinded. Bandaranaike, after unsuccessful attempts to dissuade the monks, gave in to their siege and drove to the radio station to announce that the pact was dissolved. His biographer comments: "And so, in the most grievous blunder of his career, he caved in" (ibid., p. 286). The Tamil leaders responded by preparing for a massive civil disobedience protest and planned to hold a conference in late May at Vavuniya, a town on the borderline between Tamil and Sinhalese settlements in the north (ibid., p. 287).

The deepening political crisis between the Federalist Tamils and their Sinhalese opponents was then fatefully affected by labor strikes that were extraneous to the ethnic conflict but fed into the rising storm. There had occurred a series of strikes by the workers of Colombo harbor in late 1957. Soon after Bandaranaike repudiated the pact with Chelvanayagam, internecine rivalries for increased membership between the Communist and Trotskyist trade unions at each other's expense led to a big strike among government workers. Expecting disorder, the police and army patrolled Colombo, but after an incident that provoked union protests, the army units were withdrawn, and the police were demoralized by orders to show restraint. It was in this atmosphere of the weakening of law enforcement agencies that the riots of 1958 exploded around the time that the Federalists were preparing to hold their annual convention in Vavuniya in the north preparatory to launching a campaign of nonviolent protest.

The violence between the Sinhalese and Tamils, when it broke in

late May 1958, came somewhat as a surprise because the country had been preoccupied with the contentious Paddy Lands bill in the preceding months.[6]
Manor describes the riots as occurring in three overlapping phases.

> The first extended from the night of 22 May until 25 May during which serious incidents occurred mainly in and around two places: Polonnaruwa in the predominantly Sinhalese area of the North Central Province and Eravur in a mainly Tamil section of the Eastern Province. The second phase extended from 25 to 29 May and was marked by attacks, overwhelmingly against Tamils, throughout most of the Sinhalese majority areas. The third phase, between 26 or 27 May and 2 or 3 June, took place in the Tamil-majority Northern and Eastern provinces. The violence there was directed against Sinhalese and against government personnel and installations. (Ibid.)

First Phase

The sites of the first phase of the riots were some locations in the north central and eastern provinces. We shall focus primarily on the dramatic events that took place in the Polonnaruwa region, for they illustrate the deadly effect of the kind of issues that would continue to plague the island and the nature of the homicidal propensities that its ethnic conflict could generate.

The triggering events were these. An innocuous incident that took place in Valaichennai, a new town on the east coast railway whose residents were mainly Tamil, was exaggerated and distorted by the time report of it reached the town of Polonnaruwa, a focal point of the peasant colonies, virtually a Sinhalese monopoly.

An agitated and turbulent crowd of many hundred Sinhalese massed at the Polonnaruwa railway station at midnight on 22 May and in the early hours of 23 May to attack a train believed to carry Tamil passengers. On the next night a train was derailed near Eravur in the eastern province; three passengers were killed and many others were injured. Eravur's residents were predominantly Tamil, and whether they caused the derailment is unclear. The same uncertainty surrounds

---

6. This bill, introduced by Philip Gunawardena, was to transfer ownership from absentee landlords to long-standing tenants and to set up cultivation committees made up of farmers actively involved in agriculture to oversee agrarian issues. The bill was crippled by right-wing elements of the SLFP.

the murder of a Sinhalese planter and former mayor of Nuwara Eliya who was shot to death at Eravur while traveling by car. His death, later believed to be the work of his personal enemies, was at first attributed to Tamil violence and was mentioned in a fateful broadcast by the prime minister, which ignited a spreading violence by the Sinhalese throughout the country, the subject of the second phase.

Vittachi provides this necessary setting for the tensions that were boiling up in the shatter zone between north central and eastern provinces just before the riots broke out.

In April 1958, the minister of lands authorized a plan to transfer four hundred Tamil families who had been displaced by the closing down of the Royal Navy dockyards in Trincomalee to east Padaviya for resettlement as farmers on land newly opened for colonies. But Sinhalese colonists and squatters, themselves transplanted from the southwest of Ceylon from places ranging from Veyangoda to Kosgoda, were opposed to the settling of Tamils in the Polonnaruwa or Anuradhapura districts, which were regarded by them as their traditional territory. "In fact, the field officers of the Land Development Department had reported that Action Committees had been formed and that there were open threats of violence if the transfer scheme was carried out."[7]

We need to note that the Sinhala protesters in the interior provinces were first and foremost the wage laborers recruited by the Departments of Public Works and Land Development to prepare the resettlement schemes, cutting the forests, leveling the lands, preparing irrigation channels, and so on. Only secondarily did the peasant colonist-farmers themselves become involved. Vittachi reports that in Padaviya and Polonnaruwa, these footloose and mobile laborers who usually lived in labor camps were themselves the willing tools of politicians and their local allies. "Sinhalese laborers had organized themselves as a striking force against any infiltration of Tamils from Trincomalee. This loose organization had been employed before—on two or three occasions—as shock troops which acted at the instigation of certain politicians to whom they were beholden. A year ago they had been sent as far as Maho to break up a meeting called to hear Dudley Senanayake denouncing the B-C Pact" (Vittachi, p. 34).

Following their unsuccessful attempt to attack a train arriving in Polonnaruwa railway station in the belief that it was loaded with

7. Tarzie Vittachi, *Emergency '58: The Story of the Ceylon Race Riots* (London: Andre Deutsch, 1958), p. 34.

Tamils on their way to the Vavuniya convention (in fact there was only a single passenger on board, a Sinhalese, who was mistakenly beaten up), the crowd composed of these labor gangs unleashed their violence in that formerly "historic," and now border, town. Calling themselves in epic terms the Sinhala Hamudawa (army), laborers from the Land Development and Irrigation departments and from the government-run farms went "on the rampage, raping, looting, and beating Tamil laborers and public officers" (ibid., p. 37). In the Polonnaruwa area from May 24 on Sinhalese mobs caused much damage. Vehicles were halted at main junctions and the passengers assaulted, especially if they were Tamils. Sinhalese merchants who had been asked to provision hard-pressed Tamil civil servants were successfully intimidated. On the evening of the same day, a crowd of nearly a thousand invaded the railway station and assaulted many persons and wrecked property until armed police intervened. The violence then spread to the nearby towns of Giritale, Hingurakgoda, and Minneriya (eight miles away) where men were burned alive.

On the next day (May 25) the disorder worsened around Polonnaruwa. "Assault, arson and looting continued against Tamils in broad daylight in most towns in the area. Government bungalows believed to belong to Tamil officials were put to the torch" (Manor, 1989, p. 289). The brutalities reached their climax when "large gangs of Sinhalese armed with swords, knives and clubs attacked settlements of Tamil laborers" and caused several dozen deaths (ibid). Details of these brutalities are provided by Vittachi.[8]

According to Vittachi, the element of "planning" in the riots was

8. Vittachi writes (p. 40): "On the night of May 25, one of the most heinous crimes in the history of Ceylon was carried out. Almost simultaneously, on the Government farms at Polonnaruwa and Hingurakgoda, the thugs struck remorselessly. The Tamil laborers in the Polonnaruwa sugar cane plantation fled when they saw the enemy approaching and hid in the sugar cane bushes. The *goondas* wasted no time. They set the sugar cane alight and flushed out the Tamils. As they came out screaming, men, women, and children were cut down with home-made swords, grass cutting knives, and *katties,* or pulped under heavy clubs.

"At the Government farm at Hingurakgoda, too, the Tamils were slaughtered that night. One woman in sheer terror embraced her two children and jumped into a well. The rioters were enjoying themselves thoroughly. They ripped open the belly of a woman eight months pregnant, and left her to bleed to death. First estimates of the mass murder on that night were frightening: 150–200 was a quick guess on the basis of forty families on an average of four each. This estimate was later pruned down to around 70, on the basis of bodies recovered and the possibility that many Tamils had got away in time."

conspicuously evident in the wide use of *agents provocateurs*. Many thugs—some of them well-known criminals—had shaved their heads and assumed the yellow robes of *bhikkhu*. Police reports show that the "monks" arrested for looting and arson were car-drivers by "occupation." Those phoney priests went about whipping up race hatred, spreading false stories, and taking part in the lucrative side of the game—robbery and looting (Vittachi, pp. 37–38).

The tenor of the "righteous" attitudes of the Sinhala rioters who had converged on Polonnaruwa from the colonies of Minneriya, Giritale, and Hingurakgoda and were fighting for the cause of "our government" (*apey anduwa*) can be sensed from this incident. When in the course of rioting the armed forces of the government finally turned a Bren gun on the rioters in order to defend their own men and fellow police, all Sinhalese, from being attacked, the rioters expressed their outrage to the minister of lands in the form of the question, "Why is the army killing Sinhalese?"

Second Phase

It was clear by May 26 that the riots had spread to many other localities and threatened to be virtually an islandwide upheaval. The prime minister failed to act decisively by declaring an emergency, and "the second phase of the disturbance began, with attacks on Tamils throughout the Sinhala-majority areas. Incidents occurred at intervals along the main road linking Polonnaruwa with Colombo. Very severe violence occurred in the capital itself and spread—mainly in the form of looting of Tamil shops—down the coast to Panadura, Galle and even to Weligama, near the southern tip of the island" (Manor, 1989, p. 289). In the city of Colombo itself, predictably small gangs of Sinhalese committed arson, looting, and theft in the commercial and shopping centers of Pettah and the Fort, and passengers in cars and buses were dragged out and beaten. The worst violence against Tamils in greater Colombo took place in the southern residential districts, especially Ratmalana, where Tamils resided in some numbers and whose enviable middle-class status was resented. "Railway stations and bus depots in that area yielded tales of violence from throughout the capital and from further south, and at Ratmalana airport, passengers disembarked from Jaffna with stories of 'outrages' there" (ibid., p. 292).

In other towns, police stations were attacked and the police had to open fire; and it is reported that in the town of Kutunegala "*bhikkhus*

led a procession through the streets to protest the arrest of a man who
stoned Tamil shops" (ibid., pp. 289–90).

> On the evening of the 26th, Bandaranaike made a radio
> address to the nation to calm fears and stress the govern-
> ment's intention to act firmly. But he mistakenly said that
> the first serious incident had been the death of the Sinhal-
> ese politician Seneviratne in a predominantly Tamil area.
> . . . The next morning, attacks on Tamils resumed in
> many parts of Colombo. Hysterical rumors of Tamil atroc-
> ities against Sinhalese and cries of vengeance for Sene-
> viratne were heard amid dozens of cases of maiming,
> murder, arson, rape and looting both in the capital and
> southward along the coast to Galle and Matara, up country
> at Kandy and numerous towns in the Central Province and
> at Kurunegala, Polonnaruwa and even remote Badulla
> (ibid., p. 290).

Only after four days of ethnic violence, around noon on May 27, did
the prime minister and the governor-general, Sir Oliver Goonetilleke,
agree to declare a state of emergency, to impose press censorship and a
dusk-to-dawn curfew, and to ban public meetings, processions, and
strikes in essential services. At the same time, two political parties
were singled out for proscription—the Federal party, which represented the dominant Tamil views, and the Janatha Vimukti Peramuna,
which voiced extreme Sinhala populist views. These measures seemed
to be effective in the Sinhalese majority areas where after two days
violence had become a spent force. But the Tamil backlash was yet to
come.

Third Phase
Violence in the Tamil majority areas rose in intensity after
the full force of Sinhalese aggression had been disclosed and news of
"horrors" inflicted was received. The locations where violence
erupted were the most populous Tamil towns of Jaffna in the northern
and Batticaloa in the eastern provinces.

In Batticaloa by May 27 there had occurred a number of attacks on
Sinhalese residents and the murder of some Sinhalese fishermen on the
coast about 25 miles to the south of the city. The passion and cruelty of
the Tamil vengeance is described by Vittachi (pp. 51–52). Migrant
Sinhalese fishermen were killed or driven out to sea by Tamil fishermen. Many Sinhalese living as a minority fled their homes, which

were put to the torch, and the official report lists 56 cases of arson and 11 murders.

In Jaffna a crowd attacked a Buddhist temple, and when the police who saved the sole Buddhist monk there removed him to the hospital, the hospital in turn was attacked, but the police successfully protected it without loss of life. The main targets of Tamil vengeance, however, were government property and police stations. Customs and excise offices in the coastal trading port of Kayts were raided or demolished, while in Valvettiturai, also an important location for sea trade and smuggling, fierce attacks forced the police to abandon many stations and to concentrate their strength. Finally, on May 30, the offshore Buddhist temple at Nainativu, long regarded as a sacred place of pilgrimage among the Buddhists, was leveled and the Buddha statue shattered. By June 3 martial law was imposed on Jaffna and Batticaloa districts, and order was soon restored.

Participants

The evidence regarding the actual participants in the ethnic riots is not ample or specific on an islandwide basis, but it is clearest and least ambiguous in that part of Sri Lanka where the violence began and was most extensive and destructive, namely, in the Polonnaruwa region and other parts of the north central province.

The Sinhalese aggressors, as we have seen, came primarily from the large peasant colonization schemes. They were mainly of two sorts: men from the laborer gangs who had access to and knew how to use heavy vehicles and explosives were the major assailants; the other, less virulent, kind of actors were drawn from Sinhalese squatters, from footloose transients from the market settlements, and on a lesser scale from among the more fortunate peasant colonists themselves.

For the other arenas of conflict the faces in the crowd and the organizers and collaborators are not very discernible, though the evidence on the sites where riots were staged and the pattern of destruction are clearer. Manor advanced the conspiracy theory, which he acknowledges to be impossible to prove on available evidence, "that interests which had suffered during Bandaranaike's two years in power contributed to the rioting in order to destabilize the government. Prominent among the candidates are former bus owners whose vehicles had been nationalized and retail traders, money lenders and notables who felt threatened by Philip Gunawardena's proposal to create new and well-funded multi-purpose cooperatives" (Manor,

1989, p. 293). If this is likely, it affirms a point I have made before that the riots have to be linked to the larger context of political and social issues and the play of competing interest groups.

It would seem that in Jaffna, Kayts, and Valvettiturai a good many of the Tamil assailants who attached government property and customs offices were smugglers in whose interest it was to join their personal business interests with the larger Tamil political causes: they appropriated arms and ammunition and destroyed incriminating documents when they attacked customs stations. Attackers of the Nainativu temple were also probably drawn from the same interest groups because boats and explosives were used in that operation. It also seems that in Jaffna "educated youths who had earlier defaced number [license] plates were active in the attack on the city's Buddhist temple and hospital and early attacks on Sinhalese shops" (ibid.). Educated Tamil youths facing increasing discrimination and frustrations with regard to higher education and employment would figure importantly later in the country's ongoing ethnic conflict.

Evidence of the sort presented, though incomplete, lends support to the thesis that frequently those complexes of events that come to be labeled the ethnic riots of a specific month and year can be seen to be an aggregation and chainlike connection of locally organized operations and local conflicts engaging different categories of participants with their particular agenda, which over a short period of time feed into one another and create a widening conflagration of regional and even countrywide proportions.

8 The Restoration of Buddhism and the Transformation of Education in the 1960s and 1970s

When one scrutinizes the 1958 riots—the participants, their locations, and their acts—and places them in relation to the preceding events and issues, such as the official language controversy, the Tamil pressure for a federal solution to their felt underdog status, the demonstrations and fasts staged by the EBP monks and lay Buddhist nationalists to protest concessions to the Tamils, together with labor strikes that had their origins in the rivalries of left-wing parties and weakened public order, and finally, when one contemplates the fact that the riots themselves occurred at their worst not in Colombo and Jaffna but in the far provinces of peasant colonization resettlement, one is puzzled about how to identify in any meaningful way the "Buddhist" components as such that inform them in contrast to other components, whether economic, territorial, or political.

Since these components are difficult to disaggregate, I want to approach the question of Sri Lankan Buddhism as a religious, social, and political complex differently. I want to substantiate the argument from now on that as the energies of Sinhala Buddhist nationalism were translated into concrete policies and programs of language, education, employment, peasant resettlement, territorial control of the island and so on, the substantively soteriological, ethical, and normative components of doctrinal Buddhism qua religion were weakened, displaced, even distorted, while the religio-political associations of Buddhism as set out in the monkish chronicles (the *Mahavamsa, Culavamsa,* and so on), which bound it with the Sinhala people, with the territory of the entire island, and with a political authority dedicated to the protection of Buddhism, assumed primacy. Thus Buddhist fundamentalism and revivalism progressively transformed into Buddhist nationalism ends up as a political Buddhism from which the religious core and inspiration as set out in doctrinal Buddhism are either privatized or leached out in favor of a political affirmation of a collectivity that sees itself as homogeneous and majoritarian and for whom doctrinal Buddhism is a possession owned as a legacy, an object that is appropriated or (to use a Freudian term) "introjected," but not more generally serving for many persons as an ego-ideal and mental discipline for personal salvation. To put the matter in another way: Sinhalese revivalist Buddhism with nationalist overtones that had an upsurge toward the end of the nineteenth century and the beginning decades of the twentieth did contain an appeal to a selective scripturalism that placed an accent on certain doctrinal tenets and on the devaluation of "superstitious" accretions and practices. But inevitably this purification of the religious field involved a process of popularization, whereby the Buddhist doctrine and message was carried to the people in simplified cathechistic terms leavened with mytho-historical claims culled from chronicles such as the *Mahavamsa*. This propagandization and popularization entailed the acquisition and use of modern media of communication such as the printing press, of new educational institutions and organizational forms, and of effective techniques of dissemination like sermons and pamphlets in the vernacular.

But these activities of revivalism and reform, including scripturalism, led progressively to the ideologization of religion as a charter which represented a shift from "religiousness" to "religious-mindedness," from religion as moral practice to religion as a cultural and political possession. Finally, as we saw in the developments of the 1950s, nationalism, which grew out of the revivalism, advanced further by encompassing and then superseding it in substantive terms. We enter (arguably) the climactic phase of a political Buddhism or a Buddhist nationalism and chauvinism, which could in its collective manifestation have little links with the major tenets of canonical Buddhist ethics, and, because of its hegemonic, preferential, and exclusive claims vis-à-vis other collectivities in its midst erupt as periodic overflows of violence in its alleged defense.

There are two changes and distinctive features that can be associated with political Buddhism, or alternatively, Buddhist nationalism. Progressively removed from its original inspiration, both the doctrinal texts and the mytho-historical chronicles come to have value as sacred objects, serving as fetishes imbued with power and acting as markers of special ethnic entitlement, self-respect, and identity. We may say that when religion reaches this form it has been to some degree "objectified" and "fetishized." By a process of inversion, collective ethnic interests and concerns are projected onto a Buddhist cultural capital which in turn is then seen as requiring and justifying certain forms of political action to ensure its preservation.

But there is another trend which gives a substantive and structuring content and an ideological potency to political Buddhism as it has developed in recent times. While many of the "truths" of doctrinal Buddhism at the level of the individual that are recommended to be studied, interiorized, and applied to life's tasks fade in urgency, a collectivist conception of Buddhist "nationalism" and Buddhist "democracy"— even Buddhist "socialism"—sketched and preached by both lay and clerical ideologues and activists progressively suffuses and becomes the dominant public consciousness. This in many ways is a "positive" ideological project, despite its limitations and its creative misreadings of the past. It refers back to certain canonical *suttas* dealing with ideal righteous rulers in the form of *cakkavatti* and sees in them the attainments of glorious welfare-oriented rule. It refers back to the regimes of great Sinhala kings of *Mahavamsa* and *Culavamsa* fame, who allegedly constructed an "egalitarian" rural society focused on the triad of temple (*stupa* and *vihara*), the irrigation tank, and rice fields. It sounds a clarion call for Sinhalese unity and berates the contemporary Sinhalese for their divisiveness. It criticizes present-day divisive party politics and present-day hankering after West-inspired materialist, consumerist, and capitalist self-seeking goals and proposes in their place a simpler, harmonious "Buddhist way of life" in a "Buddhist democracy." This call to a Buddhist way of life does invoke some of the precepts and admonitions suitable for lay householders set out in doctrinal texts. Finally, and most significantly, it envisages a central role as political advisors and counselors for activist monks at all levels of the Buddhist polity.

Both these trends are interwoven in political Buddhism. Its trajectory and the crystallizing shapes are what I shall now sketch in the rest of this study. Since the subject of Buddhist nationalism and democracy as an ideological construction frames, structures, and motivates in important ways the voices of many contemporary activist monks, it will be given a special elucidation in the last section of this study.

Let us begin this trajectory by first focusing on some relevant developments in the sixties and seventies. If the mid-fifties constituted a watershed in the politics of postindependence Sri Lanka, when the arguments for a Buddhist restoration, for the dethronement of the English language and the elevation of the Sinhalese language, and for the recovery of Sinhalese majoritarian influence had been accepted as legitimate through the electoral process and entrusted to Bandaranaike and the MEP for implementation, then the sixties and seventies represent a different trend by virtue of both the major parties—the SLFP and the UNP—attempting to implement those objectives, and largely succeeding in that task (though there were many other issues of reform and reconstruction that had been stalled or evaded).

The story of these two decades for the theme of this essay is that the UNP saw its way in the sixties to accepting these objectives as essential planks in its party platform, and therefore the two major Sinhala political parties, the UNP and the SLFP, not only grew closer ideologically regarding Buddhist restoration but also became alternative choices at subsequent elections. Sri Lankan politics, we might say, is enacted in an arena where the majority group, the Sinhalese, has a "bipolar" division within and is ranged against a minority which according to context is regarded as an enemy and an ally.

Paralleling this process toward a dual balance was the progressive bifurcation of the support of the Buddhist monks for the two major parties. If in 1956 the enormous groundswell of monks led by the progressive monks of the EBP overshadowed the rest of the *sangha* and decided an election, in the sixties and seventies the monks of all sects, temples, and status tended toward a spectrum of parallel support for the two main Sinhala parties.

Let me now document this more fully and then elaborate their further implications.

As a matter of fact, the salience of, and public support for, the politically active monks suffered a traumatic setback in September 1959, when Prime Minister Bandaranaike was assassinated by a monk, whose accomplice and sponsor turned out to be Buddharakkhita, the chief incumbent of the famous Kelaniya temple and a leader of the EBP. So in the elections of 1960 the monks were not by and large visible and active.

The setback was, however, temporary and the monks were active again during the elections of 1965. And an issue that engaged them and caused division within their ranks was the character and structure of the *sangha* itself, and its willingness or not to tolerate governmental and lay Buddhist actions to "reform" it.

The Buddha Sasana Commission, following a recommendation made in 1956 in *The Betrayal of Buddhism,* had made certain regulatory proposals regarding the reorganization and unification of various chapters of monks—a move designed to stem the alleged increased fragmentation of the *sangha* and to give it organizational strength to compete with the challenge of Christian missions—and regarding the question of monks receiving salaries for filling certain positions, especially in schools. The SLFP government felt obliged to move toward the implementation of these proposals, and this generated a wave of resistance against government "interference." Thus, for instance, the All Ceylon Buddhist Congress protested that antireligious and antidemocratic Marxists were influencing the government. It was clear that by now the SLFP of 1965 had tarnished its reputation among some circles as the defender of Buddhism.

We are here encountering one of the central obstacles to any return to government regulation and "purification" of the *sangha*'s internal organization, which was achieved with varying efficacy in the precolonial political regimes and was abandoned by the British as part of their policy of the "disestablishment of Buddhism." Disestablishment entailed the withdrawal of state support and protection of Buddhism as the official religion of state. The monks and laity might collaborate in general in "restoring" Buddhism to its previous preeminence, but would diverge sharply about the concrete need for administrative regulation of the *sangha* and its temporalities. And this issue would split the *sangha* itself and also create differences and tensions between lay Buddhist leaders and establishment monks.

So when large numbers of monks began to canvass in the March 1965 elections, there was parallel support for the UNP and SLFP, which signaled the emergence of a political dualism within the *sangha* matching the polarization between the two major political parties.[1] The modes of mobilization of support, through rallies, meetings, and pamphlet distributions were replicated. As Phadnis put it: "1965 could be termed as the point when the Bhikkhus' participation in electoral politics had turned full circle. Political polarization of the Bhikkhu community had reached its high water mark as both the major parties were supported by a conglomeration of Bhikkhu groups who, whatever their nomenclature, could be easily identified in their political alignments" (Phadnis, p. 195).

1. Thus Phadnis, *Religion and Politics in Sri Lanka* (London: C. Hurst & Co., 1976), pp. 19–92, writes that while the Lanka Eksath Bhikkhu Mandalaya (LEBM) and many teachers of the Vidyalankara and Vidyodaya universities supported the coalition between the SLFP and the LSSP (Marxists), the UNP drew support from newly formed Colombo-based monk organizations such as Maha Sangha and Maha Sangha Peramuna as well as the chief monk of the Malvatta chapter of the Siyam Nikaya.

In 1965 the UNP won the election. In 1970 it lost it again to Sirimavo Bandaranaike, widow of the assassinated prime minister, to win it again in 1977 under the leadership of J. R. Jayawardene, who was in power until 1987, having changed the government to a presidential form and maintaining control through a referendum rather than elections. In December 1988 in a new presidential election, R. Premadasa was elected to power, and soon afterwards the UNP won the parliamentary elections in March 1989.

The seesaw victories of the SLFP and the UNP between 1960 and 1977 did not change the now established pattern of the monks' now customary participation in electoral politics and their divided support for these two main parties. For some 16 or 17 years, from 1960 to 1977, there were no anti-Tamil riots or any form of collective violence against ethnic minorities. The period was, however, punctuated by the 1971 insurrection of the Sinhalese youth (JVP) against an SLFP government which at that time was inspired more by grievances against the government than against the Tamils. (But as we shall see later, in 1977 and again in 1981 and 1983 there was a recurrence of anti-Tamil riots in quick succession with the last in 1983 being the worst).

In terms of our theme of Buddhism, politics and violence, we thus have to answer two questions: Why was there a period of quiescence from 1960 until 1977 as far as ethnic violence and Buddhist militancy were concerned? Why did ethnic riots resume in 1977 and reach a level of violence never before witnessed, and thereafter plunge the country into a prolonged civil war?

A good part of the answer to the first question is that between 1960 and the early 1970s the aspirations and objectives of militant lay Buddhists and politically ardent Buddhist monks with regard to the restoration of Buddhism to a preeminent place had been largely addressed and fulfilled. The symbolic high point of this era, when both the SLFP and the UNP collaborated in its acceptance, was the inclusion in the country's constitution in 1972 the formal declaration that Buddhism would have the "foremost place" as the religion of the majority. After the victory of Bandaranaike and the MEP in 1956 the Department of Cultural Affairs had been set up to sponsor Buddhism. The Buddha Jayanthi celebrations had been successfully staged with pomp, fervor, and piety in that same year, and the characteristic projects of all politically sponsored Buddhist revivals in the traditional Buddhist polities of Southeast Asia were undertaken. They were projects to collate and edit the texts of Pali canon, the *Tripitaka,* and also to translate them into Sinhalese, to publish a number of Buddhist literary texts, to compile an encyclopedia in Sinhalese and English, and to restore the Dalada Maligawa (the temple in Kandy where the Buddha's tooth relic, the palladium of the precolonial Sinhala kingdom resided) and other famous Buddhist monuments in Anuradhapura, Polonnaruwa, and elsewhere. In the mid-fifties similar projects celebrating the restoration of Buddhism were undertaken in Burma by Premier U Nu.

Indeed the architectural restorations of the ancient capitals and other famous monuments, accompanied by extensive Sinhalese peasant colonization and resettlement of the ancient lands that lay in their hinterland, and the popularization of pilgrimages to these sites restored and made accessible must be judged to be important contributions to the stimulation as well as appeasement of Sinhalese desires to regain their past glories.[2]

But it is education that has been at the heart of postindependence politics. Education is the umbrella term under which were grouped a set of interlocking issues and interests: the animus against the Christian schools which taught in English and produced a largely Christian elite; the restoration of Sinhalese as language of administration and education, and thereby the opening of opportunity for social mobility to the lower classes who could learn in the vernacular language; and the restoration of Buddhist and other orientalist studies to a position of eminence in the universities, and so on.

A conspicuous step taken was the creation of two Buddhist universities—Vidyodaya and Vidyalankara—in 1959 by act of Parliament at the very sites of the island's two most distinguished *pirivenas,* which had dispensed education to monks. (The staff of the parent *pirivenas* were absorbed into the universities, and many other *pirivenas* were affiliated with the universities as their colleges.) These two universities, as we have already seen, were the seat of and the breeding ground for the scholarly activist "progressive" monks who led the EBP. Indeed, the intensified political participation of the monks in the sixties was itself a barometer of their faith in achieving results through political participation, and their political relevance and strength as championing "Buddhist" social welfare issues were harnessed to the full by both the UNP and SLFP during the 1965 and 1970 elections.

2. See Elizabeth Nissan's "The Sacred City of Anuradhapura" (Ph.D. diss., London School of Economics, 1985).

In both ideological and practical terms, probably the most important measures taken related to the school system and the teachers' training colleges of the island. As we have indicated before, the Buddhist Commission of Inquiry report, *The Betrayal of Buddhism* (1956), had leveled the warning that "what Buddhism has to protect itself from today is not the Catholic Church, but Catholic Schools," and had urged the nationalization of all schools. The SLFP promise to bring the schools under a central system that would give a national stamp to the education imparted was fulfilled by Mrs. Bandaranaike in the sixties. All private schools had previously been assisted by the state, and now it was declared that all Grade III assisted schools (primary and post-primary) would be taken over by the government; all Grade I and Grade II assisted schools would be similarly taken over, unless they chose to remain private without financial assistance. The net result was that the majority of schools so nationalized were those previously run by Christian organizations, though the latter did decide to retain some of their best secondary schools as private fee-paying schools. The Catholics were the major losers, especially the poorer amongst them. The beneficiaries of education in the private fee-paying Christian schools came mostly from the elite and wealthy families. Hence Christian privilege though diminished was not eradicated. The majority of private teachers' training colleges run by Christian bodies were also similarly surrendered to the government. By comparison with the Christian schools, the private schools run by Buddhist organizations readily participated in the takeover, because now under governmental sponsorship their Sinhala-Buddhist identity would be further enhanced.[3]

The takeover of the majority of schools, combined with the switch to the mother tongue as the medium of instruction which was by 1967 achieved in all primary and secondary schools, was perhaps the most substantial accomplishment of the program dedicated to restoring the rights of the religion and language of the majority.

---

3. The number of private Hindu schools was small by comparison with Christian and Buddhist schools, and most of them were taken over by the government.

9 The 1970s and 1980s: The Deepening Crisis

The next question to pose is this: if by the early 1970s the program of Sinhala Buddhist nationalism on which most segments of the laity and all the clergy could agree had been largely achieved, then why did the Sinhala-Tamil conflict flare up again and produce the riots of 1977, 1981, and 1983, the last being the most violent and destructive so far experienced?

The answers are complex, but the following are important ingredients.

At the core of the Sinhala-Tamil ethnic conflict since the seventies which invoked and generated the passions of Sinhala Buddhist nationalism and the separatist claims of Tamil homelands are two clusters of interest-based issues. One cluster concerns the official language(s) of administration and the linguistic media of education and their linkage with the issues of educational opportunities, including admissions to universities and places of higher learning, and of recruitment to administrative services and the professions. In the long run the Tamils have lost out on these issues, which the Sinhalese majority decided in its favor by the imposition of quotas and discriminatory policies.

I have already outlined the changes in the educational system that resulted in changes in the medium of instruction and the takeover of the majority of private schools. Aside from establishing Sinhalese as the official language and the principal medium of instruction, there were other measures adopted that affected the Tamils drastically.

The skewing of higher education in favor of the Sinhalese majority was a climactic step of felt discrimination among the Tamils and finally drove the Tamil youth movement for Eelam to take up arms and engage in militant confrontation.

In Sri Lanka the facilities for training in the sciences, both theoretical and applied, are limited. There is heavy competition to enter the universities and find places especially in the natural sciences, engineering, and medicine. By the mid-seventies less than 9 percent of those taking the entrance examinations were admitted to the universities. A so-called policy of standardization that adjusted the examination scores given scripts written in the Sinhalese and Tamil languages and a quota system with special concessions for "backward" districts ultimately worked first against the educated Tamil youth of the north and second against the educated youth of Colombo. The details of those policies are as follows. In 1970, different minimum standards for the Tamil and Sinhala media, with the bias in favor of the latter, were arbitrarily set as entry requirements. In 1974 to the standardization by medium was added a modified district quota system, and in 1975 this quota system was extended. In 1976–77, admission to the universities was based on this formula: 70 percent of the admissions to be on raw marks, and 30 percent on a district basis, of which 15 percent was reserved for backward districts. The final step taken in 1979 restricted still further the admissions allowed on merit and performance: only 30 percent of the admissions were allowed on an all-island merit basis, 55 percent on a district basis, and 15 percent allotted to backward districts.

Bastian sums up the consequences thus:

> The introduction of the standardization and district quota systems, which are essentially methods by which the proportion of Tamils in much sought-after science facilities were reduced in favor of Sinhalese, had its political implications. Discrimination in education had become one of the key slogans of the Tamil minority of Sri Lanka agitating for its rights. It became a main subject for the resolutions adopted by the TULF at Vaddukkodai when the demand for a separate state was proclaimed. The discriminatory measures imposed by the Sinhala-dominated governments of Sri Lanka in the field of university admission had helped to politicize and radicalize the Tamil youth.[1]

1. Sunil Bastian, "Education and Social Conflict in Sri Lanka," unpublished essay. For an analysis of admission policies until 1975, see also C. R. de Silva, "The Impact of Nationalism on Education: The Schools Take-over (1961) and the University Admissions Crisis, 1970–1975," in Michael Roberts, ed., *Collective Identities, Nationalisms, and Protest in Modern Sri Lanka* (Colombo: Marga Institute, 1979), chap. 15, pp. 474–99.

It is significant that the Tamil youth resistance became militant around the mid-seventies, as their higher educational opportunities were perceived to be irretrievably eroding.

The second complex surrounds peasant resettlement in "colonization schemes" in the sparsely populated Dry Zone of Sri Lanka, which covers regions in the north central, northern and eastern provinces. This is currently at the heart of the ongoing conflict and involves the vexed and contested issues of devolution of powers from the central government to provincial/regional councils, the ethnic quotas to be allocated to colonization schemes under central and local control, the degree to which regional autonomy is to be granted in matters of local government, education, land alienation, policing and so on.[2]

While the colonization of the Dry Zone was begun before independence, it has since the fifties been continuously implemented on a large scale as the major form of agricultural development. Large, capital-intensive, multipurpose enterprises such as the Gal Oya Scheme and the Mahavali Program are part of this developmental thrust. The Dry Zone was the ancient site of a much glorified Sinhala Buddhist civilization centered in Anuradhapura and Polonnaruwa, and a return of Sinhalese peasantry to the area is seen as a recreation of that past. But the northern and eastern provinces in the historical present have as their majority populations Sri Lankan (and Indian) Tamils, with the Muslims as the next largest group. Peasant resettlement has involved the migration and transplantation of poor peasants from the densely populated and land-hungry parts of the country, primarily the central, south, and southwestern parts of the island, where Sinhalese vastly predominate. And successive Sinhalese majoritarian governments have virtually occupied themselves with catering to the needs of the Sinhalese peasantry, while either discriminating against or being less caring about the interests and needs of the minorities who are the major native populations of the northern and eastern provinces. Given the ethnically preferential policy and the manner in which the Sinhala-Tamil conflict was developing, it was inevitable that the Sri Lankan Tamils would see the massive migrations of Sinhalese into the Dry

2. On the Bandaranaike-Chelvanayajam pact of 1956–57 and subsequent discussions on devolution, see Stanley J. Tambiah, "Ethnic Fratricide in Sri Lanka: An Update," in *Ethnicities and Nations,* ed. Remo Guidieri, Francesco Pellizzi, and Stanley J. Tambiah (Austin: University of Texas Press, 1988). See also James Manor, *The Expedient Utopian: Bandaranaike and Ceylon* (Cambridge: Cambridge University Press, 1989), chap. 8.

Zone as an intrusion into their alleged "homelands," and as attempts to swamp them. The separatist claim to Eelam is the stance taken by the most radical and militant of the Tamil dissidents. The unfolding pattern of Dry Zone colonization has fueled the ethnic conflict. The patterns of internal migration have produced dramatic growth in the population of the Dry Zone, which in turn has seen a spectacular transformation into a rice-producing economy as a result of the peasant resettlement schemes implemented since independence. Currently in Sri Lanka the Grand Accelerated Mahavali Program is viewed as the climactic achievement.

The whole program of agricultural development has been plagued by the political issue of ethnic preference and quotas with regard to the composition of colonists and by tendentious appeals to historical precedents by both sides. Peebles has documented "the transformation of the Dry Zone from a sparsely populated and unhealthy, but ethnically diverse, region to a rapidly growing, and almost exclusively Sinhalese and Buddhist, one. Tamil protests against this transformation have been followed by intensification rather than moderation."[3]

Peebles makes this judgment on the vexed issue of colonization: The Sinhalese predominance in the colonies and the Buddhist character of the settlements are by themselves not objectionable. But the "insistence that such colonization is a Sinhalese entitlement on historical grounds, in which the resources of the state are dedicated to one community with no comparable benefits to others is intolerable."

In a remarkable essay Amita Shastri attempts to explain the circumstances and considerations that led the Sri Lankan Tamil "ethnoregional movement" to demand in the mid-seventies a separate state of Eelam.[4] The Tamil separatist demand progressively emerged not merely because of cumulative grievances of discrimination. More important, the forging of a positive separatist vision was undergirded by the realization that the northern and eastern provinces could constitute a viable autonomous political and economic entity. Shastri thus sketches an arguable geopolitical rationale for separatism, which emerged from the dynamics of various political and economic processes. The chief of these was the peasant resettlement in and coloni-

3. Patrick Peebles, "Colonization and Ethnic Conflict in the Dry Zone of Sri Lanka," *Journal of Asian Studies* 49, no. 1 (1990): 30–55.

4. Amita Shastri, "The Material Basis for Separatism: The Tamil Eelam Movement in Sri Lanka," *Journal of Asian Studies* 49, no. 1 (1990): 56–77.

zation of the Dry Zone: she reiterates the conclusions already mentioned by Peebles that it led to a major stream of Sinhalese from the center and southwest and a smaller stream of Tamils from the north migrating into a less densely populated region and competing for a limited set of opportunities there and that the colonization policy, which favored the Sinhalese, dramatically changed the population ratio among the Sinhalese, Tamils, and Muslims and thereby deepened the ethnic divide.

Shastri argues that the very agricultural prosperity created in the Dry Zone, especially the rice surpluses resulting from irrigation agriculture, made the Tamils conscious of the agricultural possibilities and economic viability of their alleged "homelands" supplemented by an industrial hinterland around Trincomalee as harbor. Shastri thus expounds, from the perspective of Tamil secessionists, the case for Eelam as a positively viable project, and not merely as a negative refuge.

From the Riots of the Eighties to the Indo–Sri Lanka Peace Accord

The riots perpetrated by the Sinhalese upon the Tamils in 1981 and 1983 were a result of the collision between an emphatic, but still unsatiated Buddhist Sinhala nationalism—which had, nevertheless, as we have seen, secured since 1956 more and more benefits for the Sinhalese majority—and a rising, desperate, and confrontational Tamil nationalism, which threatened secession and a separate state of Eelam, objectives that were bound to infuriate and inflame Sinhala chauvinists.

While at no time has the Tamil civilian public as such initiated riots against the Sinhalese public, an armed insurrection of the Tamil youth was begun in the early seventies. It was the end result of many developments: their feeling of hopelessness caused by the discrimination practiced against them in higher education, the Tamil politicians' intensified objections to the pace and magnitude of resettlement of Sinhalese peasants in the "homelands" of the Tamils, and finally the TULF's declaration of its commitment to Eelam.

The government's reaction to the Tamil militants, whose first victims by homicide were some Tamil politicians and policemen who were singled out as "collaborators," was to send an army of occupation (the army is virtually a Sinhalese monopoly) to the north and the east to stamp out the insurgency.

It is relevant to keep in mind the following chronology of events that escalated to produce the riots of 1983. In 1977, after seven years of

SLFP rule, the UNP was reelected under the leadership of J. R. Jayawardene. In 1979 this government passed the Prevention of Terrorism Act with its draconian provisions,[5] and this allowed the security forces to take punitive actions in the north that would progressively alienate the Tamils there. Then, in 1981, the elections to the District Development councils were seriously disturbed by violent Tamil insurgents, and the Public Library in Jaffna was burned. Thereafter while a string of encounters between the army and the insurgents were taking place, the atmosphere was further poisoned by the punitive actions of Sinhalese civilians against Tamil civilians in many towns throughout the country. These mounting tensions finally escalated into the riots of 1983.[6]

The Colombo Riots of 1983

Here let me summarize what we know of the locations at which the arson and violence took place and the kinds of participants— "the faces in the crowd."

The 1983 riots began in Colombo, the capital city, on July 24 and lasted until August 5. They spread to other parts of the country from this point of origin, especially to the towns of Gampaha, Kalutara in the southwest; Kandy, Matale, and Nuwara Eliya in the central tea plantation districts; and Trincomalee in the eastern province. The death toll was between 350 (the government figure) and 2,000 (Tamil estimate). Large numbers of refugees fled their homes: in Colombo itself the number of refugees ranged from 80,000 to 100,000. Arson and property destruction were extensive. In this account I shall limit myself to happenings in Colombo, because the worst damage was done there.

The conventional and accepted story is that the most proximate triggering event was the ambush of an army truck and the killing and mutilation of thirteen soldiers at Tinneveli, in the heart of Sri Lankan Tamil territory in North Sri Lanka, which had been occupied by a Sinhalese army for some time. The ambush was the work of Tamil insurgents belonging to the Liberation Tigers of Tamil Eelam (LTTE). This was certainly a mo-

---

5. This act for instance allowed the army and police to hold prisoners incommunicado for up to eighteen months without trial, thus creating conditions for the practice of arrest on suspicion, incarceration, and even torture and killing. See Stanley J. Tambiah, *Sri Lanka: Ethnic Fratricide and the Dismantling of Democracy* (Chicago: University of Chicago Press, 1986), pp. 19–20.

6. For an account of the escalation of violent incidents between the Tamil insurgents and the government's security forces that led up to the 1983 riots, see Tambiah, *Sri Lanka*, chaps. 2 and 3.

ment of escalation in the ethnic conflict. India had begun to supply the Tigers with Claymore land mines as a way of better withstanding the Sinhalese army's superiority in mobility and its increasing resort to a military solution. Though skirmishes had taken place before, never had so many Sinhala soldiers been killed at once. On July 23 certain elements in the army decided to bring the corpses in their mangled state to the capital city and display them publicly in Colombo's central cemetery of Kanatte (in Borella) prior to a military burial.

The preparations for the burial were complicated and plagued by adventitious and uncontrollable factors. One of the soldiers killed was a young second lieutenant who had apparently been a popular student at Ananda College, a premier Buddhist school, located in Maradana. Many pupils of this school together with their parents and teachers had gathered at the cemetery and awaited the arrival of the bodies.

In the meantime the plane transporting the bodies to Colombo from Jaffna was delayed, and the waiting crowd, increasing in size, also became increasingly restive. The bodies were being prepared at a funeral home next to the cemetery after arrival, and during this additional delay, the police and army who had gathered in numbers at Borella also became emotionally agitated. As may be expected, the Sinhala media added further fuel to the mounting grief and rage. (It is important to note that since there are newspapers, radio, and television channels that relay separately to both Sinhalese and Tamil language groups, their slanted reports intensify the ethnic conflict.)

A review of the riots suggests that there were two phases. The first phase began in the vicinity of the cemetery in Borella as more or less a result of an overflow of heightened emotions on the part of the crowd gathered there—the schoolboys and friends and relatives of the dead, some of the security forces, plus some of the local populace in Borella.

Soon after the mortuary rites, violence broke out in Borella, Thimbirigasyaya, Nugegoda, Wellawatte, and Bambalapitiya, in the form of street fighting, stopping traffic, and physical attacks and almost a whole day passed before the army and police were called upon to intervene. Subsequently the riots took a form that was decidedly more destructive and homicidal and showed firm evidence of planning and direction, of participation of politicians, government employees (minor staff, laborers, technicians), and of the use of government vehicles and buses.

A conspicuous feature of the 1983 riots was that the mob violence, especially from the second day onward, was organized and for the most part purposeful. The crowds came armed with weapons, such as metal rods and knives, and carrying gasoline that was frequently confiscated from passing motor vehicles. Evidence of the rioters' prior intent and planning was their carrying voter lists and addresses of Tamil owners and occupants of houses, shops, industries, and other property. Moreover, the gangs frequently had access to transportation; they arrived mostly in government-owned trucks and buses or were dropped off at successive locations by the Colombo coastline trains.

A well-informed friend of mine has pointed out to me that the "liberalized economy" introduced from 1977 onwards had opened up new commercial and business opportunities. Many shops selling imported and local goods had opened. New business premises and houses had been constructed in Colombo, and higher rents had become possible. At the same time, this context had aggravated competition, so that the riots could be the occasion for Sinhala businessmen to wipe out their competitors, for landlords to get rid of unwanted tenants and so on. It has also been suggested that Cyril Mathew, the chauvinist minister of industries, was vociferous that Tamil businessmen in Colombo were working both sides of the street—collaborating with the government and the Tamil insurgents in Jaffna—and therefore deserved to be "taught a lesson." Mathew's ministry was the repository of knowledge about businesses, their locations, and owners. Its employees also provided the manpower for the government union called the Jatika Sevaka Sangamaya, which was involved in punitive actions. And it was the source for vehicles that were used for political purposes.

The following is a list of the locations and the kinds of property methodically burned, destroyed, and looted in Colombo:

1. Tamil houses in Colombo's middle- and lower-class residential wards of Wellawatte, Dehiwela, Bambalapitiya, and Kirillapone.

2. Tamil shops—groceries, textile shops, tea boutiques—lining Colombo's principal waterfront thoroughfare, especially in Bambalapitiya, and also in well-established residential and business zones like Borella and Kotahena. In the most dense shopping district, called Pettah, Tamil shops and shops of Indian merchants, selling principally cloth and wholesale foodstuffs were targeted. Moreover, shops located in the city's newer and expanding residential areas such as Timbirigasyaya and Nugegoda were also affected.

3. Textile mills, garment factories, rubber goods factories, coconut oil distilling plants at Ratmalana, Ja-ela, and Peliyagoda, at the edges of the city, owned and managed by Tamil entrepreneurs and large businessmen.

4. Indian Overseas Bank, the principal bank of Sri Lankans of Indian origin and of Indian citizens in Sri Lanka.

The victims in Colombo were Tamil shopkeepers; Tamil homeowners, especially of the middle class and administrative, clerical, and professional categories; large Tamil business capitalists and entrepreneurs; and Indian merchants, both Tamil and non-Tamil.

These facts clearly indicate that the locations were central market and business zones, locations of new industrial development stimulated by the new "liberalization policy" in economic activities initiated by the Jayawardene government in 1977, and middle-class residential areas. Arson in slums and working-class residential zones was practically absent.

We now turn to the all-important question of the participants. At the most general level the rioters on the Sinhalese side were all male and virtually all drawn from the urban population of Colombo and its suburbs. Those who engaged in acts of aggression, arson, property destruction, and looting as well as those who actually took human lives and inflicted bodily injury were typically drawn from the urban working class, particularly those in government factories, the laborers, small businessmen, and others employed in the congested bazaars and markets, secondary school students and recent school dropouts, the urban underclass of unemployed and underemployed, the residents of shanty towns.

A more detailed enumeration includes the following "occupational" categories: wage workers in factories and mills; transport workers, such as bus drivers and conductors, workers in railway yards and electrical installations; petty traders and workers in markets, including fish mongers and market porters; small shopkeepers and salesmen in government corporations; hospital workers and attendants; high school students and students of technical institutes and tutories[7] including recent school dropouts. The literacy explosion and the poor employment prospects of school graduates and dropouts are potent factors in motivating the last category.

It would be a mistake to exclude from the list of participants those whose involvements were less "visible" but important in the initiation, the organization, and the direction of the riots. Certain Sinhala politicians and their local managers and bosses, entrepreneurs of organized crime and smuggling, small businessmen (the *mudalalis*) and their

---

7. Small academies—some not very reputable—that prepare students for exams.

henchmen figure prominently as the directors and manipulators of mass violence. Some of them could be described as "riot captains" who were experts at arousing a mob. We cannot leave out of account the role of some militant Buddhist monks in inciting crowd action, sometimes as active witnesses and orators. Nor can we discount the calculated support rendered by some businessmen who took this opportunity to eliminate their business rivals. Finally, it has been well attested that many members of the police force and security forces stood by during the 1983 riots—unwilling to restrain the rioters, showing sympathy for their actions, and in a few instances actively participating in the work of destruction.

The Mounting Violence and the Indian Intervention

While some activist monks participated in the riots as agitators, it can definitely be said that the vast majority of monks were by and large not directly involved in the riots, nor in the immediately preceding events, when the issues that now engaged the Sinhalese and the Tamils seemed to be more "political" and "territorial," focused on secession and "homelands," peasant colonization and discrimination, than directly "religious" in the sense of "the restoration of Buddhism," which had been the dominant rhetoric of the late fifties and the sixties. But soon they would reengage in politics in large numbers.

The years 1984–87 were largely a time of the engagement of the government's army and security forces with the Tamil militants of the north and east. But surely and unavoidably civilians on both sides became aroused. During these years certain incidents took place which would periodically inflame the Buddhist and nationalist sentiments of the public at large, including many sections of the Buddhist *sangha*. In 1985 Tamil militants took the fateful step of attacking for the first time Sinhalese civilians in the vicinity of the sacred Bo Tree in the historic city of Anuradhapura, a city that is not merely a reminder and repository of ancient glory, but also the focus of pious and celebrated pilgrimages, and at the heart of the region of expanding peasant resettlement, and the "reclamation" and "repeopling" of the ancient kingdom immortalized by the *Mahavamsa*. Increasingly, Sinhalese civilians, monks, and Buddhist temples became the targets of Tamil militant attacks. A particularly notorious case was the brutal killing at Arantalawa in 1986 of a busload of monks returning from a pilgrimage. The Sinhalese army had previously not only killed many Tamil civilians but also demolished Hindu temples and killed their priests. Now the Tamil rebels began to do the same, hitting the Sinhalese at their sacred sites, thereby making a statement that they were prepared to indulge in the same kind of violence against civilians, bystanders, and nonmilitary targets as the armed forces did. The Sinhalese civilians became themselves directly implicated in the civil war in the northern and eastern provinces, when the government distributed arms to Sinhalese civilian home guards and encouraged them to engage with the Tamil dissidents because its own army was unable to contain, let alone defeat, the Tamil militants.

Thus, by the mid-eighties, as we shall see in the following chapters, various protest organizations and movements made up of varying numbers of members of political parties, Buddhist monks, and concerned laymen were being formed not only to support the war against Tamil separation but also to protest against any tendency on the part of the UNP government to negotiate a peace with the Tamil insurgents on the basis of a devolution of powers to provincial councils. At the same time the Indian government's support for the Tamil "rebels" and application of pressure on the Sri Lankan government to cease its economic blockade of Jaffna, and its army's determined last push, called the Vadamarachi Operation, to eradicate the rebels, finally forced Jayawardene to sign the Indo–Sri Lanka Peace Accord in July 1987.

The peace accord allowed for the entry into Sri Lanka of a large Indian army (estimated at its maximum to be around 55,000 troops) to enforce the accord and to pacify the north and the east, and to achieve what the Sinhalese armed forces had hitherto failed to accomplish. It seemed that the Sri Lankan government had on its side, apart from the threat of an Indian armed invasion, good reasons for signing the accord: with the increasing destabilizing and oppositional militancy being mounted by the JVP (which was banned in 1983) in the core Sinhalese majority provinces (in central, southwestern, southern parts of the island), the government felt the need to withdraw its troops in order to deploy them against the insurrectionary threat in its own midst.

But the accord stirred the fears of Sinhalese nationalists on many grounds. While affirming the need to preserve the unity and integrity of Sri Lanka, the accord acknowledged that Sri Lanka was "a multiethnic and multilingual plural society," that each ethnic group had its "distinct cultural and linguistic identity," which had to be nurtured, and that "the northern and eastern provinces have been areas of historical habitation of the Sri Lankan Tamil-speaking peoples" while sharing "this territory with other ethnic groups." This was tantamount to recognizing the north and east as the "homelands" of the Tamils, subject to the residential rights of other groups.

The accord also stated that once peace was restored, a single provincial council consisting of both the northern and eastern provinces would be formed; it was understood on the basis of previous negotiations that this provincial council would have all powers held by a state in the Indian union. Elections to the council were to be held before the end of 1987. The president of Sri Lanka was authorized to hold a referendum in the eastern province in the course of the following year to determine whether the people in that area (the Muslims were nearly a third of the population) wished to remain united with the north or have a separate provincial council of their own.

The annexure to the accord provided for an Indian peace-keeping contingent, as and when requested by the Sri Lankan government, to help in terminating the hostilities and to implement the terms of the agreement. This agreement to an active Indian presence and intervention in Sri Lankan affairs (which in fact did happen subsequently) was further complicated by an agreement between the Indian and Sri Lankan governments in an exchange of letters that neither the port of Trincomalee nor any other part of the island will be made "available for military use by any country in a manner prejudicial to India's interests."

While some ministers even within the UNP government (like Prime Minister Premadasa and Minister for National Security Athulathmudali) thought that their leader President Jayawardene had conceded too much, opposition forces quickly coalesced, however tenuously and intermittently, to create an uproar. They were led by the SLFP, the main opposition party and supported by the MEP and the JVP. The objections, which exploited the most unfavorable readings of the terms of the accord, were that the government had acceded to the Tamil extremists' demand for their separate "homelands," that the island had thereby been dismembered and partitioned, and that Sri Lanka had become a pawn and a client state of India, which had geopolitical ambitions of exercising hegemony over the Indian Ocean. The actual presence of a large Indian army was an effective stick to beat the UNP with and to play upon all the historic fears of old about marauding Tamils invading the island and threatening the unity and sovereignty of a beleaguered but twenty-five-hundred-year-old Sinhala Buddhist polity.

One of the complicating factors in Sri Lanka's current conflict is that the issue of devolution itself is a highly emotional and explosive one, carrying different meanings for different individuals and groups. A separate state of Eelam; a federal union between Tamil and Sinhalese states; a unitary state with devolution of power to regional or provincial councils; the recognition of a merger between existing northern and eastern provinces, or portions of them, so as to constitute "Tamil homelands"; the exact powers and functions with regard to security, defense, taxation, peasant colonization, education, and so on that are to be reserved to the center and allocated to the regional or provincial councils: these are only some of many issues which have been periodically discussed by the Sri Lankan and Indian governments, with or without Tamil representatives of the TULF and the militants being present.

Especially since 1985, prodded by the Indian government, which wanted Sri Lanka to settle its ethnic conflict, President Jayawardene engaged in a series of dialogues and negotiations. Thus in June 1985 under Indian auspices, the Sri Lankan government directly negotiated with the Tamil insurgents in Thimpu, the capital of Bhutan. This dialogue was derailed when the Tamil insurgents walked out because the Sri Lankan government rejected the recognition of Tamils as a distinct nationality and of the territorial integrity of their "homelands." Then in September 1985 discussions were held between Sri Lankan and Indian officials in New Delhi, the chief topic being the establishment of elected provincial councils and the powers to be given them. The issues broached included the fiscal, legislative, and executive powers to be given the councils; the role of the center and the provinces in controlling the police; the control of land grants in irrigation schemes on an ethnic basis in major (national) projects as opposed to minor schemes left entirely to the provinces; and the terms on which Parliament could amend the legislation relating to provincial councils. But the TULF politicians at this time in exile in Madras as well as the Tamil militants rejected these provisions—they had been excluded from the negotiations—and reiterated their demand for a merger of the northern and eastern provinces to form a Tamil homeland and favored a less powerful and more power-sharing federal government.

Then again in July 1986, after a visit by an Indian delegation led by India's Minister of State Chidambaram, the Sri Lankans countered with the concession that the separate provincial councils of the northern and eastern provinces could consult each other and act in coordination in matters of common interest and that they would have more or less the same powers enjoyed by the states of the Indian Federal Union. Subsequently, in December, after the Bangalore talks between Rajiv Gandhi and Jayawardene, the possibility was discussed of detaching Amparai district from the eastern province to ensure that Tamils would form a majority in that province. These were the successive dialogues and bargaining regarding the terms of a possible settlement that had been engaged in, until after further deterioration in the ethnic conflict, the imposition of an economic blockade, and the launching of a determined push by the Sinhala army in the North in 1987 (the Vadamarachi operation), the Indian government decisively intervened to lift the blockade and to sign the Indo–Sri Lanka Peace Accord.

All these deliberations I have outlined were concerned with specifying terms of a devolutionary solution, and no doubt much progress had been made toward a solution that was finally embodied in the Indo–Sri Lanka Peace Accord. But this accord was an agreement between two governments. And the interpretation and implementation of its terms would provide plenty of contentious space for the Sinhalese parties and interest groups in opposition to the UNP government, on the one hand, and to the Tamil dissidents and militants whose participation in the negotiations was irregular, discontinuous, and not binding, on the other. In this situation of ambiguity, disagreement, misperception, mischievous exaggeration, and bad faith among the Tamil dissidents, the Sinhala political parties, and various pressure groups, "devolution" was a rallying cry of hope and reconciliation for some, or a warning slogan of dividing and dismembering the country for others, or a talking point for stretching out the conflict and regrouping for still others.

10 The Mavbima Surakime Vyaparaya (MSV): The Movement for the Protection of the Motherland

In two informative papers, Schalk and Amunugama describe and discuss how the Buddhist *sangha* engaged in political action and exercised power through linkages with political parties and, indirectly, through monks' participation in intersecting, joint, intermediary militant movements composed of laity and monks.[1] These movements and organizations, militantly Buddhist, have proliferated in the eighties and focused on the Sinhala-Tamil ethnic conflict allegedly in order to protect the rights of "the sons of the soil," the native Sinhalese, heirs to the island, and protectors of the Buddhist religion. These movements harked back to, and reactivated, on the one hand, the enduring slogans of the remote past enshrined in the *Mahavamsa,* such as Dhammadipa, the island's unification under King Dutthagamani, and the more recent Sinhala Buddhist nationalism and revivalism of Dharmapala. On the other hand, they reacted to and addressed proximate and immediate events of the present-day ethnic conflict and its "murderous" Tamil separatism. They warned against the dangers of a devolutionary solution to the ethnic conflict which they interpreted as the partition of a unitary island, and, finally, opposed the terms of the Indo–Sri Lanka Peace Accord of July 29, 1987, which they interpreted as the ignominious capitulation to the designs of imperialist India and its sponsorship of the Tamil cause.

Schalk enumerates some seven leading organizations formed since 1979, with members drawn from political parties, lay circles, and the ranks of Buddhist monks, which had as their principal purpose the

1. Peter Schalk, "'Unity' and 'Sovereignty': Key Concepts of a Militant Buddhist Organization in the Present Conflict in Sri Lanka," *Temenos* 24 (1989): 55–82; Sarath Amunugama, "Buddhaputra and Bhumiputra? Dilemmas of Modern Sinhala Buddhist Monks in Relation to Ethnic and Political Conflict," *Religion* 21 (1991): 115–39.

promotion of the interests of Sinhala Buddhists as the true "sons of the soil."[2] We are here primarily concerned with one of these organizations, the Mavbima Surakime Vyaparaya (MSV), founded in July 1986. It was a wide-ranging umbrella organization, which in turn included many of the new lay and clerical Buddhist organizations such as the Sinhala Bala Mandalaya and the Jatika Peramuna. Through demonstrations, rallies, and printed tracts, the MSV conducted a most vigorous campaign for maintaining the "unity" and "sovereignty" of Sri Lanka.

I shall try to give an account of the MSV with regard to its (1) membership and organization; (2) ideology and propaganda; (3) and its political activities, primarily in order to tease out and evaluate its "Buddhist" impulsions and content and to focus on the nature of the involvement of Buddhist monks in the political turmoil of the eighties, including the practice of collective violence.

The MSV's Membership and Organization
It is worth listing the organizational components and leading figures in the MSV, which is an amalgam of both laity and monks in their professed identity and unity as Buddhists and as non-Marxists, but anti-UNP political oppositionists. This broad coalition against the UNP is constituted of three entities: members of political parties, members of the *sangha,* and individual lay Buddhist enthusiasts and special cause activists.

1. From the political parties, we have in the forefront of the MSV, the SLFP led by the former prime minister, Sirimavo Bandaranaike, the MEP led by Dinesh Gunawardena (the son of Philip Gunawardena, the founder), and a front organization of the banned JVP called the Sri Lanka Deshapremi Peramuna.[3] Other conspicuous politicians involved were Rukman Senanayake, who started his political career as a UNP member of Parliament and has drifted into the opposition. He was for a time an advocate of JVP views, but later distanced himself from the JVP; he also lost his seat in the 1989 elections. Prins

---

2. Other organizations in existence and concerned with political-religious causes are the All Ceylon Buddhist Congress and the national branch of the World Fellowship of Buddhists.

3. There were two other smaller parties listed by Amunugama, namely, Sinhala Bala Mandalaya, led by Nath Amerakone, and Sinhala Janata Peramuna.

Gunasekera is another former member of Parliament, who began with MEP affiliations, shifted to the SLFP, and later left it to lead the Human and Democratic Rights Organization concerned with civil rights. He became a radical nationalist and a civil rights defense lawyer, especially on behalf of defendants belonging to the JVP.

2. In understanding the participation of Buddhist monks it is relevant to note that they have many organizational identities, and according to context and cause they might mobilize in terms of one or the other. At the same time it is noteworthy that these multiple memberships, identities, and interests may sometimes work at cross purposes, and thus also lead to fragmentation, weak organizational structure, and lack of sustained activity.

Their first organizational identity is "sectarian" stemming from their *nikaya* membership in the Siyam, Amarapura, and Ramanna nikayas that are distributed in various strengths throughout the island. The next is the separate territorial grouping on a district (*palata*) basis of the monks belonging to each *nikaya;* these are smaller locality groupings that are more solidary and face to face. Each of the three sects has its head monk (*mahanayake*) and a working committee (*karaka sabha*) who speak officially on the entire *nikaya*'s behalf. The sect leadership appoints a monk to be head of each of its "district" groupings.

Buddhist monks belonging to all three *nikaya* may band together to form special-interest associations with a political agenda. Their membership is therefore tri-*nikaya,* and they have known links to political parties and may thus be acknowledged as branches or components of the UNP, SLFP, MEP, JVP, and so on. These special-interest political associations of monks on a tri-*nikaya* basis may be organized at local, regional, or national levels and may be mobilized at all these levels for rallies, meetings, and launching movements.[4]

Just as named political parties and their members were represented in activist coalitions of both lay and monk associations, so were monks and their voluntary tri-*nikaya* groupings. Moreover, as we shall see shortly, some of the politically active monks leading lay and monk movements also have their lay followings in their capacity as leaders of other causes and platforms (e.g., temperance and even a nurses

4. Amunugama, "Buddhaputra and Bhumiputra?" p. 119, names three such national organizations, two of which are JVP-oriented and the third MEP-oriented. They are Sri Lanka Deshapremi Peramuna and Deshapremi Taruna Bhikshu Sanvidanaya (both JVP-oriented), and Samastha Lanka Pragatisili Bhikshu Peramuna (MEP-oriented).

trade union). Buddhist monks have participated as officials (chairmen, board members), not only in the associations limited to themselves, but also in these coalition organizations where politicians, monks, and lay activists join hands.

It is relevant to focus on some of the leading Buddhist monk political activists of the eighties to illustrate their multiple identities, constituencies and causes, and their functioning within the coalition represented by the MSV.

Two of these prominent monks came into the MSV in 1986 as leaders of pre-existing organizations combining politicians, monks, and lay activists. One was Sobhita Thero, a charismatic and rousing preacher and propagandist leader of the Sinhala Bala Mandalaya, founded earlier in 1982, and in sympathy with the SLFP.[5] The other was Palipane Chandananda Thero, the head monk of the historic Asgiriya chapter of the Siyam Nikaya in Kandy, a leading founder of the Jatika Peramuna in August 1985, and who in alliance again with Mrs. Bandaranaike of the SLFP has offered powerful resistance to the peace accord.

Certain biographical details of these two monks—Sobhita and Chandananda, and a third called Muruttetuve Ananda Thero—who, in the eighties, were the leading political activists drawn from the *sangha,* are useful in understanding the way in which personal ambitions, political patronage, and contemporary concerns and opportunities intertwine and cause inevitable disappointments and entanglements and become the ingredients of and impulsions for another "level" of action which we can label national religio-politics.[6]

Sobhita Thero, the head monk of Naga Viharaya in Kotte, was in earlier years sponsored by Ananda Tissa D'Alwis, a member of Parliament for Kotte constituency, who was minister of information in the UNP-controlled government from 1978 to 1987. Sobhita, a university graduate, became a popular preacher in the seventies on Radio Ceylon. When he began to voice some sentiments critical of the UNP, however, President Jayawardene ruled that his connection with Radio Ceylon be discontinued. This was an important ingredient in his later support of the SLFP and his strong criticism of the president's attempts

---

5. Nath Amerakoon was a lay leader of this organization at this time. With a Sinhala educational background, he was trained as an engineer in England. He became secretary of the Ministry of Housing under Mrs. Bandaranaike and lost his job when her government fell in 1977.

6. I am indebted to Sarath Amunugama for these details (personal communication).

to settle the ethnic conflict. Sobhita is also chairman of the Youth Temperance Movement.

Chandananda Thero's social origins are in the lower levels of Kandyan rural aristocracy. He was ordained young and he has climbed the ladder of the Siyam Nikaya hierarchy. Earlier he, too, was a supporter of the UNP, but his relations to a local UNP member of Parliament and minister, E. L. Senanayake, cooled. And he seemed to have more sympathetic support from Mrs. Bandaranaike, who also stems from the Kandyan aristocracy, than from Jayawardene, and became pro-SLFP. There is also the factor of rivalry between the two branches of the Siyam Nikaya located in Kandy, namely, the Asgiriya chapter which Chandananda leads and the Malvatta chapter which is currently more pro-UNP. Being of the Goyigama caste and a leader in the Siyam Nikaya, Chandananda is structurally in the right position to lead all sections of the Buddhist *sangha* engaged in political protest against the alleged impending division of the country and compromise of the supremacy of Buddhism.

Muruttetuve Ananda Thero is the incumbent of a temple called Abhayarama, located in Narahenpita at the end of Thimbirigasyaya Road, almost at the edge of the city of Colombo. The locality has a mixed middle-class, working-class and a poor underclass population. This temple, too, is considered today a locus of anti-UNP sentiments and is even alleged to have had connections with the youth insurgents of the JVP.

Once again, we find that this monk had earlier enjoyed UNP support: his temple lay in the constituency of M. D. H. Jayawardena who was minister of health in the UNP government and who appointed Ananda Thero as chaplain to the Nurses Union. He proved to be a successful counsellor and, because of factional rivalries within the union, was, as an "outsider," deemed suitable to be made president of the Nurses Union. Muruttetuve became opposed to the UNP when President J. R. Jayawardene thought it improper for a monk to be president of such a union and wanted him removed.

Muruttetuve's career took a radical activist turn, and he led several militant strikes staged by the nurses union, a notably successful one being that conducted in 1978. He engaged in other trade union actions as well. His temple was a venue and host for large meetings staged by strikers and attended by many young monks at which, aside from himself, many lay speakers gave voice, including feminist leaders of women's organizations supporting the cause of the nurses. A

Women's Day, falling on March 8, was once celebrated in the temple premises. Because the temple was considered a safe place, many small leftist groups used it for their meetings and had access to its telephone. When a banned rally that formed outside the temple was broken up by the police, a student was shot and killed. Muruttetuve's sympathies ultimately gravitated toward the radical but chauvinist rhetoric of the JVP. The more orthodox left-wing groups drifted away from him, and at the end of the eighties he became a leader of the MSV.

The Ideology of the MSV

The members of the MSV, like many "patriotic" Sinhalese, reject the claim of the Tamil insurrectionists and politicians to their own "homelands" and are totally opposed to any devolutionary solution to the conflict (equating and exaggerating any notion of provincial councils as a "division" of the country). The MSV's special Buddhist dimension comes from its plea that a "division" of the country and the weakening of its sovereignty would also diminish, even doom, Buddhism and the Sinhala culture that it supports. These are not specifically "monkish" preoccupations or slogans, but today monks are proclaiming these views and waving these banners as participants of clearly "political organizations" and even as adherents of different political parties, while also keeping their membership in purely *sangha*-linked organizations. If the Vidyalankara monks of the 1950s first asserted the rights of the monks to engage in politics, and the Eksath Bhikkhu Peramuna, as a canvassing phalanx of monks, largely won the elections for Bandaranaike in 1956, and if in the sixties and seventies we saw a bipolar division within the *sangha* paralleling the contest between the two political parties, the UNP and the SLFP, today we see a further transformation of the *sangha*. The monks are more differentiated, having pluralistic affiliations, and participate not only in coalition groups composed of politicians, laity, and monks, but also as branch units and wings of political parties as encompassing units.

The affirmation and nonnegotiability of the unity and indivisibility of the country were not solely addressed against the alleged dangers of Tamil secession and the threatening and humiliating presence of the Indian army. They are also directed at another suspected enemy—the Catholic Church, which is thought to have made inroads into the Sinhalese population and as proselytizer might steal more Buddhists.

This animus against the Catholic Church should be linked to previously discussed themes of "betrayal" and "restoration" of Buddhism and the government takeover of the majority of denominational schools (the Catholic Church being the biggest loser), the termination of Catholic nuns working in government hospitals, and the parallel policies to strengthen Buddhism in schools.

The ethnic conflict had, in fact, split the Catholic Church into two camps—one championing the Sinhalese nationalist claims and the other defending the Tamil opposition and its political aspirations. Bishop Fernando of Chilaw and Bishop Deogupillai of Jaffna publicly engaged in both accusatory and defensive pronouncements on behalf of their own Catholic flocks. Moreover, the Roman Catholics in the Sinhalese electorates had traditionally supported the UNP, and this support lent further credibility to the Buddhist nationalists' allegations that President Jayawardene was not firmly committed to the support of Buddhism and to keeping the island undivided. Thus successfully "mixing" and "conflating" issues and messages the *Vinivida,* the only journal published by monks, had this to say in 1988: "A dangerous leopard has donned the white cassock to convert impoverished Buddhist villagers to Catholicism. This is only the first step on the road to Eelam."[7]

Now let us look more closely at the actual verbal expressions, slogans, memories, and symbols invoked by the patriotic campaign.

The expression "sons of the soil" (*bhumiputra*) is widely used in India and elsewhere in Southeast Asia (for example, in Malaysia) as an emotionally charged overriding claim of the "indigenous" people to their territory, in preference to "alien" and "immigrant peoples" who have come later. In Sri Lanka today, many Sinhalese patriotic groups freely use this slogan. In turn, two key concepts of the MSV (and other "sons of the soil" Sri Lankan organizations) are "unity" (*ekiya bhavaya*) and "sovereignty" (*svairi bhavaya*). These terms revive, says Schalk, the "one umbrella" (*eka chatta*) imagery used in the ancient *Mahavamsa* chronicle to represent the unification of the country under the glorified hero Dutthagamani. Today, aside from the flag itself, the words "lion flag" are also used to symbolize unity and sovereignty, and they figure prominently in martial songs propagated through youth organizations. The pure lion flag of Dutthagamani (which lacks the green and orange stripes in the present-day flag meant

7. Cited in Amunugama, "Buddhaputra and Bhumiputra?" p. 127.

to represent the Muslim and Tamil minorities) is fused with the notion of "Sinhala race" (*hela jatiya*). A medieval Sinhala expression *tun sinhalaya*, standing for three provinces (Rajarata, Mayarata and Ruhunarata), which as a unity constituted the precolonial Kandyan Kingdom, is also used nowadays to express the unity and indivisibility of the motherland (*mavbima*) that is the birthright of the sons of the soil.[8] When we discover that the head monk of the important Amarapura Nikaya, Madihe Pannasiha, pronounces that the "Sinhala Buddhist flag" (which has deleted the stripes for the minorities) is the only flag that reminds people of their essence and identity as Sinhalese and Buddhists, we realize to what extent fetishized nationalism compounded of race and territory—"the sons of the soil" ideology—has suffused the vocation of monkhood as set out in doctrinal Buddhism. This is one half of the story of Buddhism transformed. The monk ideologues, who include leaders of other branches of the *sangha*, speaking in the name of the Ramanna Nikaya, the Malvatta and Asiriya chapters of the Siyam Nikaya, have also primordialized and romanticized the "unity" of the country to a pristine homogeneity devoid of differences of political party and the divisions of party government. At the other end influential preacher monks like Sobhita Thero, leading rallies of the MSV, using the language of militancy and trading on holy war resonances, have condoned as righteous the campaigns launched against "the Tamil terrorists." They also preach the need to safeguard the Sinhalese of the hill country from the creeping nationalism of the Indian Tamils so as to secure a "Sinhalese peace" premised on a country under one umbrella, saved from the peril of "federal states based on racial division."[9] And they have argued that the provision of the Constitution of 1978, which gave "Buddhism the foremost place" in the republic, would be threatened by the equality granted to all religions as a necessary accompaniment of a divided (federalized) country.

As Amunugama sums it up:

> The 1980s see the rapid politicization of the Sinhala Sangha. . . . All Sinhala-based political parties have established support organizations among the sangha. They

8. Schalk, "'Unity' and 'Sovereignty,'" pp. 64–66. A youth organization song translated by Schalk has the title "by the Lion Flag"; its first two lines are: "By the lion flag, under the white parasol of the Sinhalese, We would bring together the three Sinhala [regions]."

9. The government's proposal of devolution of powers to provincial councils is thus turned into the stronger notion of federal states.

compete for the monks' favors by offering them material
benefits—official residences, Mercedes Benz cars, trips
abroad, state appointments and construction of temples.
Pirivenas and universities became recruitment centers of
monks for different political parties. The ethnic conflict
provided an opportunity for monks to openly engage in
social and political activity since it was presented as a national concern. (Amunugama, 1991, p. 127)

This was taken to its logical extreme when later the JVP viewed and
recruited the monk "as another foot soldier in the revolutionary
struggle."

Thus, after the signing of the Indo–Sri Lanka Peace Accord, the cry
first coined by the JVP—"Motherland above all"—became a generalized battle cry, and was suitably (and humorously) adapted to their
needs by university students, secondary school students, and scholar-
monks in seminaries as "Motherland first, degree second"; "Motherland first, school second"; and "Motherland first, pirivena second"
(ibid., pp. 126–27).

The Activities of the MSV

On paper the MSV, which in November 1986 claimed to
have some forty affiliated organizations, has constructed an elaborate
organizational chart: a board of secretaries, both lay and clerical, at
the top to direct administrative activities, and at the base, at the district
level, the formation of units of no less than one hundred persons,
drawn from "youth, women, peasants, laborers, and students." It was
the stated intention that these "sections of society" would be organized
as separate "fronts" of youth, women, peasants, laborers, and students
"for protection of the motherland . . . and in order to face the threats
that might come from [Tamil] terrorists to the rest of the people living
in the village" (Schalk, p. 76). It is noteworthy that in this mobilization
plan for the defense of village and mother country, the MSV regarded
the focal entity at the grass-roots level to be the "temple" (whether
Buddhist, Muslim, or Hindu) and its surrounding "parish." The primary point to extract from this is that the MSV automatically regarded
monasteries and their incumbents, surrounded by outer circles of lay
parishioners and congregations, themselves organized as sectional
fronts, as the battle plan for positive action for saving the Sinhalese
people from terrorism, division of the country, drugs and liquor, and
for islandwide propagation of Buddhism.

There is no doubt that this paper plan was more utopian than realistic, and under the present circumstances could not be realized as a sustained grass-roots movement. As Schalk has demonstrated, the effectiveness and visibility of the MSV lay in its short-term spasmodic capacity to organize "colorful rallies all over the country led by famous and heart-stirring speakers who can stimulate and mobilize the masses. The MSV has only one aim, to counteract the government's proposals of provincial councils. This aim may be achieved through mass meetings, but it is scarcely adequate as a program on a long-term basis. . . . As soon as the government has made a final decision about the provincial councils . . . there will no longer be any need for the MSV. It is only in the present situation of conflict and contingency that the MSV can flourish" (ibid., p. 77).

Thus, the campaign of the MSV in our era of participatory politics and crowd formations consisted in its devotion to and expertise in mobilizing masses for rallies and demonstrations. Emotional slogans, stirring rhetoric from the mouths of impassioned speakers, the massing of people amidst flags and loudspeakers, the converging of linear processions in a central arena to fuse into a milling mass—these episodic, short-lived spectacles were and are effective in putting pressure on the leading politicians and their parties. They have the impact of opinion polls and instantaneous media transmission.[10] How sensitive and vulnerable politicians are to them is well portrayed in James Manor's biography of S. W. R. D. Bandaranaike.[11] Schalk reports that "between the end of August and the middle of September 1986 as many as sixteen rallies were planned—almost one daily" and that by November of the same year thirty rallies had been held. We can take the story further where Schalk leaves off—the story of how on the eve of the actual signing of the Indo–Sri Lanka Peace Accord on July 29, 1987, an accord which for members of MSV coalition conceded to the Tamils and to the Indian government the very "unity" and "sovereignty" of the country, a mass rally of protest organized by the MSV deteriorated in a horrible riot in Colombo.

On July 28, 1987, the major components of the MSV—the SLFP with Mrs. Bandaranaike and other leaders of that party, the MEP led

10. Schalk, pp. 57–58. One document published by the MSV claimed that "These rallies have given to the country a correct understanding about the provincial council ordinance which has been proposed by the President, Mr. J. R. Jayawardene, and which aims to divide the country." Schalk, p. 64.

11. James Manor, *The Expedient Utopian: Bandaranaike and Ceylon* (Cambridge: Cambridge University Press, 1989).

by Dinesh Gunawardena, the banned JVP represented by university student supporters, and finally monks numbering at least two hundred from virtually all their member organizations—staged a procession and assembled under a sacred Bo tree in Pettah, Colombo's "native" commercial center. The location, adjacent to the central bus station and near the Fort Railway Station, was chosen so as to enable the commuting participants to congregate easily. A huge crowd had formed, and the monks as well as the lay leaders waving black flags urged the people to protect the motherland from division and to oppose the accord which would pave the way for India to take control of the island. Jayawardene's government in turn was prepared to disperse the crowd by force. The positioned police fired canisters of tear gas into the crowd, which breaking out in different directions went on a destructive rampage. According to one report, during this riot which lasted one day, nineteen civilians were killed and more than a hundred were reported wounded when the police fired into the crowds.[12] The mobs set fire to eighty buses, scores of cars, and a number of buildings, including shops, hospitals, and other government property. The government then took the step of sealing off the major entry points into the city, when it was heard that crowds were massing in the immediate suburbs with intent to march to the city center.

This political demonstration deteriorating into a riot was the climactic point in the political rallies mounted by the MSV as well as the beginning of its disarray. Many participants were put off by the violence itself. The monks had been publicly, rudely, and summarily put in vans and taken away. The JVP and its youthful enthusiasts would now turn to the practice of their own brand of insurgency marked by terrorism and violence.

Recapitulation

This essay has spanned a fairly long period of time, from late colonialism through independence and the alleged "social revolution" of 1956 to the late eighties, when the island of Sri Lanka was racked with serious internal conflict.

The primary issue has been the role of Buddhism itself as a religion, and of Buddhist monks as the "exemplars" of that religion, and of lay activists who identify themselves as espousing "Buddhist" causes, in the unfolding politics and the mounting violence associated with the

12. See Seth Mydans, *New York Times,* July 29, 1987.

ethnic conflict between the Sinhalese and Tamils and, most recently, with the insurrectionary movement of the JVP within the Sinhala body politic itself.

In my narration of events from the late forties onward, I placed in the forefront the ideological work focused on three objectives: the construction of the monk as a political actor from early times; a critique of British rule and the Christian missions as injurious to Buddhism; and a program for the restoration of Buddhism to its rightful place. I highlighted two moments when the political activism of the Buddhist monks peaked, first in 1956 and in the years immediately following, and then in the mid-eighties, when resolution of the ethnic conflict was sought through a political agreement interpreted by its opponents as a dismemberment of a country that must remain under Sinhala Buddhist control and domination.

But there is a big difference between the late fifties and the late eighties. In the earlier climactic phase the "restoration" of a "betrayed" Buddhism was couched and implemented in ways that could be seen as the strengthening of Buddhism and the eradication of inequalities resulting from colonialism: the recognition of Sinhala as the official language, the creation of Buddhist universities, the takeover of most of the Christian mission schools, the creation of a ministry to promote Sinhala culture, the formal recognition in 1972 of Buddhism as having "the foremost place" in the country, and so on. Many of these positive measures were actually implemented in the SLFP government of S. W. R. D. Bandaranaike's widow and successor, Sirimavo, and these restoration goals had been virtually achieved by 1970. Moreover, the UNP had progressively fallen in line with the SLFP's policy on these matters. Many activist monks, under the umbrella of the Eksath Bhikkhu Peramuna, had become sufficiently focused to help Bandaranaike win the 1956 elections, and to influence political decisions directly for a while. But by the seventies the *sangha* had returned to a steady state of differentiation and divided affiliations distributed between the two major parties, the UNP and SLFP ranged in a bipolar contest.

In the late 1980s many monks, more divided and bearing multiple cross-cutting identities, did enter into a coalition movement with laity for political purposes. But this time the primary slogans, for monks as well as laity, were the unity and sovereignty of the "motherland," and their major identity was as "sons of the soil," whose political legacy was Buddhism. The Buddhist content and impulsion in a strictly doctrinal sense here is different, if not more distant, than in the fifties; in the latest phase there is substantively no concrete and plausible Buddhist program to implement, although there exists a "Buddhist" critique of the political economy of the country and the present social order which is important to take into account. The phenomenon of the late eighties may be seen by some observers as the final shift of "political Buddhism" from a more localized religiosity of earlier times primarily enacted among monk-laity circles in villages and towns in terms of ethical teachings, moral concerns, and gift-giving (*dana*) to a vocal and sloganized "religious-mindedness," which has objectified and fetishized the religion and espoused a "Buddhist nationalism," even as regards the monks themselves, so that important tenets of their religion regarding detachment, compassion, tranquility, and nonviolence and the overcoming of mental impurities are subordinated and made less relevant to Sinhala religio-nationalist and social reform goals. In this changed context, Buddhism in its militant, populist, fetishized form, as espoused by certain groups, seems to some observers to have been emptied of much of its normative and humane ethic, denuded of its story-telling homilies through the Jataka stories, and to function as a marker of crowd and mob identity, as a rhetorical mobilizer of volatile masses, and as an instigator of spurts of violence. As Newton Gunasinha has remarked, the monk who previously preached to village congregations now commands the limelight in the media as a representative of the *sangha,* which claims to be "the guardian of the nation," and "myths of how the sangha stepped forward when the Sinhala nation was in danger are daily recounted in the populist media."[13] Though this judgment is on the mark, it is incomplete. A serious study of the polemical comments and critiques of activist monk-ideologues definitely reveals that there is a Buddhist content and a Buddhist-inspired evaluation that colors the Buddhist nationalism advocated today. This topic will be given full attention later.

It may be that a homogenizing national identity indexed to an objectified Buddhism, whose universalistic ethical message is temporarily repressed, is consonant with new directions and magnitudes taken by popular Sinhalese religiosity in the guise of ecstatic cults and *bhakti*-type worship of gods, such as Kataragama, and in the form of mass

---

13. Newton Gunasingha, "The Symbolic Role of the Sangha," *Lanka Guardian,* October 15, 1986, pp. 9–10.

rituals addressed to the *bodhi* tree as a cult object. The intensified pre-occupation with spirit cults and seeking favors from deities, documented by Obeyesekere (and others), may well signal a religious change.[14] But an account of the transformation of Buddhism is gravely distorted and deficient if there is no account of the political direction and transformation taken by Buddhism in this century. This account must show the trajectory and changes in the *sangha*'s involvement in politics in alliance with the lay supporters and the substantive and pragmatic issues that were embedded in the phases manifested by political Buddhism. These phases are the "Buddhist revivalism and nationalism" spearheaded by Dharmapala and his successors in earlier decades; the "restoration" of a Buddhism "betrayed" in the late fifties and the sixties, and the "protection of the Motherland by sons of the soil" in the eighties.

The Buddhist *sangha* in Sri Lanka is a long-lived institution that has experienced discontinuities and upheavals as well as revivals and reactivations. Certain members or segments of the *sangha* may mobilize and coalesce temporarily for pressing their causes and interests in the political domain. But the larger truth about the *sangha* in this century is that it is differentiated on sectarian and regional bases and further fragmented by ordination lineages and property interests. There is no long-term discernible correlation between the political preferences and activities of monks and their differentiated and intersecting associational identities. Of the three sects, the Amarapura Nikaya, whose main sphere of influence is in the south and southwest ("the low country") remains the most fractious and volatile.[15] This sect consists of between thirty and forty splinter groups, whose fragmentation is in part due to the play of caste solidarities (e.g., the Karava and Salagama identities being the most salient) and to the divisive consequences of the support and patronage given temples by their local lay "parishioners" (*dayakas*). The older and larger Siyam Nikaya has had its up-country Kandyan branch in contrastive and competitive relation to the low-country branch, centered in Kotte and Kelaniya. And even in Kandy, as the most recent politics showed, the Malvatta and

14. See Richard Gombrich and Gananath Obeyesekere, *Buddhism Transformed* (Princeton: Princeton University Press, 1988).

15. For their origins and organizational history in the nineteenth century, see Kitsiri Malalgoda, *Buddhism in Sinhalese Society, 1750–1900: A Study of Religious Revival and Change* (Berkeley: University of California Press, 1976).

Asgiriya chapters could diverge. Blessed with temporalities and land endowments, the Siyam Nikaya is capable of a lethargic conservatism and inaction especially on the part of its elderly monks. The Ramanna Nikaya is the smallest, most localized (mainly based around Colombo and its environs) and the least fractious.

The *sangha* has never acted as a unified monolithic agent; all shades of political preferences are reflected in its ranks. And perhaps most important, for the present and the future, it shows no sign of declining or withering away.[16] It would seem that over the decades of this century, the number of monks being recruited to serve in the *sangha* has been stable. The *sangha* is thus reproducing itself. It is still the village youth who comprise the pool from which recruits come. The poorer and more excluded these youth, the more they are attracted by the educational opportunities and material support provided by the *sangha*.[17] There is today the drawing power of acquiring a higher education at the Buddhist universities, and thereafter deploying that cultural capital in educational and other professions. It is true that many of the modern educated monks disrobe and seek white-collar employment, but there is also the growing voice of young monks, who want to remain in robes, while being eligible to practice secular salaried occupations. Finally, by virtue of their social origins, and their commitment to the rightful place of Sinhala Buddhism as the majority religion in the island, many members of the *sangha,* especially the younger cohorts, will tend to be moved by political causes that seek to elevate the status of the underprivileged and the marginalized. In short, the *sangha* necessarily reflects the dynamics and complexities of the larger social, political, and economic context in which it is situated.

16. For these and other remarks on the current state of the *sangha,* I am indebted to Professor H. L. Seneviratne.

17. The *sangha* has by and large recruited its novices and monks "from the middle-peasant/small cultivator layers of rural society, but very rarely from the ranks of the landless rural workers." "The younger monks of today come from social strata less privileged than the rural petty bourgeoisie proper"; Gunasingha, "The Symbolic Role of the Sangha."

Fig. 1. A march and meditation staged by Buddhist monks to protest the Anuradhapura Massacre committed by the Liberation Tigers of Tamil Eelam in 1985.

Fig. 2. Monk students at Colombo University.

Fig. 3. A protest march by young Buddhist monks at the funeral of a university student, Kitsiri Mevan Ranawaka, who was killed at Abhayarama on May 1, 1987.

Fig. 4. A young monk addressing the crowd at Ranawaka's funeral.

Fig. 5. The Reverend Maduluwave Sobitha, president of Sinhala Bala Mandalaya, addressing a May Day rally at Abhayarama, at Narahenpita, Colombo.

Fig. 6. Two oratorical postures of the Reverend Maduluwave Sobitha, president of the Sinhala Bala Mandalaya.

Fig. 7. The Reverend Muruttetuwe Ananda, president of the Nurses Union of Sri Lanka.

Fig. 8. A demonstration for Peace with Justice, consisting of Buddhist monks, Christian priests and nuns, and others. So far a forlorn hope.

11 Monks and Violence Face to Face

The politically active monks of the 1980s, consisting of many established leaders known for their orthodox adherence to rules pertaining to the monastic life and, even more, the young monks, a great number of whom were at the universities and *pirivenas* or had recently left them, were, by virtue of their political commitments, confronted with the matter of having to come to terms with the violence generated by the Tamil-Sinhala conflict, and later by the civil war unleashed within the Sinhala society itself by the JVP. As stated before, Tamil guerrillas had attacked Buddhist temples and killed monks. Sacred pilgrimage sites were being made inaccessible. In this charged atmosphere, it was possible to fling the ancient epithet of *mlecca* ("savage") at those committing heinous crimes against Buddhism.

By and large the Sinhalese army's operations in the north and the east, especially after 1983, when the Tamil insurgents themselves became committed to counterviolence, had been supported by the majority of the Sinhala public. With some notable exceptions, the majority of monks explicitly or privately supported and condoned the Sinhalese army's killing of Tamil guerrillas and had not felt the moral imperative to object to the tribulations imposed on Tamil civilians.

Increasingly in the late eighties, as we have seen, as popular movements composed of politicians, lay enthusiasts, and activist monks formed for protesting against the so-called murderous Tamil Eelamism, and the suspected and feared devolutionary solution to the conflict, the more Buddhist ceremonial and ritual and the preachings of monks invoking allegedly Buddhist concepts and justifications informed and colored and legitimated the public posture. Slightly changing Amunugama's title, I find it necessary to pose the question of how the "sons of Buddha"—ideally dedicated to nonviolence and required by disciplinary rules to abstain from killing and to be no-

95

where near marching armies and the traffic in arms—have taken on the more compelling identity of "sons of the soil," which entails militant and violent politics. The most dramatic illustration of this transformation came in a May day parade in 1982, when about a thousand young monks affiliated with the JVP "clad in their distinctive saffron red robes walked under the banner of the socialist Bhikkhu Front."[1]

In the charters and propaganda sheets of these movements, "Buddhist" aims and objectives are inserted and interpreted as consonant with the preoccupations of the sons of the soil. Monks recite *pirit* at the public ceremonies and rallies; they present staged sermons and give them the inflated name *dharmadesanaya;* the "commemoration" and recall of the Buddha's enlightenment itself may precede the campaign rhetoric of fighting Tamil terrorism; and finally, the newly prominent *bodhipuja* (worship of the *bodhi* tree) cult may again be a part of a rally to protect the motherland.[2] Moreover, "Bodhipujas were held in leading temples to seek the blessings of gods in ensuring the safety and success of military personnel. Monks officiated at military functions and the central army cantonment at Panagoda saw the erection of an impressive 'chaitya' (pagoda)" (Amunugama, p. 129). If in previous times prime ministers and ministers of state did this, now military commanders too worship at the Temple of the Tooth Relic in Kandy upon appointment and obtain blessings from the head monks of the Asgiriya and Malvatta chapters.

The JVP Monks: Alienation and Violence

Until the end of the year 1989, the story of the monks' involvement with militant politics is best told by reference to the JVP. Among all the Sinhala political parties it was the JVP that most systematically and deliberately set out to mobilize monks as an essential militant support group. The JVP membership itself was drawn primarily from Sinhala Buddhist male youth of rural social origins. And the movement sought to infiltrate the universities, where young monks have increasingly come to constitute an important segment of the student population. The egalitarian, populist, nationalist, anti-Tamil (and notably anti-Indian estate labor), Sinhala-Buddhist charter of the JVP appealed to young monks. In fact, in the 1971 insurgency some Bud-

---

1. Amunugama, "Buddhaputra and Bhumiputra?" *Religion* 21 (1991):126.
2. On the *bodhipuja* ritual, see H. L. Seneviratne and Swarna Wickremaratne, "Bodhipuja: Collective Representations of Sri Lanka Youth," *American Ethnologist* 7, no. 4 (1980):734–43.

dhist temples in the interior had been used to store arms and ammunition and as hiding places and outposts for the insurgents.[3] But it was in the late eighties that monks became an integral component of the JVP. Accusing it of participating in the anti-Tamil riots of 1983, the Jayawardene government had banned the JVP, which thereafter had to resort to front organizations through which to operate. Aside from lay university and upper school students, young Buddhist monks provided this shield and outlet.

The JVP attempted to operate through national committees and territorial organizations at zonal, district, and subdistrict levels, and it appears that an attempt was made to form a JVP monk branch at each territorial level. As Amunugama remarks, this was a comprehensive hierarchical organization of monks created *outside* the grid of the formal *sangha* organization on the basis of *nikaya* (sects) and locality (*palata*) and acting parallel to it (ibid., p. 131). Monks of all sects were invited to join the JVP branches. While other political parties had also, as we have seen, organized similar cohorts of monks crosscutting *nikaya* differences, it was the JVP that achieved the most effective and widest tri-*nikaya* formation of politically activist monks.

These monks were particularly useful in the canvassing of views on issues that were favorable to the interests of youth at large. Monks were in the forefront of agitation against the White Paper on Education, the formal recognition of a private medical college which would cater to the rich, and the Indo–Sri Lanka Peace Accord. They lent support to demands for increasing the money value of university scholarships, and the salaries of university teachers. And they joined all opposition groups in the cry for early general elections.

These monks also criticized the increasingly visible "consumerism"— a negative judgment on the growing importation of Western goods into Sri Lanka and the intensified adoption of Western life styles and recreational patterns—ensuing from the "liberalizing" of the economy and the establishment of the free-trade zone and the expansion of tourism under the UNP regime. The Buddhist emphasis on muting worldly desires and the nostalgic fiction of a simple, homogeneous, and egalitarian precolonial Sinhala Buddhist peasant society were the themes preached against consumerism and against deepening divisions between the rich and the poor.

The most crucial dilemma facing the JVP monks concerned their

3. See A. C. Alles, *Insurgency—1971* (Colombo: Colombo Apothecaries' Co.), 1976.

party's decision to engage in "revolutionary" violence to put right these wrongs. Officially this violent activity was said to be the work not of the JVP but of another organization called the Deshapremi Janatha Vijayaparaya (DJV), but despite the disavowal, the public knew the DJV to be an armed division of the JVP, implementing the latter's decisions.

The engagement in militant violence by the JVP, which in the event was directed not so much against the distant Tamil insurgents and the alien Indian army but at chosen targets among the security forces of the government, its administrators, and local as well as national political agents of the UNP—all Sinhalese in identity and living in Sinhalese majority areas—drove the stakes of division and divided loyalty into all the groups and parties which saw themselves as opposed to the UNP government in power.

Cracks began to appear in the umbrella organization MSV, which opposed the Indo–Sri Lanka Peace Accord and consisted loosely of the major opposition parties—SLFP, MEP, JVP—and several lay and monk Buddhist organizations. The representatives of the SLFP and MEP and leading monks such as Chandananda, the mahanayake of Asgiriya, now saw the need to dissociate and distance themselves from active involvement with the MSV first and even more emphatically from the young monks committed to the JVP's militant nationalism, which was now creating havoc within the Sinhala body politic. The argument of the JVP that its violence was a response to the government's prior use of force and repression against civilians provided no balm to those who were disassociating themselves.

Many of the JVP monks, faced with what they construed as abandonment and even betrayal by their senior monks and sectarian leaders and compelled by their political commitments, became condoners of, even collaborators in, acts of violence against senior monks. Within their own temples and within their own sects, they mounted criticism against their elders and their clerical authorities; they advocated that these monks in authority should sever their political connections with the major Sinhala parties, the UNP and the SLFP, both of which were construed as willing to live with the accord; they passively condoned, perhaps even collaborated in, the assassination of recalcitrant senior monks by JVP/DJV executioners.

In turn, the government forces and paramilitary agents were involved in the counteraction of mass killing of suspected JVP insurgents. Their victims included many alleged JVP monks, who were treated unceremoniously, chased, degraded, arrested, and tortured, and in some cases killed. The JVP monks in reply organized many fasts and nonviolent protests at Buddhist temples (the most massive of them was staged at the Temple of the Tooth) that were intended to put pressure on the senior monks of the Asgiriya and Malvatta chapters, the highest establishments of the Siyam Nikaya. "Soon after this demonstration the highest decision-making bodies (Karaka Sabha) of these two establishments passed resolutions condemning the Accord and seeking protection for the monks who had been taken into custody by armed services. When the JVP escalated their terror tactics leading Buddhist monks were characterized as 'traitors' and sent 'death threats'. As a result some left the island and others drastically curtailed their religious and social activities" (ibid., p. 134). The JVP radical monks' basic stand was that the religion of the Buddha and the language and culture of the Sinhalese could not flourish without a sovereign territory, which was the motherland of Sri Lanka, and their uncompromising judgment pronounced on their elders was that they had been slothful in patriotic obligations and become trapped in worldly interests of property, rank, and temple-building.

By late 1989 and early 1990 (the time of my writing), fortune had turned against the JVP as a whole, and also therefore the JVP monks. The government of Premadasa, the security forces, and their paramilitary organs have succeeded in killing the leadership ("the Politburo") of the JVP and have followed that with the final decimation and capture of the dispersed JVP rank and file. The JVP monks have paid the price of this awesome show of force by the state: being readily recognizable in their robes, many have been killed; many have surrendered or disrobed and become laymen; some have confessed and turned informer. Many obviously have retreated with lay members to jungle camps and hideouts. The monk who has finally taken to the gun can no longer be considered a vehicle of the Buddha's religion; moreover, he is unlikely to survive physically as a rebel in the jungle, the same jungle that had fostered the wandering, meditating renouncer of the world, the highest achiever in Buddhism.

Have we in Sri Lanka today arrived at a critical turning point? Large numbers of the young monks, more widely drawn than before from the lower reaches of rural society, are recruited into the *sangha* and find themselves on the upward path of education in monastic colleges and at higher levels of education, including the national universities. Being in much the same situation as the young men and women who joined the JVP, they are alienated more than ever before from the system of politics and the politicians who participate in it and are frustrated by their inability to create a political economy and a public culture in which they can participate. At the same time, they are more fully involved in public politics in larger numbers than at any time in the history of the *sangha*, and this involvement makes them less distinguishable from the laity participating in politics. The questions we are compelled to pose but cannot answer are: Will the *sangha* renew and reproduce itself, and what might its possibly transformed shape be, when the present generation of more "orthodox" monk-elders and *mahanayakes* pass away? What would be the structure of the *sangha*, its public presentation of itself, and the substance of the monk's vocation? What would be the activities and functions of the temples and the pattern of transactions between monks and laity?

To many of us who live in the glow of the classical Buddhist heritage, witnessing the increasing participation of monks, especially young monks being educated in monastic colleges and national universities, in violence, whether directly or indirectly, is a disturbing experience. Amunugama's essay "Buddhaputra and Bhumiputra?" is a poignant account of the concerns and predicament of young monks who had joined the JVP.

The participation of monks in rebellions and millennial movements in precolonial times against the British raj, and subsequently in postindependence times, is not new. Burma has perhaps the most impressive evidence of this. Examples are the Saya San rebellion in the 1930s and the most recent uprisings in 1988 (and continuing to this day) by the students and young monks of Rangoon and Mandalay against an oppressive military regime. And, as Kumari Jayawardena has reminded us, in Sri Lanka, too, monks were involved in the rebellions and protest movements during the time of the Dutch in 1760 and even more prominently in British times during the period 1816–48.[4] Jayawardena has also brought to our notice the involvement of monks like Boose Dhammarakhita and Udakandawela Siri Saranankara in the trade union politics and labor strikes that took place in the 1920s under the leadership of A. E. Goonesinha.[5] Saranankara subsequently became vice-chairman of the Communist party and was awarded the

4. Kumari Jayawardena has written four articles entitled "Bhikkus in Revolt" in *Lanka Guardian*, May 15, June 15, July 1, and July 15, 1979.

5. Examples cited earlier are the general strike of 1923, the harbor strike of 1927, and the tramway strike of 1929.

Lenin Peace Prize. Between these involvements and the political activism of the Vidyalankara group of radical monks in the forties there is some continuity.

So it is important to recognize, especially in connection to all those Pali text puritans who give only sanitized accounts of Buddhism in Sri Lanka and would prefer to ignore, even in modern times, the *sangha*'s involvement in politics, that some Buddhist monks have played a role "in anti-imperialist peasant struggles of the nineteenth century, and in nationalist and working class protest movements in the twentieth century" (Jayawardena). We may add that in important ways the *sangha*'s involvement in politics from the forties to the eighties that I have related here bears testimony to the vital concerns monks have had in national political, educational, and social issues and may push us into understanding why monks, whose origins primarily are in the rural peasantry (and urban working class), are touched by, and want to be involved in, causes and issues that are relevant to the place of Buddhism—as religion, civilization, and way of life—in the life of its adherents, both lay and clerical.

Nevertheless, it is necessary to realize that many Buddhists among the ranks of the laity as well as the sectarian communities of monks must necessarily experience a profound misgiving, even consternation, when monks become caught up in political violence. There are central normative rules linked in doctrinal terms to the monks' vocation, which advocate nonviolence and the necessity to repudiate and to be distanced from all forms of taking life and inflicting injury. There is an inescapable dilemma here which surely must tug at the conscience and moral sensibilities of all Buddhists. It cannot be ignored; it has to be confronted, even if it cannot be satisfactorily resolved.

12 The Parameters of Buddhist Nationalism and Buddhist Democracy

It is important to reiterate that the ideological work begun by Bhikkhu Rahula and the Vidyalankara group of monks in the 1940s, which took as its task the construction and legitimation of the monk as a political actor, has by now become an established and accepted norm for many, if not most, monks today. Rahula argued that since classical times the monk has participated in the island's politics as advisor, mediator, and guide; that he has always been actively involved in the achievement of the island's welfare and prosperity; that Buddhism has always been the national religion of the people, hence the label "religio-nationalism" aptly described its role; and that it was a result of British colonial policy of divide and rule that the bond between the *sangha* and the laity was severed, and the monk was confined to, and retreated to, the temple to perform rituals and recite sermons.

This study has documented how from the forties onward monks have participated in the politics of the country; it has traced the shifts that have taken place in their causes and their political affiliations; and it has evaluated the efficacy of their political participation. One thing is clear—the Buddhist *sangha* has never functioned as a wholly united and monolithic entity. Indeed, we have seen that the monks have always been fragmented and segmented by sectarian, caste, and regional interests and ties of pupil succession, and by different linkages with lay political parties, though at critical times they have mobilized in numbers for action.

Many of the prominent monk-ideologues and propagandists, some of them recognized scholar-monks (with the title of *rajakiya panditha,* or "king's scholar," conferred upon them), others recognized as public figures who have served on national committees dealing with public issues, have engaged in criticism and moral evaluation of contemporary politics, as practiced today in Sri Lanka, and the kind of economic and social order that has developed on the island in postindependence times. It is worth noting that despite the divisions within the *sangha* and despite individual differences among these monk-ideologues, there are some themes and issues that they emphasize which seem to derive from their common understandings about the contours and valuations of Buddhism as a religio-political totality in the life of the Sinhalese people since ancient times. Such deep-seated attitudes and world views necessarily take us to the constantly reiterated and reinterpreted "truths" about the destiny of Buddhism and the Sinhalese enshrined in monkish chronicles like the *Mahavamsa* and the constantly invoked "precedents" concerning the orientations and organization of the pristine *sangha* as set out in the Pali canon.

In reviewing these themes that inform the critique of prominent Buddhist monks, I shall primarily refer to the views expressed by two monks who, despite their quite significant differences, meet on common ground when it comes to the basic themes of current Sinhala Buddhist nationalism. And these common themes are shared and voiced by many contemporary activist monks.[1]

The two monks are Madihe Pannasiha Thero and Henpitagedera Gnanasiha Thero, and they have been illuminatingly compared by Steven Kemper.[2]

Madihe Pannasiha was first introduced in the early part of this study as one of the members of the Committee of Inquiry, convened in 1954, which composed the explosive report *The Betrayal of Buddhism* (1956). At that time he already had the reputation of being a strong nationalist and a critic of the Roman Catholic Church and its activities.

1. For example, see Mark Juergensmeyer, "What the Bhikkhu Said: Reflections on the Rise of Militant Religious Nationalism," *Religion* 20 (1990): 53–75. I shall also cite shortly as a supplement a pamphlet written by a scholar-monk teaching at a university, namely, Ariyasena Maha Thera.

2. I am much indebted to Steven Kemper for making available to me "Nationalist Discourse," chap. 7 of his forthcoming book *The Presence of the Past: Chronicles, Politics, and Culture in Sinhala Nationalism.*

Kemper has also kindly given me his unpublished English translation ("Why Do We Need a Buddhist-Administered Country?") of Henpitagedera Gnanasiha Thero, *Apata Bauddha Palana Kramayak Avashy Ayi?* (Ratnapura, Sri Lanka: Samupakara Mudranalaye, 1982). Gnanasiha's political tract, written in 1969, was originally given the title "Buddhist Socialism." All citations of Gnanasiha are from Kemper's translation.

While I make use of Kemper's information and elucidation, I also discuss some issues, express views, and cite other sources which are not in his chapter "Nationalist Discourse."

He came as a novice from Matara to Colombo to be fully ordained and to take up residence at one of Colombo's most famous temples, Vajirarama, which belonged to the Amarapura sect. It was a center of Buddhist revivalism. When the monk who ordained him died in 1955, Pannasiha succeeded him as the head of a small sect within the larger Amarapura Nikaya. This sect was distinctive as a body dominated by the *durava* caste (a low-status group by traditional reckoning). Later Pannasiha was elected *mahanayake* of the entire Amarapura Nikaya, a position that is filled in rotation.

Pannasiha has been an important public figure, has voiced many statements on platforms and in the newspapers, but has not been identified with any political party as such. Though not an acclaimed scholar, he has been active on government committees advising on matters concerning the relationship between monks, the laity, and the state. He has also been involved in organizational work such as the founding of the Dhammavijaya Society, to which I shall refer shortly.

Among Pannasiha's writings is a collection of essays, *Sinhalayage Anagataya*, which Kemper cites effectively. As Kemper puts it: "Pannasiha is the foremost exemplar of a monkly activism that has monks giving advice without being dragged into partisan politics, and he calls other monks back from party involvements."

Gnanasiha, by contrast with Pannasiha, has had a more volatile and a more "political" career as a monk. Until his death in 1981, Gnanasiha seems to have combined political activism with scholarship. He has written some forty books, including an esteemed work on the life of King Dutthagamani, the hero of the *Mahavamsa*. Kemper notes that at the same time Gnanasiha was "an active participant in a series of political incidents, the most significant of which was his involvement in an unsuccessful coup in 1964." In fact as a result of this involvement in a conspiracy to overthrow the government, he was held in Colombo's Magazine Prison for a while, and it was during this detention that he composed in mid-1969 the tract on Buddhist socialism which I shall cite later.

Gnanasiha belonged to the Ramanna Nikaya. Apparently early in his career he was a supporter of D. S. Senanayake, the first prime minister and leader of the UNP, but Senanayake was not, as we have seen, sympathetic to the political activism of monks. Gnanasiha became an active campaigner on behalf of S. W. R. D. Bandaranaike during the historic 1956 elections in which the Eksath Bhikkhu Peramuna played a critical role. Later, although he supported Mrs. Banadaranaike, he fell out with her, and was kept at a distance by the SLFP.

Gnanasiha was an active political propagandist who incorporated "radical" socialist ideas into his political theorizing of a better "Buddhist-administered society." However, it seems that over the last ten years of his life, this erudite, engaged, and polemical monk disengaged himself from party politics and devoted himself to social service by working for the Sarvodaya Shramadana movement (a movement for rural uplift and development started by A. T. Ariyaratne, whose philosophy of action consists in an adaptation of Buddhist scriptures to affirm this worldly action and in an idealized conception of traditional village life revolving around tank, temple, and rice fields).[3] As an advocate and theorist of Buddhist nationalism and socialism, he fully deserves a hearing.[4]

The Discourse on National Unity

The need for and benefits of Sinhala national unity (in today's language *jatika samagiya*) has been an ever recurring theme in Sinhala political discourse for over a century. In the 1880s during the momentous time of Buddhist revivalism, Olcott preached about the need for the Sinhalese Buddhists, especially their *sangha* divided by sectarian, caste, and regional interests, to unite so as to combat the Christian challenge. Dharmapala never tired of berating the Buddhists for being divided and for being slow to reform. Since then politicians of every decade have bemoaned the divisiveness and lack of unity of the Sinhalese, which made them prey to colonial domination. And once again in the eighties we saw how salient the call for "unity" under one umbrella and for the exercise of sovereignty under one flag was for the MSV. But in fact the theme of Sinhala unity, and of Sinhalese achieving unification of both people and the entire island, had already been broached in the *Mahavamsa* and other chronicles. And especially since the second half of the nineteenth century, one of the heroic themes read into the chronicles was how great heroes like

---

3. For sympathetic accounts of this movement, see George Bond, *The Buddhist Revival in Sri Lanka* (Columbia: University of South Carolina Press, 1988), chap. 7, and Detlef Kantowsky, *Sarvodaya: The Other Development* (Delhi: Vikas, 1980).

4. Richard Gombrich and Gananath Obeyesekere, *Buddhism Transformed* (Princeton: Princeton University Press, 1988), pp. 229, 253. In a curiously inconsistent set of references to Gnanasiha, Gombrich and Obeyesekere call him "an outstanding modernist monk" and "one of Sri Lanka's most erudite and influential monks," and yet not worthy of consideration in their book because they did not know of "anyone who was influenced by his idiosyncratic opinions." I do not agree with this latter dismissal which seems to have been inserted in order to excuse their lack of a serious discussion of the role of the monk-activist in the current politics of Sri Lanka.

Dutthagamani and Parakrama Bahu the great united the entire island, which was fragmented and in part under enemy (Damila) occupation, through a series of military campaigns. The dual patriotic task of these heroes was the protection of Buddhism and the recovery of the entire island for the Sinhalese. One could not be achieved without the other. It is believed that, starting from the periphery of southern Lanka, these heroes progressively conquered, subdued, and aggregated the kingdom, with their celebrated capitals based successively in the cities of Anuradhapura and Polonnaruva. This unification then provided the capacity, under the aegis of enlightened kingship, to create and achieve great works of civilization in religion, literature, architecture, and art, as well as irrigation and agriculture. Bruce Kapferer has suggestively argued that this powerful cosmology of unification, domestication of the rebellious agents, and their hierarchized inclusion structures contemporary Sinhalese nationalism in a deep-seated way.[5]

Politically active monks like Pannasiha, Gnanasiha, and many others do not tire of preaching the need for overcoming Sinhala disunity, which prevents the people from achieving a righteous and prosperous society. Pannasiha, for example, founded the Dharmavijaya Society in 1974, whose motto "unity is good" also resonates with and exploits the great Asokan slogan of conquest and victory through the vehicle of righteousness.[6]

The Utopian Past: A Beacon for the Future

The theme of unification of the island—realizing the unity of the Sinhala people, now glorified as a nation existing from pristine times, and through that the initiation of a golden age—was concretely realized in the eyes of many present-day Sinhala Buddhists in the ideal reigns of great monarchs who were *cakkavatti*s (wheel-rolling universal kings) and *dharmarajas* (righteous monarchs). This vision of a utopian past invoked as a vision of a utopian future embodies, as present-day ideologues see it, precedents for instituting a welfare state and a social and economic egalitarianism in a noncompetitive agricultural society of villagers. The villagers of earlier times led simple lives, and the focus of their communal and religious lives was the Buddhist

---

5. Bruce Kapferer, *Legends of People, Myths of State* (Washington, D.C.: Smithsonian Institution Press, 1988).

6. As Kemper explains, in practice, this movement consisted of establishing local branches of the society in some fourteen Buddhist temples, to distribute milk and other food products to needy children.

temple, whose monks guided them in all matters. If the monks were the moral guides at the base of the society, the monks were the political and moral advisors of the monarch and the ruling chiefs at the top. In fact Gnanasiha's text on Buddhist socialism (or "Why Do We Need a Buddhist-Administered Society?") not only recapitulates this romanticized and idealized vision but, perhaps even more important, uses it as a yardstick for criticizing and evaluating the present and for projecting a democracy of the future.

Gnanasiha's text describes an ancient Sinhala past that is projected on what I surmise to be three axes, which are components of the ideology of Buddhist nationalism.

1. With canonical references to the *suttas* in the Pali canon that deal with the ideal world rulers (such as the *Cakkavatti Sihanada* and *Kutadanta Suttas*), Gnanasiha paints the regime of Parakrama Bahu I of Polonnaruwa as a collective welfare–oriented dispensation, indeed as a kind of "socialist welfare society" where the monarch was the chief holder, developer, and distributor of land, resources, and rewards to all the people, while at the same time being a liberal supporter and protector of the *sangha,* and a propagator of Dhammic virtues. In two of my works (Tambiah 1976 and 1987) I have given an exegesis of the *suttas* concerning the *cakkavatti* and how they have influenced the Buddhist polities of South and Southeast Asia. These *suttas* are frequently referred to today by monks who are politically active. The *Kutadanta Sutta,* which tells the story of how a chaplain advised a king on how to improve the condition of his people who were suffering from civil disorder and insecurity, is interpreted today as a precedent for a monk's rightful role as an advisor to present-day political authorities.

Gnanasiha in fact simplifies the ancient regimes which clearly manifested differentiation and hierarchy of power and well being to this model: In ancient Sri Lanka the economy showed a tradition of equal income. The land belonged to the king, and except for those who received land from the king as gifts, all others participated in an economy of equal living. The farmer who cultivated his land sent half the produce to the treasury, and the other half he used for his livelihood. Money was rarely used, and there were no landowners as we have today. That the economy was organized to produce equality, which people today take to be a principle enunciated by communism, is a Buddhist tradition that has existed from long ago. Gnanasiha writes, "In ancient law, all land belonged to the king. The subjects cultivated

it, paid rent to the state, and used the balance for their livelihood."
Russian socialism is based on similar principles of state ownership and
equal living.

While Gnanasiha's "socialist" reading of the regime of Parakrama
Bahu may be more innovative and radical than is generally prevalent,
yet the contours of the utopian past, in which the political authority
actively intervened and "planned" for the elimination of poverty and
to create general prosperity is widely shared by prominent Buddhist
monk-scholars today.

It is worthwhile making a digression here, to illustrate this point by
citing a pamphlet in English on "the Buddhist philosophy of state" by
Pundit Kamburupitiye Ariyasena Maha Thera, a monk-scholar at the
University of Peradeniya.[7] For his exposition he resorts to what have
by now become standard canonical citations for those theorists who
see in certain *suttas* Buddhist precedents for, indeed explicit formulations of, democracy, equality, rule by popular consensus, a contractual
theory of elective kingship (as opposed to a divinely appointed institution as in Hindu traditions), nonrecognition of caste distinctions, social welfare policy, the need to eliminate poverty and unequal
distribution of wealth, and so on. Indeed in Ariyasena's later exposition, we see possibly most of the original "sources" for the even freer
modernist interpretations in the form of radical politics propounded by
Gnanasiha.

Thus in the *Agganna Sutta* Ariyasena finds the Buddhist exposition
"of the source of political authority." He asserts that "the Buddhist
concept of the origin of kingship not only emancipated the ancient Indian philosophy of kingship from theology, but it also tried to correct it
by criticizing its unethical activities from the Buddhist point of view."
Citing B. C. Gokhale's statement that *dhamma* as understood in the
Buddhist literature "is equated with justice (*naya*) and equity (*sama*),"
Ariyasena asserts that the Buddhist conception which frequently pairs
dhamma with *sama* (equality) as a synonym is the opposite of *dharma*
in Brahmanical tradition, which "always signifies inequality when it is
used in relation to society (*varnadharma*)."

The *Agganna Sutta* is explicit that "the source of political authority
lies in the collective consent of the people." In the *Kutadanta Sutta*

---

7. See Venerable Pundit Kamburupitiye Ariyasena Maha Thera, *An Introduction to
Buddhist Philosophy of the State* (Colombo: Lake House Printers, 1986). The quota-
tions from Ariyasena in this section are taken from this pamphlet.

"the Buddhist chaplain advises the king to consult the people irrespective of caste distinctions." The *Cakkavatti Sihanada Sutta* establishes that "the possession of political authority becomes valid in so far as the principles of *dhamma* are not neglected by the ruler," and that "the political participation of citizens is very essential for the valid existence of authority of the state."

Indeed the *Kutadanta Sutta* proposes a "policy or plan" which would enable the king to suppress the unlawful activities "of the oppressed people" (*dassukhilas*). It consists of provisions such as: promoting production by providing agriculturists with seeds, manure, cattle, and the necessary agricultural implements; providing essential capital to the trading section of the society so that "it may desist from commercial misbehaviour"; suitably rewarding the employees of the state so as to prevent them "from indulging in malpractices."

Again, the *Cakkavatti Sihanada Sutta* is discussed as explaining the "factors which bring forth revolution in society." This *sutta* states that "the immediate cause of social upheaval or revolution seems to be the mode of distribution, that is, the inequitable distribution of wealth, and the accumulation of wealth in the hands of a few on the one hand and increasing poverty of the majority on the other. It emphatically states that increasing poverty is a result of the accumulation of wealth in the hands of a few."

All the *sutta* he has cited, asserts Ariyasena, establish "public opinion as the decisive and essential factor in the conduct of the affairs of the state" and the people who make up the society in the land (*janapadika*) as "the ultimate wielders of political authority," should the rulers fail "to follow the accepted policies of the [Buddhist] State." It is not without interest that Ariyasena cites the Oxford-trained Sri Lankan analytical philosopher with logical-positivist leanings, K. N. Jayatilake, as observing that "According to the Buddhist theory of social contract, sovereignty in the sense of supreme legislative power is vested in the people as a whole."[8]

2. There is an equally well-entrenched and widely shared second axis, on which the Buddhist society of the past is projected. It is a conception of a rural society, whose base is a community of egalitarian peasant owners and cultivators. The irrigation "tank" watered their

8. The source cited is K. N. Jayatilake, "The Principles of International Law in Buddhist Doctrine," *The Hague Academy of International Law Collected Courses* 11 (1977):527.

green rice fields, and the Buddhist temple in their midst served as the religious, moral, and cultural center, and its inmates, the monks, acted as their "advisors." Despite well-known traditions of "feudal" hierarchy, overlords, and differential privileges in Sri Lanka, especially in the last precolonial Kandyan Kingdom, this conception of a village community of ancient times—in which the irrigation tank and its surrounding rice terraces, the village community of peasant owners, and the combined duality of *vihara* and *stupa* constituted focal points of "moral" existence—has a powerful stereotypical hold in modern Sri Lanka, even among the urban middle classes and the proletariat.

The greatest Sinhalese novelist of this century, Martin Wickramasinghe is credited with this formula of Sinhala cultural identity: *vava* (tank), *dagaba* (temple), *yaya* (paddy field). So important is this imprint that both in novels and in television dramas, the impurities and immorality of current urban life are uncritically castigated, while out there in the newly created peasant settlements and colonies, in the sites of ancient glory such as Anuradhapura and Polonnaruwa, might be found the ideal harmonious life. The new colonization schemes hold the prospect of regaining the lost utopia. This devaluation, if not rejection of urban existence as a necessary contemporary fact of life, may impede the literati and the ideologues from formulating and envisioning a "plausible" satisfying and creative urban form of life for Sri Lankans. And the fixation on an idealized mode of rural, "egalitarian," temple-focused community life may also act as a brake on thinking innovatively about agro-industrial forms of rural life that transcend the limits of imagined village republics.

Let me illustrate this point by referring to the language of political rhetoric and the symbolism of the rituals of development that are currently enacted with respect to Sri Lanka's largest agricultural-industrial development, the Mahavali Project. This grand project is estimated to cost some U.S. $1.5 billion and is expected to irrigate 130,000 hectares of new agricultural lands and 37,000 hectares of cultivated lands and to double the hydroelectric capacity of the country. On the one hand, as Tennekoon puts it, the program is oriented toward establishing "the material conditions of modernization as well as a correlative system of modernity that privileges science and technology and a centralized state bureaucracy, and incorporates agro-industrial production into a capitalist market-economy."[9] But on the

9. N. Serena Tennekoon, "Rituals of Development: The Accelerated Mahavali Development Program of Sri Lanka," *American Ethnologist* 15, no. 2 (1988):294–310.

other hand, following the format of all previous resettlement schemes, the Mahavali Project will continue to reproduce the pattern of peasant families conducting small-scale agriculture (by 1987 some 18,000 families had been settled on this basis). Moreover this form of irrigated agricultural development is officially presented in political speeches, in radio programs and television dramas, in posters and advertisements, and most dramatically of all, in the grand "opening ceremonies" staged to inaugurate the completion of a component project as "a reincarnation of an ancient, indigenous, national culture whose features are indisputably ethnic (Sinhala) and religious (Buddhist)" (Tennekoon, p. 297).

Indeed the minister for Mahavali Development, Gamini Dissanayake declared in 1983, when ceremonially commissioning the first of these projects, the Maduru Oya reservoir, these stereotyped sentiments: "The soul of the new Mahavali society . . . will be the cherished values of the ancient society which was inspired and nourished by the tank, the temple and the paddy field." And recycling a rhetoric that recurs throughout modern agricultural settlement policy, the same minister declared the Mahavali program as "a return of the people to the ancient homeland . . . in the Rajarata" (ibid., pp. 297, 298). Tennekoon explicates with interpretive virtuosity how the water-offering ritual (*jala puja*), performed in August 1985 to mark the successful completion of the Kotmale reservoir and powerhouse, linked the tank and the temple, and by extension, water (irrigation) and religion (Buddhism).

Let us return to Gnanasiha, who has this to say of the past: "Accounts in books and commentaries on Buddhism quote instances which show that the livelihood of the people was determined by the principles of Buddhism, following instructions received from the Temple in each village." In the communities of monks (*sangha*) discussions devoted to clarifying misconceptions were scheduled to take place once in fifteen days. This rule of the *vinaya* brought the monks into unity. In a similar way the people of the ancient village communities were kept united by the monks. "The village temple was the place where villagers and the monks met. The ancient Sinhalas went to the temple on *poya* days; and the Bhikkhus who chaired the meetings unravelled the disputes and misconceptions of the villagers."

It does not matter whether this format is old or new—the point is that it is a good form of social and political life. We have witnessed, says Gnanasiha, how, under a new form of government that is in place today, man's inner qualities have deteriorated. "We have declined to such a state that is is doubtful whether we could protect our Sinhala Nation and Buddhism in the future as we have done during the past two thousand five hundred years." The existence of political extremists and the faithless in our society, of those who are corrupt, and engage in robbery and cheating, are signs of decline.

Long ago the development of the country was conceived on a village basis and it progressed from village to village. The village was considered a small-scale kingdom, and it became a habit to make it self-sufficient. The village temple safeguarded the interests of the village and developed the living conditions of the people. Gnanasiha writes,

> In ancient Sri Lanka, *viharas* were built in every village not merely to collect merit, but also for the benefit of life both in this world and the next. The tank, the temple, the physician, the headman played useful roles in the village. Living in quiet surroundings, villagers were free from external disturbances and misfortunes. The village was not a busy place and unity prevailed. Everyone was engaged in agriculture. Then there were no people mad with greed to collect wealth and land. The temples were responsible for creating among the people unity, righteousness, piety, and fear of unjust actions.

Today the village has fallen prey to dispute. "Party politics has destroyed village unity." The existing disunity sabotages village development. Moreover, the monk in the temple might favor a certain political party, and the people of the village opposed to that party would boycott the temple. Such situations make it difficult to organize development programs in a village.

During the twenty years parliamentary politics has existed, the political parties, divided amongst themselves, have created divisions in the villages as well. The party system has destroyed the unity of villagers and caused both indifference and actions of revenge among them. While professional politicians in Parliament dispute their party differences and can behave as friends after their debates, in the villages party rivalries are continued as enduring rifts.

Gnanasiha's assertions are both a critique and an apocalyptic vision of the present form of life. The critique itself, undeniable in some respects, will be elucidated more fully later. What we should note here is that this fixation on a romanticized past of a coherent, integrated, harmonious Buddhist culture, nation, and religion is in danger of producing the conservative attitude that there is no reason to want to change from the past forms of life and that new forms and developments endanger Buddhist principles.

3. The third axis of Buddhist nationalism, which is particularly emphasized by the monk-ideologues and activists who propose that monks have a legitimate political role to enact, refers back to certain passages in the Pali canon where the Buddha is alleged to have laid down certain admonitions and rules for the constitution and conduct of monastic communities. These canonical precedents are well known, and monk advocates cite them in order to lay claim to their appropriateness as advisors in political life, and even as alternatives to the lay politicians themselves, whose alleged "self-interested" motives are deemed suspect.

One oft-repeated precedent which I have referred to before is the case of the chaplain in the *Kutandanta Sutta* who, as one modern scholar-monk puts it, advised the king "to consult people irrespective of caste distinctions" and "the country became prosperous and peaceful after the implementation of the economic policy proposed by him" (Ariyasena, p. 9).

Rahula, Pannasiha, Gnanasiha, Chandananda, and many other leading monks refer to the following features as evidence for the unselfish advisory vocation of the monks and the exemplary "democratic" constitution of the monastic communities. A precedent frequently cited is the Buddha's recommendation of the Vajjian "tribal republican model" as a pattern of organization for the *sangha*.

In tandem with this is invoked the famous episode when the Buddha told Ananda that after his death the *dhamma* (doctrine) alone should bind the *bhikkhus*, thereby repudiating the idea of a successor who would be their leader or head. Thus it is said that in the early *sangha* there was no hierarchy or locus of authority; while the older monks and elders deserved respect and privilege in etiquette, they could only advise and instruct, not legislate or compel.

There is a strong tradition transmitted from early times that the monastic brethren formed decentralized communities whose "democratic" traditions were exemplified by the concept of *sanghakamma*, transactions of the *sangha*. These transactions were and are held in "full and frequent assemblies" according to carefully defined procedural rules. The ordination of monks, the inquiry into infringements against the disciplinary rules of order, and the settling of schismatic disputes are examples of matters of concern to the assembly. The conventions are that decisions are made by all the members together in assembly, that the members are equal, and that they arrive at a decision through consensus. The tradition of reciting the *Patimokkha* confessional by the full assembly of monks living as a community semimonthly on the sacred *uposatha* days (at full moon and new moon) is also cited as a marker of the monastic mode of life.

Finally, there are the norms against individual accumulation and possession of property by the monks beyond the bare minimum. The term *bhikkhu* means one who is without possessions and lives on alms. And the corporate communal (even "communistic") stamp of monastic communities is reflected with regard to the ownership and use of property. Whatever the later developments in Buddhist countries with regard to the ownership of property by individual monks and by individual monasteries, early Buddhism's stress that the *bhikkhu* went from home into homelessness, rejecting the householder's values and attachments, implied that he possessed only the minimal material requisites for following the path—such as three robes, begging bowl, umbrella, needle and thread, packet of medicines, and so on, making some eight requisites in all. These are the minimal possessions which are still given him at his *upasampada* ordination. And the norm that all offerings made to the *sangha* should be shared equally and that all increase goes into a common fund again underscored the collective orientations of monastic life.

These classical features of the monastic communal life and of the monks' unselfish vocation, no matter what deviations have taken place in practice, are powerful reminders when they are invoked in modern political discourse as a critique of contemporary politics. Moreover, reformist monks effectively invoke them to criticize those establishment monks whose temples are endowed with much property and who lead comfortable lives and consort with the rich and with right-wing politicians.

The Critique of Parliamentary Party Politics

The voices of Gnanasiha and Pannasiha are powerful when they condemn the present system of parliamentary politics in Sri Lanka for the divisiveness and rivalries it encourages among competing parties so that no national consensus can be reached. Gnanasiha, for example, complained in his text that party politics can never create unity and that the very notion of an "opposition" to the "government" made up of the party or parties in power, which is taken to be essential to the practice of Western-style democracy, is inadmissible in his conception of a "Buddhist democracy." What is necessary for democracy to function is not simply the existence of an opposition, but the liberty of every member of Parliament, not to act in conformity as a party member, but according to his conscience and in support of principles that are just and good. Pannasiha similarly held that Sinhalese unity was undone by party politics; Kemper describes his view as being that "without political parties in the past, Sinhalas were unified; without political parties in the future, they could be unified again." Similar denunciations of the divisiveness of party politics have been expressed by other monks who are public figures.

In disagreeing with the view that democracy cannot function without an opposition, Gnanasiha cites the era of the Donoughmore Constitution in the thirties and early forties as proof that government without a party system is feasible in this land. At that time every member of the legislature belonged to a committee, which elected a chairman who also became minister. Individual members were not bound by party affiliations.

In a Buddhist democracy there exists only one party and there is no opposition. The members meet in unity, discuss and arrive at a settlement in peace, and disperse in unity. The party system is not suitable to Sri Lanka, where many races and religions exist. In other countries the opposition helps the government to function well, but in Sri Lanka it genuinely opposes the ruling party, and thereby makes citizens contemptuous of the government's actions. In the end there is deep enmity between the groups, and the enmity spreads and penetrates the villages.

Elections do have a place in a Buddhist administration, but if a majority (in Parliament) votes against the principles of *dhamma*, the Buddhist administration will not allow it to be defeated.[10] "The present democratic system has not given pride of place to *Dhamma* and Justice." It is a system which has allowed powerful and unjust people into the governing party. "In such a government corruption and misdeeds reign." Nor are the laws in force today framed according to the principles of *dhamma* and justice. "Thus when Buddhism obstructs the implementing of unjust laws, how can one say that this action is wrong?" The *Kalama Sutta* teaches "how to determine good and bad,

10. This is a curious statement and a piece of fuzzy political thinking that credits "a Buddhist administration," seemingly existing apart from democratic parties, with the power to authoritatively override a majority government. What it demonstrates is the view that the *dhamma* is an absolute and enduring norm, and overrides erroneous human views.

right and wrong, justice and injustice." "Our teacher [the Buddha] is
not the creator of *Dhamma* and Justice. But *Dhamma* and Justice exist
in the world. What our teacher did was to distinguish justice from injustice, *Dhamma* from evil." We can prove how justice and *dhamma*
are of value to society as the principles required for good living.

The divisiveness and unproductivity of party politics is, in the eyes
of the Buddhist clerical critics, intimately tied to the self-seeking of
the politicians themselves. The frequent complaints from present-
day monks are that "the politicians are ruining the country," that they
are "the enemy of Buddhism," and that parliamentary democracy and
the party system serve the interests of the politicians, not the people.
Gnanasiha for instance launches this salvo at "the so-called great men
of the country—politicians who indulge in licentiousness, government officers . . . who pose as the rich," and at their indulging in
drunkenness, racing, and bribery. While a poor man may rob and bribe
through need, the vices of the great men have little to do with gaining a
livelihood. By various devices they steal the wealth of the government, but government officers turn a blind eye to their actions, while
the police are prevented by their superiors from taking action against
them.

Moreover, while professional politicians, rivals, and enemies in
parliamentary debate frequently socialize and make their compromises and deals, the divisive issues of party politics once they penetrate village life, create enmities and rivalries which are not
overcome. In this sense, party politics played out at one level in Colombo corrupts and divides the village folk in the interior.

Gnanasiha graphically condemns the parliamentary system as an
urachakramala, a circular saw which looks like a garland to the observer, but cuts the wearer's neck. The observer begs to possess it, but
the wearer is unable to part with it and does not want to. The parliamentary system in place destroys the rights of the people, erodes justice, good behavior, and the unity of the people, but is difficult to
dislodge in present circumstances.

These criticisms of present-day democratic politics as divisive and
self-seeking are linked to another domain of conduct which critics feel
is integrally linked to the present dispensation, namely, self-interested
economic conduct that produces great disparities of wealth and well
being and elevates external (material) values of wealth accumulation
and consumerism. These values and mode of life are seen as antithetical to the "Buddhist way of life." We might call this a critique of the
excesses of "possessive individualism" and of "capitalism."

Gnanasiha, for example, while accepting features of capitalism as a fact of life today in Sri Lanka, points out that in a country with a teeming population and a high unemployment rate, one man should not be allowed to be a millionaire while another remains a pauper. These conditions of inequality create the class system, which is abhorred by Buddhism. While stating that elders and superiors deserve respect, Buddhism does not ascribe high or low status to people. Buddhism differentiates people into high and low on the basis of their righteousness and not according to their external differences, such as those based on caste, ethnicity, and the like. When the Sakyans (the Buddha's relations) presented themselves for ordination, the Buddha robed the barber, Upali, of low caste, first and made the Sakyans pay their respects to him. The Buddha said that it is by action that one becomes an outcast or a brahman. This enduring truth cannot be subdued by heresy or alien faith.

The class system existing in our society today can only be destroyed by a Buddhist administration. The socialist countries like Russia and China have destroyed the class system by instituting an economy that provides "equal living" to all people. This is in accord with Buddhist law. Thus we arrive at Gnanasiha's concept of Buddhist socialism, which he sees as consistent with norms already present in classical Buddhism and with some principles which socialist countries, such as Russia and China, have instituted. (Though the latter systems are preferable to capitalism and party politics, Gnanasiha will fault them, as we shall see later, for not developing the "inner features of man.")

The ancient Sri Lankan political economy which instituted "the Buddhist tradition of equal income" is no more. The conditions today are different. "Each man controls his private income. There are landowners possessing thousands of acres, and people without land to even build a house to live in." But this does not mean that corrective action cannot be taken. Gnanasiha reminds the reader that the *vinaya* code limits the monks' material requisites and disapproves of hoarding. "It is hoarding that opens the door to corruption." The same lesson applies to lay society.

> Once the extent of land and income available to each individual is limited, competition in society disappears. If personal income is limited, the plundering of others' wealth and corruption will disappear. Income gained above the limit imposed will be handed to the state. Thus capitalism built on plundering other people's wealth will come to an end. The winning of democratic elections

through bribes will also disappear. The state will be in a position to give houses and lands to the needy people to cultivate. On five hundred acres previously owned privately, the state could settle peasants with their own land, and they could pay a share of their earnings to the state.

Gnanasiha concludes that these types of suggestions, which are considered the latest principles of politics, were actually proposed to the *sangha* by the Buddha two thousand five hundred years ago.

As commentator it seems to me quite clear that the majority of monk-ideologues who formulate a theory of Buddhist politics read in the Buddhist canon and in later Buddhist chronicles a clear endorsement of welfare politics and state planning and redistribution. They also interpret Buddhism as being against "self-interested action," which leads to greed, competition, and even exploitation, and therefore as being against capitalism, which leads to inequality. This is a critical parameter of a type of modern interpretation of the relevance of Buddhist norms for life today.

The Buddhist Way of Life in a Buddhist Democracy

The "Buddhist way of life" as a conception has been consciously invoked for many decades, at the height of the Buddhist revivalism and reformism propagated by Dharmapala at the turn of the century and until the 1930s, again during the first two decades of the century by leaders of the temperance movement, and finally since independence, by numerous public figures, both lay and robed. It has at least two sides. The conception is on the one hand a critique of the kinds of "vices," style of life, and cultural "deracination" that are seen as introduced by Western colonial powers, especially the British, and aped by their collaborative "English-educated Sinhala elite." It is, on the other hand, a positive effort to sketch a mode of life that claims to draw on timeless values enshrined in early Buddhism, but which also incorporates traditional features associated with precolonial rural Sinhala life.

The Committee of Inquiry that on the eve of Buddha Jayanthi wrote *The Betrayal of Buddhism* was by no means indulging in mere formulaic rhetoric when, after blaming colonialism and Christianity for undermining Buddhism and the *sangha* and for introducing false values and life styles, it declared: "The real and final remedy is the displacement of Western materialistic, social and individual values and the establishment of genuine values founded on the Buddhist Dhamma."

George Bond summarizes well the report's recommendations concerning the promotion of a more authentic Buddhist life style. "The first recommendation was to ban the publication and importation of obscene books and magazines, and to appoint a National Film Board of Censors. . . . the report favored outlawing all forms of alcoholic drinks and enforcing total prohibition. . . . Horse racing, too, should be banned since the gambling associated with it led to 'the greater gain of the wealthy few and the further degradation of the poverty-stricken.' "[11] The Buddhist *poya* days should replace Sundays as days of rest, and lay people should be encouraged to attend the temples and observe *sil* regularly. There was a call for a "movement for plain living" that involved a simplicity in dress and lifestyle; Western outfit for men should be replaced by cloth and long-sleeved banian.[12] Buddhists should not imitate colonial overlords by maintaining servants. The recommended features of a "Buddhist mode of life" was "early rising, invoking the Triple Gem and practicing mental concentration, diligent and speedy execution of one's duties, and retiring to rest early."

These features of a simple "Buddhist way of life" are regularly repeated in the political tracts of activist monks. Thus Gnanasiha attacks the prime minister of his time (Dudley Senanayake) "who advocates morality, but allows intoxicants in big cities." He remarks on the number of juvenile delinquents he met in Magazine Prison who had taken to liquor and crime. "People drink intoxicants [as if they were] water. The police are unable to stop the trade in *kasippu* [illegally distilled local liquor]. Even the school-going youngsters have become drunkards. This is a result of abandoning Buddhist culture."

He continues: "In a Buddhist-administered country the action of man is directed to a good path not only by advice, *but by closing the avenues that lead to wrong actions.* It is due to this that bribery, horse racing, intoxicants, bad behavior, and stealing, which corrupt the society, should be eliminated."

In elucidating the Buddhist way of life, Gnanasiha resorts to a characteristically well-established Buddhist praxis that a person must cultivate his inner virtues and dissolve mental defilements and base

11. Bond, *The Buddhist Revival,* pp. 87–88.

12. In Sri Lanka, as in India, the majority of adult women have worn "traditional" clothing right through modern times whether it be cloth and blouse, or the sari. Men of the middle classes engaged in the professions of civil administration and business largely took to Western clothes in their public appearance.

intentions in order to act successfully upon the external world. Gnanasiha deploys a distinction between a person's "internal" and "external" qualities and uses this dichotomy and yardstick to criticize Western orientations—whether capitalist or socialist—as concentrating on the latter only. Gnanasiha asserts that the "external" qualities are connected to material well-being only, and that modern inventions exist to create material comfort only. Present-day orientations do not address the development of man's inner qualities, which are concerned with the aims of man's life. According to Buddhism, man is the greatest being, superseding the gods, because he has the capacity to end the cycle of rebirths and because he alone can think beyond himself to serve others. "One becomes a righteous man and makes others righteous." It is because contemporary man lacks "righteousness" that he is to be rated an "animal," in spite of his scientific discoveries and his creation of material well-being.

It is for this lack of attention to the "internal" qualities of man that Gnanasiha faults not only the existing Western-oriented ruling government in Sri Lanka, but also the left-wing parties advocating Russian-type socialism. While creating "equal living," as in the regime of ancient *cakravartins,* the latter lacks belief in the inner qualities of man and also does not tolerate criticism. Once the mind is trained, it can train the whole world: "it is difficult to discipline the world without this prior discipline of the mind." It is difficult to develop a nation "without developing both internally and externally; it is this attention to internal behavior that is distinctive of our culture and tradition." "In the past the Buddhists in our country led a peaceful and simple life with humility. Even today the villagers love this form of living. *The urban life is a hindrance to him.* This village life is the result of an experience that is two thousand years long. We have to recover and rehabilitate this wonder before it falls into decay." Incidentally, "an articulate *bhikkhu* who is a leading member of a major monastic sect" expressed this sentiment in graphic terms when he told Mark Juergensmeyer recently: "Dhamma has gone to the forest, and ad-hamma has come to the city."[13]

So what is the Buddhist way of life for a layman? Gnanasiha says: Leading a Buddhist way of life does not mean the attempt to attain Nibbana. It means "to make people pious, peaceful and humble. Not to be proud or lazy, to be happy with little and living a simple life are

---

13. Juergensmeyer, "What the Bhikkhu Said," p. 57.

the aims of Buddhist life." A man fears sin and sin makes him shameful. He is not greedy. He lives in peace with his neighbor. "These are inner qualities that our forbears possessed. We are aping the West and leading the life of the licentious, destroying our habits and culture. . . . Our people today have resorted to a complicated life that exists in the West. . . . To show our greatness, we have become indebted to foreign countries. And thousands of families in turn spend more than their income and will be beggared in the future. This is the result of our overstepping the simple lives we led in the past."

When rich and poor resort to a simple life, it becomes popular. To live within limits, to minimize one's accumulation of wealth, and to make do with what is left, these are features of the Buddhist way of life. "When entanglements are minimized, the mind becomes less worried, and more composed." This is referred to in the *Karaniya Metta Sutta* as *appakichcho*—which has different applications for the layman and monk. For the layman it means fulfilling his portion of his responsibility to his family and his mindful orderly attendance to his delimited duties to family and occupation.

The Buddhist way of life translated into state politics should remember and implement the rule of *cakkavatti* in the past when people observed the five precepts. There was no slaughter of animals, and the rulers created numerous avenues of employment, which eliminated robbery and limited licentious living and drunkenness. This is the concept of "righteousness," and in a Buddhist-administered state "righteousness" (which separates man from animals), simple living, and equal living are all brought into line.

As a critique of contemporary life in Sri Lanka, the invocation of a "Buddhist way of life" and "Buddhist democracy" is powerful. These concepts indict the gap between the rich and the poor, the vices of public and personal life, the attraction toward "consumerist" values, the desertion of simple living, and the noncultivation of moral values, the enormous unemployment, the divisiveness of party politics, the lack of unity, and the disconnection between the governing politicians and bureaucrats and the governed. They touch on emotional and moral evaluations that were developed to counter the debilitating effects of colonial domination and to renovate a form of life which while harking back to the past incorporates active ingredients from a contemporary historical and religio-political consciousness.

But for the anthropologist interpreter as well as commentator there remain the questions of the limits of this genre of Buddhist ideological thought and the degree to which it has realistically developed a blueprint of "democracy" to address the problems of contemporary Sri Lanka.

The Limits of Buddhist Democracy and Buddhist Nationalism

There is first of all the unfinished business of the role of monk as a political actor. We have seen, starting with Rahula, the arguments made for legitimating the Buddhist monk's participation in politics. We have seen how monks with varying degrees of success have mobilized to canvass at political elections, to preach at rallies, stage demonstrations, and so on. Indeed the arguments of Rahula, Pannasiha, Gnanasiha, and other monk-activists—that the *bhikkhu's* vocation transcends self-interest, that the traditions of monastic communities conform to democratic practices that ensure equality and unity, and that the monks have served in the historic past as advisors both at the highest and at village levels of society—carry with them the not-so-hidden message that the monks are not only appropriate as political advisors and mediators but also as alternatives to politicians altogether. As Kemper puts it: "By this logic the monks constitute the patriotic alternative to the self-interest of politicians, for they produce social unity by transcending interests."[14]

As a commentator, I venture the opinion that the boldness of the claim to be fit and able to participate in a "Buddhist-administered society" is little matched by any demonstration by monks of their mastery of political, economic, and administrative skills and knowledge which would enable them to be effective politicians themselves, or be advisors at the national level, in a society facing modern challenges and tasks. (The adequacy of a monk's capacities and skills to participate at a different level in village or urban uplift projects and community development schemes is a different matter.)[15]

The inadequacies of the conception of Buddhist democracy are revealed when we search for viable formulations of how to conduct democratic politics today—which all monk-ideologues accept as a necessary and inevitable format in contemporary Sri Lanka.

Gnanasiha's model of a Buddhist democracy consists in a reminder of Buddha's reference to the strength of the Vajjian polity, whose af-

---

14. Kemper, "Nationalist Discourse."

15. And as intimated before, the Sarvodaya movement today in Sri Lanka has tried to co-opt monks in the work of rural development.

fairs were conducted by a tribal council of 7,000, and the suggestion that a democratic model for Sri Lanka might consist of a conference of 7,000 members drawn from the village councils.

Pannasiha's blueprint, though more elaborate, is also improbable and probably unworkable. Kemper describes his scheme as follows: six months before elections, a committee of educated men versed in political science and other subjects, and not belonging to any party, should propose a five-year development plan and a manifesto stating how to execute that plan. It is this plan and manifesto that should be presented to the people, who will be called upon to vote for the parties, who are expected to accept the plan. The government would be formed by the elected members of all the parties that have promised to implement the plan. The prime minister would be chosen from the party that has the largest number of representatives. Finally, keeping in mind the Donoughmore Constitution of the thirties and forties, Pannasiha suggests that each ministry should be composed of ten members of Parliament.

In this muddled proposal, it is difficult to see how any panel of educated men who have no party preferences can be chosen or to see what the purpose for the formation of political parties could be if they have to accept a plan already drawn up for them by others, or to see how members can be assigned to ministries, while at the same time taking into account their party affiliations. Moreover, national coalitions, even if possible, do not live long.

Buddhist Nationalist Hegemony and Minorities

Finally let us test the limits of the discourse of Buddhist nationalism and national unity, when it comes to attending to the rights and needs of those who are not Sinhala Buddhists in a country that has minorities.

The vexed problem of the ethnic conflict between the Sinhalese and the Tamils, as we have seen in this study, has revolved around the capacity of Sinhala Buddhist nationalism to grant equal democratic rights to those outside its fold. We have seen that this ideology is so hegemonic that it has led to the inferiorization of a minority in Sri Lanka and to the generation of a resistant attitude among many Buddhist nationalists toward any suggestion of devolution of authority, let alone the division of the island.

Let me conclude with what the two monk-ideologues, Pannasiha and Gnanasiha, have to say about minorities within the scope of Sinhala Buddhist nationalism. Pannasiha, who has taken part in many government and nongovernment deliberations on the ethnic problem, seems unable, finally, to get outside the language of Sinhala Buddhist hegemony and of Sinhala Buddhists as an endangered species. To achieve unity, the Sinhalese must exploit their numerical advantage: "when 74% of the population is united, what can the other 26% do?"[16] He has exaggerated when he has written that Tamils are favored in the distribution of Grade 1 schools and teachers' training colleges. He has objected to the enfranchising of upcountry estate Tamils because that would change the electoral arithmetic. He has accused "power hungry" Sinhala politicians of making deals with non-Sinhala members of Parliament. Finally, he has sounded the apocalyptic note that the Sinhalese have declined in every sphere of activity, including trade.

In his tract Gnanasiha, too, shows his unwillingness to concede that Sinhalese majoritarian rule might have contributed to the lack of national unity and that politicians on both sides might have contributed to the island's turmoil.

> Charges are levelled against Sinhalas that they subdue the Tamils and try to ban their language. According to my knowledge there is not a single Sinhala who would try to deny the rights of the Tamils or their language. They have been living in the North for generations, and they have a right to live there. . . . But the power hungry short-sighted Tamil politicians are misleading the innocent Tamils to steal the rights of the Sinhalese. This brought the Sinhalas into the fray. But it is only for their self-defense.
>
> The mistake lies not with the Sinhalas nor with the innocent Tamils, but with the short-sighted Tamil leaders who have become opportunists. Though the Sinhalese tolerate harassments by the Tamils in this country, no country in the world would allow a minority to indulge in such demonstrations. The policy of the division of this country demanded by the Federal party should be banned. This is a conspiracy to subdue the majority. It is a grave situation to witness the prime minister and his political party [the reference here is to Dudley Senanayake and the United National party] not taking in 1960 any measures against the Tamils, as he means only to remain in power.

Even more "liberal" views expressed by Buddhist monks concerning the ethnic conflict take as axiomatic that the state in Sri Lanka must

16. Quoted by Kemper, "Nationalist Discourse."

uphold the very notion of a Sinhalese Buddhist nation, and they tend to interpret and equate devolution with the partitioning of an island that has historically been a Sinhalese homeland. What then would be the democratic rights and status of Hindu, Muslim, and non-Sinhalese minorities in this hegemonic polity is difficult to address in a pluralistic way. This is not to deny that there have been other Buddhist monks who have voiced more accommodative and pluralistic views, but they are a small minority and are more definitely not mainstream.

Those who have raised the question of why "religious nationalism" could not in principle be a viable alternative to modern West-inspired "secular nationalism" and politics should ponder why in fact contemporary expressions of "religious nationalism" in Sri Lanka have found it difficult to accommodate the pluralistic coexistence of other "religio-political" communities on an equal basis within the same political fold.[17] This study, it is hoped, has thrown some light on the issue. It is worthwhile exploring the question whether the framework of current Buddhist nationalism can in the future stretch and incorporate a greater amount of pluralist tolerance in the name of a Buddhist conception of righteous rule. There is no reason to foreclose on this possibility, for there are precedents that can be positively employed to urge a new view. One of the lessons we have learned is that civilizations have multiple pasts, not a single past, and have classical precedents that are, within limits, capable of variant readings and of elaborations suited to new situations.

But new perspectives can be forged only under social and political conditions which are themselves not frozen or restrictive and are capable of inspiring new conceptions that will take hold on the public at large.

Our examination of Sri Lankan conditions has revealed the features that have made it so far a pressure chamber leading to periodic explosions that have now deteriorated into a condition of seemingly indefinite civil war fought on more than one front. Both Tamil and Sinhalese insurgents have battled the authorities in place. Even if they are quashed, there is no certainty that they will not re-emerge unless basic conditions change.

A conspicuous feature of the Sri Lankan turmoil is the attempt made by contemporary Sinhala Buddhist nationalist ideologues to bring into

---

17. I have in mind here Mark Juergensmeyer's challenging essay "What the Bhikkhu Said."

conjunction their contemporary concerns to champion "closure" and "exclusion" vis-à-vis the Tamils in favor of the Sinhala majority with their retrospective reading of the same concerns allegedly expressed in the Sinhala Buddhist chronicles of the past. I hold that it is predominantly the recent past and the present that have spawned the problems for which remedy is sought in the myths of "continuity" of Sinhala Buddhist national experience and Tamil enmity enduring over two thousand five hundred years.

There are several ways Sri Lanka today is locked into a prison house of both language and issues. Politics have so developed since 1956 that there is a bipolar Sinhalese majority, whose two divisions, exemplified by the UNP and the SLFP, have found a third group, the Tamils, as a minority, a common enemy or potential ally according to convenience, whom they can play off each other.

This pattern of political competition within the Sinhalese majority is reproduced over time by another ongoing horizontal division between the privileged elite and the vastness of rural society (and urban proletariat). It is noteworthy that family dynasties (Senanayakes, Bandaranaikes, Jayawardenes) are still influential in the two major parties (although President Premadasa has reduced the influence of old families within the UNP). This elite is drawn from and supported by a social stratum that is privileged, landed, and through access to English education occupies professional and higher administrative positions. This elite has not really lost power, and indeed its ranks have been augmented by newly mobile politicians, businessmen, and educated Sinhalese of lesser social origins. One of the changes stemming from the so-called social revolution of 1956 is the upward mobility into national politics and bureaucratic employment of some persons from the ranks of the village elite (school teachers, ayurvedic physicians), small-scale businessmen, and the lower levels of administrative service, who in the long run have fitted comfortably into the patronage system and its attendant inequities.

But the measures of the "welfare" state and its promise of wider social mobility has produced more frustrations than relief. As we have seen, the system of "free education" in the local languages created a vast literate and semiliterate pool of youth whose employment prospects were small. It is the youth of the lower levels of rural society who, having invested so much hope in education, became the rebels of the JVP as well as of the Tamil insurgency. In the meantime the old elite, and the new elite who have joined them, reproduce their educational and social advantages by enabling their children to acquire a knowledge of English, either locally or by sending them abroad to Great Britain, the United States, and elsewhere, and the technical knowledge that will secure for them the most rewarding and prestigious positions in Sri Lanka.

Insofar as Sinhala Buddhist nationalism is a gospel of excluding Tamils from competition, it is fueled by these frustrations of unemployment and poor employment, and of lebensraum in a crowded island.

The problems of this crowded island are compounded by its narrow industrial base. Its dependence on agriculture and its dedication to an entrenched pattern of agricultural expansion through newly opened settlements on a peasant basis directly feed, as we have underscored, the ethnic conflict. And the ethnic conflict in turn has slowed down economic development, derailed growing tourism, and made foreign investors nervous.

The Gal Oya Multipurpose Scheme of the fifties and the Mahavali Project of the present confront us with a cluster of curious contradictions. The elite bureaucrats of the island, the technically sophisticated economists, engineers, and architects, in collaboration with foreign experts and much foreign funding, plan highly "industrialized" blueprints and use heavy technology for building the irrigation dams, the roads, communication facilities, and the like. But this same cosmopolitan elite, together with the leading politicians, then yokes this heavily capitalized infrastructure to a peasant form of cultivation—small farms, run by peasant households, most of whom will resort to the traditional technology of cultivation. This pattern of peopling the newly developed hinterlands entails the transplantation of large numbers of peasants from densely populated areas, most of which are Sinhalese, to "border areas" and "shatter zones" of the north and east, and has led to the Tamil counterclaims of "homelands" and Sinhalese majoritarian discrimination in settlement policy.

What is of interest to us at the level of ideology which structures perceptions and frames political actions is that many of the elite planners, as well as many persons at all levels of society, especially the rural peasantry, subscribe to the vision of an idealized and harmonious society, centered on the tank, the temple, and the rice field as the most desirable form of a Sinhala Buddhist national existence. The elite, living a different style of life and reproducing a different pattern of privileged domination in their role as planners and rulers, wish upon the vast mass of the people an indefinitely expanding network of peasant "villages" as the answer to the island's demographic and employment problems. And the ideologues of the society, the activist scholar-monks, the populist literary circles, the vote-seeking politicians, and the creators of rituals of national development and television dramas unite to propagate this vision of a (utopian) past that could be a prospective (utopian) future. These are the parameters of a national perspective that at present hinder the envisioning of a more realistic and workable regime of Buddhist democracy and righteous rule that can accommodate minorities.

13 Epilogue: Sinhalese Identity and the Legacy of the Past

The Beginnings of Sinhala and Sinhala-Buddhist Identities

In my earlier book, *Sri Lanka, Ethnic Fratricide, and the Dismantling of Democracy,* I have myself cited as informative Heinz Bechert's assertion that the Sinhalese chronicles, especially the *Mahavamsa,* took a fateful step in postulating the unity of a people and religion. Bechert wrote, "The origination of historical literature in Ceylon in the existing form was an intentional act of political relevance. Its object was the propagation of a concept of national identity clearly connected with a religious tradition, i.e., the identity of the Sinhalese Buddhists. . . . without the impact of this idea, the remarkable continuity of the cultural as well as of the political traditions in spite of the vicissitudes in the history of the island would be impossible."[1]

K. M. de Silva, Sri Lanka's foremost historian, in his recent *Managing Ethnic Tensions in Multi-Ethnic Societies: Sri Lanka, 1880–1985,*[2] also reminds us of the critical importance of Bechert's assertion, but transforms Bechert's reference to a historical literature that propagated national identity into an imputation of a *historical consciousness* to the Buddhist societies of South and Southeast Asia, none more so than Sri Lanka. De Silva states: "Sri Lankan society carries a huge burden of historical memories and in this book I have tried to show how the pressure of these memories has helped to shape and distort policies and responses to policies over the last 100 years" (ibid., p. vii). A few pages later, referring to the "awareness of a common

1. Heinz Bechert, "The Beginnings of Buddhist Historiography: *Mahavamsa* and Political Thinking" in Bardwell Smith (ed.), *Religion and Legitimation of Power in Sri Lanka* (Chambersburg, Pa.: Anima Books, 1987), p. 7. Also see Heinz Bechert, "Buddhism in the Modern States of South East Asia," in B. Grossman, ed., *South East Asia in the Modern World* (Wiesbaden, 1972).
2. Lanham, Md.: University Press of America, 1986.

129

identity," he refers again to Sri Lanka as bearing "a crushing and unbearable burden of history." However, de Silva's text, *Managing Ethnic Tensions*, a comprehensive treatment of many developments, is not focused on *demonstrating* the continuous transmission of historical memories or of a historical consciousness over time. The book has other thematic and substantive interests, and the issue identified above is not one of the connecting threads that weave his rich tapestry.

Many writers on Sri Lanka in recent times have inevitably cast a retrospective look at these ancient chronicles (the *Mahavamsa* was written around the sixth century A.D.), and have remarked on their powerful message of conflating a people, religion, and territory as a historical mission. In this retrospective gaze cast upon the past, the story of the exemplary hero of the *Mahavamsa*, Dutthagamani, who is characterized as the Sinhala champion who united the kingdom by defeating the hated and marauding Tamil invaders and thereafter built edifices on behalf of Buddhism, has been examined and reexamined. In the original version, while the Tamils are regarded in this negative manner, there are two complex and moving subthemes: the declaration that the Tamil King Elara was a virtuous and just king though not a Buddhist and he was given mortuary rites with honors and a shrine built on that site; and the death scene of Dutthagamani, whose troubled conscience at having killed so many Tamils in his victorious war, was consoled by a group of Buddhist *arahants* (world-renouncing saints) that no hindrance in his way to heaven arose since in reality he had killed only one and a half human beings, one who "had come into the (three) refuges, and the other had taken unto himself the five precepts." The latter has been the theme of a meditation by Gananath Obeyesekere.[3]

Recently two Sri Lankan scholars[4] have stated somewhat different views on the origins and continuity of Sinhala, and Sinhala Buddhist, identities. This exchange is informative, merits close attention, and begins to pose the issues and problems that we have to tackle with re-

3. Gananath Obeysekere, *Meditation on Conscience*, Social Scientists' Association of Sri Lanka, Occasional Papers (Colombo: Navamaga, 1988).

4. The two essays compared here are R. A. L. H. Gunawardena, "The People of the Lion: Sinhala Consciousness in History and Historiography," in *Ethnicity and Social Change in Sri Lanka*, papers presented at a seminar organized by the Social Scientists' Association, December 1979 (Colombo: Navamaga, 1985), pp. 55–107, and K. N. O. Dharmadasa, "The People of the Lion: Ethnic Identity, Ideology, and Historical Revisionism in Contemporary Sri Lanka" (unpublished essay). A revised version of Gunawardena's essay has appeared recently in Jonathan Spencer, ed., *Sri Lanka: History and the Roots of Conflict* (London: Routledge, 1990).

gard to the formation and transmission of collective identity and of mytho-historical constructions.

Gunawardena asserts that the Sinhalese nationalist ideology as propagated today "with its associations with language, race, and religion" has been virtually constituted in the last hundred years or so. It "forms an essential part of contemporary bourgeois culture" and has "radically refashioned our view of the past" (Gunawardena, p. 55). It was during the period of British colonial rule that "the Sinhala consciousness underwent a radical transformation and began to assume its current form" (ibid., p. 87). Theories of race stemming from Europe, together with formulations that conflated "Aryan" as a language group with the speakers of the language as an "Aryan race," made their impact in the course of the nineteenth century on certain Sinhala literati who in turn forged the modern Sinhala consciousness. Thus, for example, James Alwis, writing in 1866 on the origin of Sinhala language, claimed Aryan status not only for the Sinhala language but also for its speakers. And from 1920 onward, "racialist writings in Sri Lanka take a vehemently anti-Tamil stance," and the label "Sinhalese Buddhist" receives a new valence. This was exemplified by Dharmapala, the father of the so-called Protestant Buddhism, among others: the Dutthagamani-Elara episode in the *Mahavamsa* was used by him retrospectively to celebrate the Sinhala Aryans of yore ("uncontaminated by Semitic and savage ideas") who had never been conquered and to champion the rights of Sinhala Buddhists as an underprivileged group under colonial and Christian domination. Gunawardena's documentation in support of this thesis is convincing,[5] and a number of modern scholars of Sri Lanka including myself would agree.[6]

5. Max Müller popularized the term *Aryan* in the sense of Indo-European (but was guilty on some occasions of conflating the language grouping with the Aryan race). B. C. Clough, in the 1820s and 1830s, was the first to assert that the Sinhalese language was derived from Sanskrit, and this classification was supported by R. C. Childers (in 1874–76) and others. Rudolph Virchow (in 1885–86) used the expression "the Sinhalese race," and by the end of the century the identity of the Sinhalese and Tamil speakers had taken on a *racial* dimension. In 1897 the *Buddhist* carried an article entitled "The Aryan Sinhalese." Dharmapala, as we have seen, used this "elevated" classification for his propagandist and polemical purposes. Nationalism, Buddhism, Sinhala language, and Sinhala race had been fused into a single indivisible reified entity.

John Rogers has informed me that James Cordiner, in *A Description of Ceylon* (London: Longman, 1807), argued that Sinhala was based on Sanskrit and Pali.

6. A recently published book, Jonathan Spencer, ed., *Sri Lanka: History and the Roots of Conflict* (London: Routledge, 1990), has articles by Spencer, R. L. Stirrat and Elizabeth Nissan, Steven Kemper, and John D. Rogers, which agree that the under-

If the current Sinhala Buddhist nationalism was a construction of the last hundred years, then what was the legacy from the past? Gunawardena sets out to demonstrate that the label "Sinhala" as applied to a people from earliest times, intersected in a varied fashion with people identified according to their religious identity (as Buddhist or otherwise), according to the language (Sinhala or other) that they spoke, and according to their "ritual status" (*varna*/caste). Gunawardena's conclusion which contests the popular retrospective view of the past is that: "It is only by about the twelfth century that the Sinhala grouping could have been considered identical with the linguistic grouping. The relationship between Sinhala and the Buddhist identities was even more complex" (ibid., p. 97).

As a historian, Gunawardena is guided by an expectation (based no doubt on comparative knowledge) that state formation in the island from the time of the landing of Vijaya and his followers as a colonizing nucleus and as the initial ruling circle was a gradual process of aggregation and incorporation of other settlements and categories of people unrelated to them. Aside from reviewing certain evidence,[7] Gunawardena makes a two-pronged exegesis to support the gradualism of state formation and the parallel extension of the Pali term *Sihala* (Sinhala) to embrace the circles of people brought under its canopy.

The first is that evidence from the Brahmi inscriptions found at various dispersed sites and information contained in some literary works (like the *Dhatuvamsa*, the *Sihalavatthuppakarana* and the *Sahassavatthuppakarana*) suggest that the early settlements were disparate and that petty rulers held sway over various parts of the island at "the beginning of historical times." The *Mahavamsa* should be read anew in the light of this evidence; in any case it attributes a different origin to the settlements in the eastern and southeastern regions of the island from that attributed to Vijaya and his retinue. The rulers at

---

standing of the national past as a history of warring "races" or "ethnic groups" is a product of colonial reading and interpretations of the chronicles; these readings have been used to structure the present and to pursue contemporary purposes.

7. For example, the word *Sihala* itself occurs for the first time in Sri Lankan sources in the *Dipavamsa* (fourth to fifth century A.D.)—it is said the island was known as Sihala "on account of the Lion." The expression *Sihaladipa* (the Sinhala island) occurs in a text by Buddhaghosa written around the fifth century A.D. The *Mahavamsa* (sixth century A.D.) contains the term *Sihala* only twice. The term *Sihala* is conspicuous by its absence in the Brahmi inscriptions, which are accepted as the earliest historical documents in Sri Lanka.

Anuradhapura may have been pre-eminent, but there is no evidence that these other rulers accepted Anuradhapura's overlordship, allegedly established by Devanampiya Tissa, whose consecration ceremony was sponsored by Asoka.

The second is that a close scrutiny of the Vijaya myth in the *Mahavamsa* and related early origin stories would indicate a concern to explain the genesis of the name *Sihala*. From the Vijaya myth itself one infers that the term *Sihala* embraced first Vijaya himself (and his close kinsmen) and second, his retinue and followers who accompanied him. The extension of this label to incorporate others has to be tracked.

The Vijaya myth concludes, after Vijaya's expulsion of the *yakkhini* Kuvanna and his two children by her to the Malaya region, with his sending a mission to Madhura (Madura) in South India to woo the daughter of the Pandu king for Vijaya himself, and "the daughters of others for the ministers and retainers." The king's daughter, together with another hundred maidens for the ministers of Vijaya, all fitted out, according to their rank, and "craftsmen and a thousand families of eighteen guilds" were sent across the sea and they disembarked at Mahatittha.[8] These Pandyan Tamil women as proper spouses for Vijaya and his male followers, and a thousand *families* of the guilds, men, women and children of fully Pandyan identity, in conjunction with Vijaya and his followers, the core *Sihala*, pose at the very beginning of the "official" chronicle history of the island the problems of counting "descent" and attributing identity that Gunawardena, the historian with a Marxist bent, tries to interpret in one way, Dharmadasa, his questioner, in another way, and I in a third way.

It might be supposed that with a patrilineal rule of counting descent, the children of Vijaya and his original 700 followers, by Pandyan women, and their children in turn if they married endogamously, would be counted Sihala. This is the presumption of the text *Vamsatthappakasini* (cited by Gunawardena) when it states that the seven hundred members of Vijaya's retinue and all their descendants "up to the present day" are called *Sihala*. But a conjectural puzzle is presented by that category of Pandyan newcomers described as "craftsmen and a thousand families of eighteen guilds," who to begin with are wholly non-Sihala, and would remain so if they propagated them-

8. *Mahavamsa, or The Great Chronicle of Ceylon* (Colombo: Ceylon Government Information Department, 1950) 7:48–58.

selves as a separate category, unless their incorporation into the broadened category of Sihala is effected minimally through their learning of the Sihala language. Thus it is by virtue of a linguistic incorporation, and not by descent, that they would have become Sihala.

For me, then, the problem of incorporation of incoming non-Sinhala (Pali: Sihala) people from South India—a process of signal importance to Sinhala chronicle writing and myth-making—is already posed in the foundation myth itself. For Gunawardena this puzzle has a different significance. Coming at the issue from a Marxist perspective which integrally links the process of state formation with social-class differentiation and with the interests of the dominant class, Gunawardena argues that the Sinhala consciousness and Sinhala identity in the early Anuradhapura period (the time of Buddhaghosa's writing) pertained to "the ruling class" of Vijaya and his followers, but excluded the group of craftsmen-agriculturists and others who performed ritually "low" service. (This is how Gunawardena interprets the social status of the original reference in the *Mahavamsa* to "craftsmen and thousand families of eighteen guilds.") He attributes to caste (*jati*) ideology the exclusion of the "service castes" from membership in the original Sinhala group.

In my view Gunawardena could plausibly sustain his "developmental" thesis that historically the movement of Sinhala consciousness could be seen as progressively extending from the ruling dynasty to the kingdom, and then finally to the people of the kingdom, without problematically imposing a class exclusion of the so-called low-status service castes.

Be that as it may, Gunawardena's strongest submission is subversive of the current "nationalist" reading of the *Mahavamsa*'s account of the military and political unification achievements. It is against the backdrop of the multicentric and dispersive array of settlements and principalities of that time that Dutthagamani's war, mounted from the southern extremity of the kingdom of Rohana (Mahagama) and concluding with his winning the northern kingdom of Elara (a "just" Tamil king but a man of "false beliefs"), must be viewed. The *Mahavamsa* itself contains details which show that not all the people who fought against Dutthagamani were Tamils; it also speaks of him fighting 32 different rulers before defeating Elara.[9] The campaigns do not tell the

9. I am tempted to suggest that this number may derive from the Hindu-Buddhist cosmological conception of Indra and his 32 lesser deities on top of Mount Meru.

story of a monolithic Sinhala-Tamil confrontation. "The most plausible explanation of the available evidence is that Dutthagamani was a powerful military leader who unified the island for the first time after fighting against several independent principalities" (ibid., 73).

The Sinhala ideology wishes to establish that the expansion and consolidation of Buddhism in the island gave a religious identity to the island: "Dutthagamani in the *Mahavamsa* and Dhatusena in *Culavamsa* are both presented as waging war against the Damilas to restore Buddhism to its proper position." Gunawardena's conclusion is deconstructive: "The chronicle seeks to create the impression that there was a strong anti–South Indian feeling among the dominant elements in Sri Lankan society, but it is less than convincing. . . . The claim that the Buddhist order was destroyed by the invaders is also not borne out by the inscriptional records of this period. They indicate that there were Buddhists among the invaders. Some of them were generous patrons of the Buddhist clergy and one of their kings bore the title Buddhadasa which meant 'the servant of the Buddha'" (ibid., p. 74).[10]

K. M. de Silva's agreement with this conclusion lends it solidity. Calling the *Mahavamsa* "a powerful myth," he states: "The historical evidence we have suggests that there were large reserves of support for Elara among the Sinhalese, and that Dutthagamani, as a prelude to his final decisive encounter with Elara, had to face the resistance of other Sinhalese rivals who appear to have been deeply suspicious of his political ambitions. Moreover, his eventual and historic triumph over Elara was much less of a self-conscious victory of Sinhalese proto-nationalism over Dravidian imperialism as much as it was in a very real sense the first significant success of centripetalism over centrifugalism in Sri Lanka's history" (*Managing Ethnic Tensions*, p. 11).

Gunawardena is persuasive when he states that, "It is only after the development in South India of a militant form of Hinduism, which adopted a pronounced hostile stance against both Buddhism and Jainism, that Tamils would have been considered foes of the faith by the Buddhists of Ceylon. . . . Thus while earlier, the Buddhist identity was one which linked the Buddhists of Sri Lanka with coreligionists in South India and other parts of the subcontinent, it is only after about the seventh century that prerequisite conditions matured making it possible to link the Sinhala identity with Buddhism and to present

---

10. Gunawardena refers us to *Epigraphia Zeylanica* 3:218, 4:114.

Tamils as opponents of Buddhism."[11] There is little doubt that within the critical early medieval period (seventh to tenth century A.D.) the Buddhist versus Saivite hostilities were a two-way process, and although there were Buddhist centers and interests in South India and constructive cultural and religious exchanges with the Pallavas, the polarity Sinhala Buddhist versus Tamil (Cola-)Saivite was taking stereotypical proportions in the face of political rivalries and confrontations between certain South Indian and Sinhala peoples divided by religious identity.

What is the nature of Dharmadasa's critique of Gunawardena's account of the beginnings of Sinhala, and Sinhala-Buddhist identities? It is not explained on what grounds Dharmadasa refers to Gunawardena's submission as "revisionist." (Is it revisionist because it goes against current nationalist understanding of the past?)

Dharmadasa sees no problem in the sparsity of references to the Sinhala in the *Mahavamsa, Dipavamsa,* or the Brahmi inscriptions; he agrees with Paranavitana that there was no need to underscore the identity of "Sinhala ethnics" (his words) in these contexts because they were in the majority, and the group affiliations specially designated in the inscriptions (only 14 out of 1234 inscriptions) were those of donors belonging to minorities—the Dameda (Tamils) and other named ethnic or tribal groups.

The earliest reference to "the Sinhala language," says Dharmadasa, is in the early fifth century: Buddhaghosa, for example, refers to the *Sihala bhasa;* and books in this language were written in that century. On this matter there is no difference from Gunawardena. Dharmadasa suggests at one point that by this time there had developed a distinct "ethnic identity" among the people of the island which explicitly excluded the Tamils. But this is a tenuous conjecture and what is in fact actually documented by him is the possibility that such an identity was realized much later in time. Dharmadasa's strongest claim is that "The Sinhala identity was considered as encompassing all the Sinhala speaking inhabitants of the island long before Mahinda IV [956–72] came to the Anuradhapura throne." He also indicates that Mahinda V (982–1029) was displaced by the Colas, who are described in the

---

11. Gunawardena, "The People of the Lion," p. 75. He further substantiates this thesis by reference to Tamil writings like the *Periya Puranam,* which reflect the intensity of the hostility that the devotees of the Saiva faith harbored against the Buddhists and Jainas. In the seventh century a Sinhalese contender won the throne with the help of the Pallavas, and his descendants succeeded in resisting South Indian intrusions for two centuries.

Culavamsa as the "Damilas" who "plundered the whole country like devils."[12] Thus Dharmadasa sees the Sinhala linguistic identity, embracing all inhabitants of the island but the Damilas, as well established by the early tenth century, and at this time it seems evident to him from certain other texts that the Sinhala "ethnic identity" was coalescing with a Buddhist religious identity.

Stated in this way there seems to be ultimately a greater convergence between Gunawardena and Dharmadasa than might appear at first sight, especially when their most radical claims are qualified by their sense of identity formation (Sinhala, and Sinhala Buddhist) as an expanding temporal process. Dharmadasa's early limit of the fifth century is modified in actual fact and stretched to the tenth century; and Gunawardena's terminal twelfth century can be pushed back by two centuries without doing violence to his argument. What the exchange between them really generates as a by-product is that the evidence on identity formation is complex and indirect, that a "historical consciousness" constructed by writers of texts cannot mechanically be attributed to the larger public, and that the modern interpreters of the past, while inevitably looking at it with present ideological concerns, should be open to the possibility of multiple discourses and multiple intentionalities operating at different levels. One thing, however, is clear: a primordial golden age with a perfect fit between Sinhala people, Sinhala language, Buddhism, and the entire territorial space of the island could not have existed in Dutthagamani's time, and probably did not exist at the time the *Mahavamsa* was composed. And another historical process is equally clear: the Buddhicization and Sinhalization of people has been a continuing process through the centuries right up to the present time, and the genius of the island's civilization may well be located there as much as in the classical past when certain central postulates about the mutuality between kingship and the *sangha* and their responsibility for the cultivation of Buddhist values in an agrarian society were articulated and pursued.

Clarifications and Problem Setting

Supposing we can agree that somewhere around the tenth century a collective identity of Sinhala designating speakers of the

12. Mahinda V according to the *Culavamsa* (54:57) was married to a Kalinga princess. Her son Sena was made king, and in the course of internal turmoil and intrigue, she had her second son Udaya made king. She, according to the text, supported by the *senapati,* "gave over the country" to the Damilas, who "now plundered the whole country like devils and pillaging, seized the property of its inhabitants" (54:64–66).

Sinhala language had crystallized and that an even more potent collective identity combining this language with attachment to Buddhism was also maturing. How, then, do we set about tracking the deployment and use of these labels in the succeeding centuries. Minimally we have to recognize the existence and interweaving of two strands in the trajectory of a composite Sinhala Buddhist identity and consciousness. On the one hand, it is possible to conceive of a consciousness being continuously transmitted—a consciousness fueled by a sense of a common language, a common form of religious beliefs and worship, and so on. This could be an inclusive, incorporative, assimilative, and benign sense of common sharing and becoming one Sinhala people without the need of an external enemy and threat. On the other hand, if the burden of that consciousness necessarily implies an unbroken existentially relevant sense of antagonism to the Tamils as aliens or outsiders, in both religion and language, menacing Sinhala identity and sovereignty, then this exclusionist, separatist, boundary-making, and polarizing impulse must be established as a reiterative theme in the literature, and also as a theme existentially valid and realistic for the Sinhala people at large.

Now, with regard to the second polarizing strand of a permanent threat posed by Tamils, and its validity as an experiential reality, we are faced with a discontinuity or rupture. As the Sinhalese in the late thirteenth century began to abandon the Polonnaruva region and retreat farther south, there was formed in the Jaffna peninsula and part of the Vanni a Tamil kingdom of Jaffna. "After the thirteenth century with the establishment of a Tamil kingdom in the north of the island, there was in fact a geographical separation of the Sinhalese from the Tamils. The buffer between them was the dry zone forests of the Vanni. The Sinhalese had by now, abandoned the north-central plains and migrated to the south-west quarter of the island. . . . Until the first quarter of the twentieth century a vast forest belt separated the Sinhalese from the Tamils of the north and the east; but they were not totally isolated from each other" (de Silva, *Managing Ethnic Tensions*, p. 14).

In fact as a gross statement it is not incorrect to suggest that from the thirteenth century to the time of the arrival of the European colonial powers, indeed well into British times in the nineteenth century, a social separation and a distancing rather than a steady symbiotic interaction better characterizes the state of coexistence between Tamil and Sinhala political formations inside the island. There were some episodic involvements and collisions, but they were no more than that. And the rule of a south Indian dynasty in the kingdom of Kandy from

1739 to 1815 is an interlude (whose significance for the continuing legacy of anti-Tamil sentiments will be examined shortly). Leaving aside the Nayakkar phenomenon for the moment, it looks as if this hiatus makes problematic how a historical legacy of the Tamils as the agents of enmity, intrusion, and spoliation can have had an existential reality and plausibility in Sinhalese consciousness, let alone transmitted in daily discourse, even if monk chroniclers kept reiterating old themes as part of the conventions of literary writing and of compositional repetition. The later chronicles may, working from the thirteenth century, project backwards to Dutthagamani as an unbroken thread of mythic history. But what is the evidence of persistent or traumatic struggles between Sinhalese and Tamils that could be wrought into an unbroken chain of enmity from the thirteenth to the twentieth centuries?

This is why I want to stress now, and signal as a theme to be developed, the inclusive, incorporating, and elaborative capacities of Sinhala Buddhist culture and society as a coexistent countertheme. The incorporations of south Indian elements into the Kotte Kingdom of the southwest and into the Kandyan Kingdom and its predecessors of the central region, including the incoming peoples from the Coromandel and Malabar coasts, suggest that their Sinhalization and Buddhicization are as much interesting conversion processes to consider as the theme of continuity of Sinhala Buddhist destiny allegedly inscribed at the beginning of sacred time. Indeed the process of "incorporation" of non-Sinhala people and the process of becoming Sinhala is embedded, as I have previously remarked, in the very foundation story and colonizing myth of Vijaya in the *Mahavamsa*.

The South Indian Presence in Sinhalese Texts, 1200–1700

Whatever the actual realities of Sinhala-Tamil distancing and lack of significant or acrimonious collisions between the Tamil kingdom in the north and the Sinhala kingdoms in the south, there was a chain of texts composed by a line of Buddhist monk-literati, who appended to their composite texts celebrating and enunciating the *Dharma* an enumeration of the line of kings and their meritorious works in support of Buddhism. These texts culminated in a panegyric on the king ruling at the time of composition. This literature also with varying intensity and frequency carried anti-Tamil sentiments.

There is a distinct, fraught, and probably traumatic experience between the tenth and thirteenth centuries, during the Polonnaruva period, that is continuously replicated in subsequent Sinhalese literary works. It takes on the proportions of an enduring mnemonic and re-minder, and a formulaic frame, that was activated when Sinhala Bud-dhist interests were threatened or believed to be under attack. This was the long Cola occupation of the island, spanning the tenth and eleventh centuries, and the enactment of intense rivalries between Sinhalese and south Indian polities. The regaining of Sinhala Buddhist su-premacy is historically enshrined, principally as the achievement of the time of Parakrama Bahu I (and of Vijaya Bahu I before him) which, as is well known, is marked by the creation of a unified *sangha* under royal aegis and the missionary spread of a vitalized Buddhism to Thailand and Burma. But the twelfth and subsequent centuries were subject to invasions by Tamil and Kalinga "princes" and their bands, and it was probably the Kalinga attacks and presence that became in-delibly associated with the collapse of the Polonnaruva kingdom and the movement southwards and the establishment of less glorious, and unstable polities in the hills and in the southwest. While Nissanka Malla, the first king of the Kalinga dynasty, is on record as publicizing his sponsorship of Buddhism and his claims to *ksatriya* (warrior) and *cakkavatti* statuses as fulfilling the requirements of kingship, it is the invasion of Magha of Kalinga in 1235 A.D. and the havoc that he wrought that is memorialized in the literature. It takes precedence in the texts over such prosaic features as the several waves of migration of south Indian linguistic groups and their incorporation, assimilation, and indigenization within the Sinhala polities and the actual polariza-tion between a Tamil kingdom in the north and Sinhalese kingdoms beyond the abandoned dry zone.

The *vamsa* texts also show an amnesiac silence about an earlier period of fertile and creative influence of south Indian Pallava culture on Sri Lanka. Holt has recently reminded us that "artistic similarities between insular Southeast Asia and Sri Lanka point to a common source of religious and cultural inspiration: South Indian Pallava cul-ture. . . . Of greatest cultural importance to the period from the sev-enth through the tenth centuries was the political link established between the fortunes of the Pallava Empire and Sri Lanka."[13] This

---

13. John Clifford Holt, *Buddha in the Crown: Avalokitesvara in the Buddhist Tradi-tions of Sri Lanka* (New York: Oxford University Press, 1991), pp. 80–82. Holt has traced the influence on Sri Lankan Buddhism (and sculpture) of the Mahayana cult of Avalokitesvara that probably arrived via Pallava South India, and may have spread from South India to Sri Lanka and Sri Vijaya in Southeast Asia at about the same time.

provides an explanation, says Holt, for the emergence of Pallava sculptural traditions within the context of early medieval Buddhist culture in Sri Lanka. It may well be asked whether the orthodox Mahavihara's virtual monopoly of official "historical" writing ignored, or suppressed, or edited out, this stream of influence which was Mahayana-inspired. The interchanges with those centers and places in south India where Buddhism flourished have been largely unrecorded or unrecognized as increasingly the contours of an orthodox "Theravada" *sangha* twinned with a Sinhala polity solidified.

One should read chapter 80 of the *Culavamsa* and peruse the account of the evil deeds of King Magha, who was imbued with "a great lust for power," and of his soldiers, "the Kerala devils," to realize that the charges listed comprise a litany of woes that only an anti-Buddha, a Mara, can inflict. Magha qualifies as the uncontested bogey-man in Sinhalese perceptions. "The great scorching fire," King Magha, and his warriors, "countless flames of fire," torched "the great forest," the kingdom of Lanka. They looted property, inflicted torture and "corrupted the good morals" of family life. Their destruction of religion and desecration of the *sangha* receives unsparing emphasis: "They wrecked the image houses, destroyed many cetiyas, ravaged the viharas . . . tormented comrades of the Order," tore and strewed many books. Even the proud Ruvanvali Cetiya was overthrown and "many of the bodily relics," which gave it life, were allowed to disappear. They finally put out the monarch's eyes and plundered all his treasures; and the leaders of the soldiers consecrated Magha to "the glorious royal dignity of Lanka." In the midst of this awesome account of carnage the following comparison was made which would become for the future a standard trope of denunciation of Tamils: "the Damila warriors in imitation of the warriors of Mara destroyed, in the evil of their nature, the laity and the Order."[14]

There is a sequence of Sinhalese texts, extending in time from the thirteenth century to the eighteenth century, that, serving as signposts, on the one hand signal the strong message of Sinhala Buddhist entitlement to the island as unitary territorial space and on the other involve and repeat the stereotyped negative valuation of the "Demala" (Tamils)—a label indiscriminately generalized to all south Indian elements singled out as inimical to Sinhala Buddhist interests.

In reading this literature written by a Buddhist monk-literati, one

---

14. *Culavamsa*, translated by Wilhelm Geiger (Colombo: Ceylon Government Information Department, 1953), part 2, pp. 132–33.

must bear in mind the tradition of scribal recopying from text to text of stock themes and phrases, and of an intertextual cross-referencing, irrespective of whether later contexts in which a text is written find the repetition of a stereotyped judgment situationally relevant to the issues and concerns of the people at large living at that time.

Some of the major landmark texts are:

Pujavaliya (History of Offerings) is a popular religious work written by Mayurapuda Thera in the thirteenth century. The last two chapters tell the history of the island, beginning with Vijaya, the coming of Buddhism at the time of Devanampiya Tissa, the honors paid by a chain of the kings of Sri Lanka to the name of the Buddha, reaching its climax with the offerings to the tooth relic made by Parakrama Bahu II.[15]

The *Pujavaliya* was largely meant to be a commentary on the *Dhamma,* and while exhorting readers to fix their minds on the highest Buddhist achievements in the persons of *arahant* (perfected saint), *paccekka* Buddha (the lesser Buddha who seeks enlightenment for himself alone), and the complete Buddha, even as a way of achieving lesser goals, does, however, also contain the literary module on the Tamil menace.

Dharmadasa notes in his argument favoring a continuous consciousness of Sinhala identity that the *Pujavaliya* in its course refers "to nine instances when the Tamils invaded the island. The word *demala* is specifically used at each instance when referring to the Colas, and to the invasion of Magha of Kalinga. In describing the reign of Magha, which was one of the longest periods of foreign occupation, it is said: '[He] made Sri Lanka adopt false beliefs . . . made Lanka like a house on fire . . . [and] had it plundered by the Tamils and reigned forcibly for nineteen years' " (Dharmadasa, "The People of the Lion," p. 47).

The *Saddharmalankaraya* (The Ornament of the Good Law) was composed by Devarakhita Dharmakirti of Gadaladeniya in the fifteenth century at the time of the Gampola kingdom. The author means his work to be "an exposition of the Dharma," and in fact it seems to be primarily a collection of stories about the Buddhas, and the *arahants* in ancient Sri Lanka, followed by mention of a string of kings and their acts (including King Dutthagamani's attempt to preach the Dhamma).

15. See C. E. Godakumbura, *Sinhalese Literature* (Colombo: Colombo Apothecaries, Co., 1955), pp. 61–62.

Interestingly it appears that Dharmakirti's retelling of old stories had a special edge to it which Godakumbara describes:

> Not only does one notice a devout Buddhist preacher in Dharmakirti, but one also sees in him a profound hatred towards the Saivites who may have been gaining power in the country and spreading their ways of life and their religious practices. The Saivite influence is noticeable in the sculpture of the buildings at Gadaladeniya. The serene eyes of the Buddha in the earlier statues have become fierce in the image in this temple—perhaps the very image which our author worshipped. So one can understand his displeasure at these Saivites which he expresses in no uncertain terms. He likens them *with their sacred ash to ripe ash pumpkins* [emphasis added]. In the first chapter, when he describes the Pasandas, Dharmakirti has the Saivites in mind. In the *Padapithika-vastuva* he ridicules the worship of Isvara. The author puts the words of ridicule into the mouths of the devotees of Siva themselves and provokes laughter in the reader. The clever manner in which this dialogue between the followers of Isvara and the devotees of the Buddha is composed should place Dharmakirti on a very high plane as a writer of religious stories. (*Sinhalese Literature*, p. 92)

This comment suggests two points of interest. That even in the centuries of withdrawal from Polonnaruva and the founding of Sinhala polities in the south, the coming and going of south Indian influences and persons was a fact of life. Second, for the monkish writers in particular, in some contexts at least, the Tamil menace is not so much a military one as a breach made by Hindu Saivite religious ideas and practices. The smearing of sacred ash on their foreheads by Saivites becoming a powerful visual marker and diacritic of false religious adherence, and this ridiculing trope becomes a stock element in the repertoire of invective. (One should remember this when this slur is invoked and attached to Kirti Sri Rajasinghe by the anti-Nayakkar faction in the Kandyan period.)

Now let us bring into focus a third text, *Rajavaliya* (Lineage of Kings),[16] written sometime between the sixteenth and eighteenth cen-

---

16. There were apparently various recensions of this text, and Godakumbura, who uses B. Gunasekera, ed., *The Rajavaliya* (Colombo: Government Press, 1900), places this text's composition in the eighteenth century. Obeyesekere, referring to this same

turies. This text aims to provide a continuous political history of the island, ending with the accession of King Vimaladharmasuriya II and also the arrival of the Portuguese.

The text opens in conventional fashion with Buddhist cosmography concerning the formation of the world system, an account of Jambudvipa, the visits of the Buddha to the island, the lineage of Vijaya and his arrival in the island. Its contents are relevant to us because they not only contain newer elaborations of the Dutthagamani story, but also report entanglements between Sinhala and south Indian, especially Colan, kingdoms. Among these reported engagements which celebrate Sinhala successes is that famous one which involved King Gajabahu's penetration of the Cola kingdom in the company of the giant Nila, his recovery of 12,000 Sinhala captives who had been taken away by the Colan king Cenkuttuvan on a previous invasion, and his additional bringing over of 12,000 Colans as his prize (together with the jewelled anklets of the goddess Pattini, the bowl relic of the Buddha carried away in the time of Valagamba, and the insignia of the gods of the four *devale* [temples]).[17] The interesting conclusion of Gajabahu's return was what he did with the 24,000 liberated Sinhala and Colan captives: he "sent each captive who owned ancestral property to his inherited estate, and caused the supernumerary captives to be distributed over and to settle in these countries, viz. Alutkuruwa, Sarasiya pattuwa, Yatinuwara, Udunuwara, Tumpane, Hewaheta, Pansiya pattuwa, Egoda Tiha, and Megoda Tiha."

Dismissing the Gajabahu story as an actual historical occurrence (as many scholars have done), Obeyesekere plausibly interprets it as a "colonization myth," one of its objectives being to explain "the existence of South Indian settlers in parts of the Kandyan provinces and coastal regions" (*Cult,* chap. 8).

Obeyesekere's exegesis is grist for my theme of continuous "incorporation" and inclusion of south Indian migrants into Sinhala society as a major counterpoint to the ideology of timeless hegemonic Sinhala

---

text, identifies it as "one of the Sinhala accounts composed in the sixteenth and seventeenth centuries" (*The Cult of the Goddess Pattini* [Chicago: University of Chicago Press, 1984], p. 364). The Gajabahu story is also told in variant fashion in another text, *Rajaratnakaraya,* which was written to extol Viravikrama, who ascended the throne of Kandy in 1542 A.D.

17. These four guardian gods of the island, whose temples were aggregated in the Kandyan capital (they had their regional seats as well) were Vishnu, Natha, Pattini, and Kataragama.

Buddhist sovereignty over the island. He observes that the Kandyan and coastal areas "came into prominence in the fourteenth century and after, particularly with the founding of the Gampola kingdom. The movement to the Kandyan areas was consequent on disastrous invasions by the Colas (tenth century) and later by Magha of Kalinga (thirteenth century). It is likely that this version of the colonization myth evolved after the fourteenth century (ibid.).

The myth, in fact, exemplifies a standard South Asian mode of differentially incorporating into an existing society sectarian or alien minorities:[18] inferiorize them and then place them in a subordinate position in the hierarchy. The late medieval period saw waves of settlers—whether by forced entry or by royal invitation or by peaceful settlement—come into Sri Lanka to the coastal and interior parts. (We should not forget that similar processes of peopling were taking place in the geographically separate Kingdom of Jaffna.) The major waves of *karava* immigration to Sri Lanka occurred in the fifteenth century and after. One of the methods of incorporating immigrant populations into the Sinhalese social system until recent times was in the Kandyan areas to rate some farming segments as low subcastes of the *Goyigama* (farming) caste, their inferiorization being the royal act of King Mahasammata, the mythical first Buddhist king, who in Kandyan areas is seen as the ordinator of the caste system. In the low country, there are some recent immigrant groups labelled as *demala gattara* (Tamil *gotra*) who also trace their origins to Gajabahu's captives (Obeyesekere, *Cult*, pp. 366–68).[19] (Incidentally, there is a parallel tradition in the north among the Tamils that the Koviyar caste, a clean caste of servants and allies of the *vellala* farming caste, are by origin Sinhalese captives settled in the Jaffna kingdom.)

The question remains as to why the Sinhala story of Gajabahu in the *Rajavaliya* takes the highly implausible, exaggerated, and bombastic form of Gajabahu invading the Cola country in a singular fashion, terrorizing his counterpart King Cenkuttuvan, and bringing back the liberated Sinhala soldiers as well as Colan captives? Obeyesekere's conjecture takes as its point of reference the trauma and humiliation of

18. This strategy was illuminatingly formulated by Louis Dumont in *Homo Hierarchicus*.

19. See also Bryce Ryan, *Caste in Modern Ceylon* (New Brunswick: Rutgers University Press, 1953) for many references to the *demala gattara*, especially pp. 135–37; and Ralph Pieris, *Sinhalese Social Organization: The Kandyan Period* (Colombo: University of Ceylon Press, 1956).

the last phase of the Polonnaruva kingdom, especially culminating in the havoc caused by Magha's invasion when "the Sinhalas sank to their lowest point in the history of the island." The myth then is a compensatory fantasy, "the opposite of the later 'reality,'" a morale booster at a time of sunken self-esteem, generated during this time, probably in the newly formed polity in Dambadeniya begun by Vijayabahu III, and which, under the reign of his son Parakrama Bahu II (1236–70), was the site of intense literary and cultural activity, and an attempted (but failed) political reunification.[20] It is also suggestive (though Obeyesekere does not deal with it) that the *Rajavaliya* follows up the account of Gajabahu's exploits with the Colas with others of the defeat of south Indian foes by Parakrama Bahu II of Dambadeniya and by Prince Sapumal under the aegis of Sri Parakrama Bahu of Kotte. The lively account of battles, treacheries, and stratagems thus lends an air of reality and proximity in time to events concocted to deal with a pervasive condition, the great deal of spillover in many forms from south India into the island, and to engage in the ideological work via mythic constructions in a historical mode of accounting and placing, to use Obeyesekere's words, "the constant presence in Sri Lanka of South Indians," and I would add, their practices.

If the Gajabahu myth (or mythic history) is an explication of the transplantation and hierarchized placement of south Indian settlers (presented as war captives), then the coming of the Pattini cult as a historical reality, which Obeyesekere identifies as originally a deity of the Jainas and Buddhists of south India, into the island on its southwestern front, is a story of nonproblematic venerated acceptance because of the Buddhist associations of the cult.[21] Moreover, an

20. The Gajabahu myth interestingly, suggests Obeyesekere, is a precise opposite (reversal?) of the "reality" of Magha's invasion: "Magha invades Sri Lanka with twenty-four (or twenty) thousand Kerala troops; Gajabahu brings back twenty-four thousand. Magha plunders and terrorizes the Sinhalas, killing their king; Gajabahu terrorizes the Colas; Magha populates Sinhala villages with Tamil conquerors; Gajabahu does it with Tamil captives" (*Cult*, p. 372). Obeyesekere sees a plausible parallelism between Gajabahu and Cenkuttuvan in the Sinhalese and Tamil accounts of their heroes' conquests. The Colan myth regarding their hero King Cenkuttuvan's alleged terrorizing and subjugating the despised Aryans of the North in the literature of the Cankam and post-Cankam age is a similar construction of compensary fantasy: "I suggest that Cenkuttuvan is to Southern India vis-à-vis the North as Gajabahu is to Sri Lanka vis-à-vis South India" (p. 376).

21. Obeyesekere surmises that Vanci, the capital of the old Cera kings, was a center of the cult of the goddess Pattini. With the evangelical push of *bhakti* Hinduism and the

associated parallel is the acceptance at the highest levels of the political order and social status in the kingdom of Kotte, of the Alagakkonara and Mehenevara families of Kerala origins but of Buddhist affiliations, who apparently wielded their ministerial powers, especially through their trading interests, on the west coast ports at Colombo and Beruvela. The seat of Alagakkonara family was Rayigama. This is an illustration of the hosting and flexible accommodation of south Indian mercantile families, which enjoyed a high reckoning on the island and whose overseas trading networks must have benefited the local fragmented polities.

Parakrama Bahu VI (1411–66), whom the chronicles accord the prefix "great," ascended the throne about 1411, his seats being Rayigama followed by Kotte, in the western part of the island. It is from the reign of this king that there is a clear reference to the Pattini cult in the island: The text *Kokila Sandesaya* says that the king dedicated a shrine to the deity.

Obeyesekere remarks that "From the commencement of the Gampola dynasty (1341) and the accession of Parakramabahu VI in 1411, the politics of the country were dominated by chieftains of 'Malabar' (Kerala) descent who originally came from Vanci" (ibid., p. 524). In the middle of the fourteenth century power was multicentrically distributed, and although the Sinhala areas were formally under the dominion of Gampola, in fact, "the Sinhala areas of the western, southern, and central regions were under the effective control of two antagonistic and intermarrying families who originally came from Kerala—the Alagakkonara and the Mehenevara families" (ibid.). The remarkable thing is that in the mid-fourteenth century, there are references that indicate that one member of the Alagakkonaras conducted himself as an independent ruler in a large part of the southwestern and Sabaragamuva regions, while the Mehenevaras, headed by Sena Lankadhikara, was married to a sister of Bhuvaneka Bahu IV of Gam-

espousal of high Hinduism by south Indian monarchs, the Buddhists and Jainas of south India faced accentuated difficulties in the eleventh and twelfth centuries. Sri Lanka might have been a prime place for outward migration for the south Indian, especially the Kerala, Buddhists between say the eighth and fourteenth centuries.

This section on the Pattini cult and the activities of the two Kerala families is based on the account given by Obeyesekere, *Cult,* chap. 13. Obeyesekere's account of the Kerala families owes much, as he indicates, to S. Paranavitana's discussion in chap. 2 of *History of Ceylon,* vol. 1, part 2 (Colombo: University of Ceylon Press Board, 1960). I have consulted this source also.

pola. Some of the later kings of Gampola by matrilineal succession were counted as Mehenevara (Paranavitana, *History*, 1:640).

The Alagakkonara family figured importantly in saving the weak Gampola and Dedigama principalities from the invasions into Sinhala territory by the Tamil ruler of Jaffna, Arya Cakravarti.[22] Nissanka Alagakkonara was responsible for building the fortress known as Jayavardhana Kotte[23] and for helping Vikramabahu III (1357–74) himself, possibly the son of Sena Lankadhikara of the Mehenevara family, stave off the attacks of the Jaffna dynasty and its south Indian allies.

The involvement of the two Kerala families, their intermarriage with Sinhala ruling families (Parakrama Bahu VI was related to the Mehenevara family), their producing kings through these marriages whenever matrilineal succession was recognized, and so on, need not be followed here any further, except to say that in all probability the transplant of the Pattini cult and its spread and increasing provenance coincided with the dominant role and networking of the Kerala chieftains—merchant princes in the western, southern, and some of the central parts of Sri Lanka for many decades, from the commencement of the Gampola dynasty in 1341 to the reign of Kotte's most celebrated king, Parakrama Bahu VI. It is also worth remarking that the political and economic participation of these two Kerala families—who bore names and titles deriving from Malayalam or Tamil[24] and whose affairs and kinsmen were closely interwoven with Sinhala royal houses—have *not* been brought out and compared by modern scholars of Sinhala identity with the parallel, but seemingly more problematic and much discussed, role of the Nayakkars from Madurai in south India, who after similar marriage alliances produced a solely Nayakkar line of kings in the Kandyan kingdom from 1739 to 1815.

The succeeding portions of this chapter will continue to document

22. Sri Lankan history is not without its ironies and its humorous moments. That a Tamil dynasty in Jaffna claimed this bombastic title does puncture the equally bombastic claims of Sinhala nationalists who claim to be of the Aryan race.

23. Kotte, renamed as Jayawardenapura, is the new capital of Sri Lanka and is the seat of the Jayawardena family, which has sought to link itself with these historical associations.

24. Paranavitana, *History*, 1:640 (see also the appendix, "The Pedigree of the Alakesvaras"), remarks that Mehenevara was probably derived from *menavan*, 'baron' or 'minister', and has the same significance as the Sinhalese *bandara*, given to Sena Lankadhikara's family, whose descendants bore names and titles that are Malayalam or Tamil.

the interactions between Sri Lankan polities and their people at large and south Indian migrations of people and religio-cultural infusions that integrally energized as well as made volatile the history of those regions of the island which were the centers of gravity and foci of its cultural, political, and religious life since the virtual abandonment of Anuradhapura and Polonnaruva in the thirteenth century.

One realizes with surprise that the Buddhist revivalism and the Sinhala Buddhist nationalism of recent times, mediated by European theories of Indo-Aryan languages, with "racist" connotations for those so inclined, and by the British colonial retrieval of the classical archaeological past of the ancient capitals and propelled by the colonialist and modern nationalist readings of the *Mahavamsa* (and the other chronicles), have taken a telescoped leap to the mythicized golden age to constitute their tenets of race, religion, language, and territory as an exclusive possession of founding fathers and their pure descendants. By that decisive step they also showed a myopic and amnesiac disregard of the busy times and variegated terrain immediately proximate to them, which portrayed the miracle of open-ended processes by which a multicultural and pluralistic civilization with a distinctively Buddhist stamp was shaped and reshaped throughout medieval and precolonial times.

The Processes of Incorporation and Inclusion

It is now conventional wisdom, especially since Lévi-Strauss's grand enterprise concerning mythology, even among knee-jerk opponents who have digested his best insights, that myths have their variants, that one should expect a corpus of related myths, especially if they are focused on themes existentially important to the cultures and societies where they circulate. Moreover, such are the paradoxes and puzzles posed by existential issues that one would expect the exploration of a number of solutions to them standing to one another in diverse relations of linkage, complementarity, inversion, mirror image, opposition and so on.

I would suggest that one of the major existential issues for the Sinhala, explored in a number of their myths (and rites), is the "peopling" of the island of Lanka and the colonization, development, and habitation of its empty spaces. Its territorial boundedness as an island defined by an ocean beating upon its shores on all sides, its adjacency at the same time to the vast subcontinent of India, which is its "parent" but from which it must differentiate itself to establish its identity: these two features establish a framework for various cultural and demographic processes and mytho-historical constructions. It is a general theme among many island peoples that both the good things and the bad things come from outside; heroes as colonizers as well as enemies as invaders and, more prosaically, migrants of diverse skills as well as different customs, make their entry and take their ordered place. The Sinhalese foundation myth of Vijaya and his followers is a story of colonization and conquest over indigenous nonhuman *yakkhas*, who were displaced, and the first steps toward the institution of a new human society, the future Sinhala people, set in place. We have referred above to one version of the Gajabahu myth which reverses the story of an alleged earlier invasion of the island, with a counterinvasion of south India, resulting in a version of transplantation of Tamil captives and their subordinate placement in spaces that invite occupation and development. The coming of the Pattini cult and the parallel story of Kerala chiefly families with mercantile skills in shaping the politics of the Gampola and Kotte kingdoms are entirely in another key of fruitful intervention and incorporation at the highest levels of Sinhala society. It seems, therefore, that a cluster of issues—how and why do incorporation and assimilation, or containment and insulation, or rejection and expulsion take place, with regard to outside Indian peoples and their practices, and how in due course can a narrative of composite yet distinctive Sinhala identity be evolved—is a major focus of ideological, mytho-historical, and practical work in Sinhala society over the centuries.

Let me also introduce here another focal theme of existential concern, not unrelated to the colonization and development theme above, but containing its own distinctive emphasis. It is a complex that intersects with the one we are considering and exemplifies the theme brought out by Kapferer and will be taken up later: how from the *periphery* or the far provinces of the Sinhala polity, an "unruly" ("fierce," even untamed) heroic actor, like Dutthagamani, mounts an insurrection and war of liberation and unification against a foreign presence occupying the center of the polity. Similarly, Parakramabahu launched a campaign of aggregation and unification of a polity which was fragmenting and whose center could not hold, and ends his career as the axis of a flourishing Buddhist civilization. The accent in this complex is the collective worry about the fragmenting and falling apart of a polity; it is the process of reaggregation *starting* from the periphery that eventually constitutes the whole at the *center*. And at the same time the unruly but generative hero travels on his own career path of being transformed into a benign and righteous and virtuous ruler once he reaches and reconstitutes the center. This complex thus explores two parallel trajectories and outcomes: the progress of the polity from disorder and impending chaos to order and stability and the transformation of a fierce warrior who must conquer before he becomes a righteous king. The two pillars of the polity, kingship and *sangha,* are again implanted securely and the Buddhist religion and irrigated rice-farming prosper again.

Let me return to the colonization and peopling theme. Holt provides us with some mythic creations of the early eighteenth-century Kandyan period, especially during the crucial time of the passing of the Kandyan throne from the Sinhala line to the "foreign" Nayakkar line. He presents two related myths concerning two deities, Natha and Pitiye Deviyo, who are even today of central importance to contemporary Kandyan cults. [25]

The plot movement that I want to highlight is how a foreign divine newcomer, Pitiye, defeats in an unbecoming battle Natha, one of the four guardian deities of the island in the Sinhala Buddhist pantheon. In the process Natha is bumped upward and elevated to the status of a *bodhisattva* (Buddha to be). Natha's defeat and promotion in the course of the battle is in line with his aspiration to become a Buddha and thereby "to free all sentient beings from the world." He felt he "could not commit sin by waging further war." He had to lose the war of violence in order to win his quest for salvation.

The trajectory of Pitiye's career is interesting, in comparison to the Gajabahu story whose plot consisted of foreign captives being placed in newly developing areas in a somewhat degraded or subordinate level of the farming category.

According to one of the core myths in which Pitiye has a prominent place (*Dolaha Deviange Kavi*), [26] he is a Soli (Cola) prince, born of the union of the king of Soli with a princess; he is cursed because he killed a calf, whose mother complains to the king by ringing a bell; [27] he is disgraced and assumes a demonic aspect. But laden with gifts and of-

---

25. See Holt, *Buddha in the Crown,* chap. 5, "The Mythicization of History: Natha and Pitiye in Kandyan Folklore" for a full treatment of the variant myths and the cults focused on the deities.

26. "The Poem of the Twelve Gods"; see Holt, pp. 133–37.

27. This episode is a component of what is also told of King Elara, who punished his son for a similar deed. It appears in many other stories as a triggering action.

ferings, "the prince set forth / surrounded by Vadiga Tamil priests" and reached the land of the Sinhala.

He makes his heroic progress from the east coast to the heart of the Kandyan country: through Batticaloa, Velassa, Dumbara (where he hunted), Udugoda (where he cleared the land), Mahalatenne (where he built a mansion to live). He continues through other places like Giragama and Amunugama, looking for suitable fields; when he comes to Haragama "the people, pleading for protection / Thronged at his feet." His work of making new rice fields (in places previously given to the grazing of cattle) seemed to reach its peak at Gurudeniya, where an irrigation channel was newly dug to irrigate fields. "Behold the mighty task done at Gurudeniya! / Rice sewn ripened like pearls and [shone like] gems. . . . Pitiye Devi, lord of this world, / stood on the rock with his holy feet . . . / There is a devale for him on the rock at Gurudeniya" (Holt, pp. 134–37).

Pitiye may have "defeated" Natha, but he in turn becomes domesticated and subordinate to him and takes his place as one of the twelve lesser regional guardian deities of the *bandara* class. It is this position, firmly placed in the guardianship and protection and furtherance of the this-worldly concerns of the populace, that gives him his positive energies as a powerful deity, himself in need of propitiation.

The trajectory of this myth is such that a powerful foreign deity/demon enters and makes his progress as a "colonizer" and creator of irrigated paddy fields and is worshipped as a regional deity. In the process he bumps upstairs an extant guardian deity, who finds a more elevated place in the pantheon by having refrained from violence. Pitiye represents the lesser moral truth that in order to be a worldly success the pioneer-entrepreneur has to employ force to conquer and expend energy to found rice-farming communities. In some ways Pitiye shares some likeness with the founding hero Vijaya, who as an unruly and disgraced prince also employs his lusty violence in the positive task of taming and civilizing a wild place. But whereas Vijaya and his band of followers conquer and displace savage *yakkhas* (with Kuvani, the *yakkhini*, herself with her two children by Vijaya being sent out into the wilderness), Pitiye enters a country already set in its course and displaces the benign god Natha, who is promoted upward in the pantheon and under whose aegis Pitiye takes a nativized position.

Holt suggests that at one level there has occurred a "mythicization of history" in that the mythical complex seems to indicate "the further domestication of jungle lands for rice cultivation carried on by the Kandyan kings with imported Tamil labor assistance and how rice farming supplemented hunting as the Dumbara region's chief economic vocation" (ibid., p. 138). The association of Pitiye with the expansion of rice-farming, a highly regarded occupation associated with high caste *goyigama* status, should be noted. "Functionally, then, we see Pitiye's *laukika* [this worldly] power has been put to extremely good use: his association with paddy cultivation and his cattle-protecting prowess become the rationalization for his eventual assimilation and cultic integration by upcountry Sinhalese" (ibid., p. 140).

It is, finally, relevant to bear in mind, especially with respect to the next section of this chapter, that Holt associates the generation of the Pitiye myths and associated cultic practices to a crucial time in the history of the Kandyan kingdom. It is the time of King Narendrasinghe, the last Sinhalese king, upon whose demise in 1739, the throne was occupied by the brother of his Nayakkar queen, thus initiating the rule of the Nayakkar dynasty, which will occupy us next. Holt mentions the tension and ambivalences arising in this period, which seem to be reflected in the myths relating to Pitiye.

Let me note one other trajectory in the process of incorporation, an inclusion that is the very opposite of the "degrading" incorporation at the lowest level of the farming caste (*goyigama*) traced for us in the Gajabahu myths, and a similar or even more elevated incorporation than that accorded the "development" deity Pitiye, who becomes a regional deity of the *bandara* class. This process of elevation seems not to have been mythicized, except perhaps in the recently constructed genre of family histories of Kandyan and low country aristocracy.[28] I am referring to the arrival during late medieval times of a significant number of *pantarams* (non-Brahmin priests of god shrines) and perhaps Brahmins (with ritual and scribal skills of administrative value) who in time, marrying with local Sinhala families, helped to consolidate and differentiate the highest status of Sinhala *goyigama* of the *radala/mudaliyar* rank.

28. For example, Yasmine Gooneratne, *Relative Merits: A Personal Memoir of the Bandaranaike Family of Sri Lanka* (London: C. Hurst & Co., 1986), writes that according to certain sources the apical ancestor of "the Bandaranaike family tree" was an Indian officer of high standing who, serving under the kings of Kandy and bearing the name Neela Perumal, was made high priest of the Temple of the God Saman and commanded to take the name of Nayaka Pandaram ("Chief Record Keeper in 1454," p. 3). The name Neela Perumal is clearly South Indian, as is the word *pantaram*.

Dewaraja documents many kinds of influxes of south Indian immigrants into the Sinhala kingdoms of Kotte, Dambadeniya, and Kandy, especially between the thirteenth and sixteenth centuries. Her discussion thus adds to our previous description of the entry of the Pattini cult and the prominent role of some Kerala chiefly and merchant families in the politics of the Gampola and Kotte kingdoms in the fourteenth and fifteenth centuries. Most of these immigrants were in due course incorporated into the Sinhala "farmer aristocracy," the *govikula*.[29] The Muslim conquests in south India accelerated the influx of Brahmins, who had lost the patronage of their Cola masters, into Sri Lanka. Perhaps the most interesting of the immigrants were those whom Dewaraja identifies as *pantarams,* or non-Brahmin priests usually of the Vellala caste who came from various parts of south India. In the reign of Bhuvaneka Bahu I (1272–84) of Dambadeniya, a group of *pantarams* came from the Cola country "together with all the paraphernalia, attendants, craftsmen, and mendicants connected with their Siva temples. When they were ushered into the presence of the king, they were given *radala* and *mudali* titles, such as were always given to the higher subcastes of the *govikula.* Villages were also given for their maintenance. A considerable group of immigrants headed by the *pantarams* came from Malayala or modern Kerala in the reign of Bhuvaneka Bahu VI (1470–78) of Kotte and received lands and titles from the king" (Dewaraja, pp. 47–48). Similar facts can be adduced for the time of Rajasimha I (1581–93). It is significant that the Sinhala title *bandara,* taken by princes and nobles, was most likely borrowed from these immigrant *pantarams,* and in turn by the seventeenth and eighteenth centuries "*pantarams* had become part and parcel of the Kandyan nobility, and their title too became popular among the nobles of high rank" (ibid., p. 48). Dewaraja also refers to the influx of Saivite mendicants called Andi at the time of Rajasimha I, who had embraced Saivism, and their infiltration into various parts of the Kandyan region. It is no surprise then that "the strong influence of South Indian religious beliefs and practices in Kandyan society was undoubtedly due to the absorption of [all] these immigrant groups" (ibid., p. 50).

Let me draw on one other example, this time from the domain of exorcism ritual and associated mythic representation, which again interacts at some points with the mytho-historical complexes I have dis-

29. L. S. Dewaraja, *The Kandyan Kingdom, 1707–1760* (Colombo: Lake House Publishers, 1971), chap. 3.

cussed that deal with issues of existential importance to the island people of Lanka dedicated to the preservation of Buddhism and of forging and maintaining their "singular identity," while requiring as well as staving off infusions from outside.

Kapferer gives this foundation myth of the principal sorcery rite called Suniyama recently (and currently) present in the Galle-Matara area in the south of the island. In its themes and logic it belongs with the complexes we have alluded to above.

The myth begins with the first act of sorcery, which takes as its point of departure the canonical *sutta* called the *Agganna Sutta*, the Buddhist genesis myth, which describes the creation of the world as a devolutionary process, in which the process of differentiation becomes at the same time more disorderly as human desire works its way, until the first king, Mahasammata, is "elected."

In the sorcery myth, Mahasammata, the child of the Sun and the former incarnation of the Buddha chooses as his wife, Manikpala, the sister of Vishnu. Mahasammata, after making joyous love to Manikpala, leaves his palace to fight the Asuras. But Devadatta, alias Vasavarti Maraya, lusts after Manikpala and, taking the form of a fire viper, enters her womb and makes her incurably ill. (Mara in Buddhist mythology was Buddha's arch enemy who attacked him and tried to seduce him from reaching the final enlightenment.)

The second myth recited in the sorcery rite relates the story of the birth of Suniyam Yaka, who is also known as Oddi Raja. It is this personage who in the ritual cures Manikpala.

Oddi Raja, who is referred to as a lustful demonic form of Vishnu, was born in the city of Vadiga in south India (the Vadiga Tamils occur frequently in the myth complexes of late medieval times, and especially in reference to the Nayakkar dynasty's occupation of Kandy, a time when Vadiga Tamils are alleged to have been brought over.)

The queen of Vadiga, in much the same way as Manikpala of the first myth, was possessed and sexually taken by Vasavarti Maraya. The queen, given to pregnancy cravings (the desire to walk naked in the city with serpents coiled about her body) eventually gives birth to a son, who, fulfilling the omens at his birth, goes to the jungle when he turns sixteen, drapes his body with cobras, returns, kills his father the king, and overruns Vadiga and its neighboring kingdoms.

Prince Oddissa then crosses the sea to Lanka and causes havoc and cannibalizes the people. Finally, the Buddha himself intervenes and has Oddissa bound in iron by Vishnu. The compassionate Buddha

frees him provided Oddissa bows to his authority. "This Oddissa says he will do; and he declares, furthermore, that he will cure disease and give protection to human beings."
In this myth then Suniyam or Oddi Raja, whom Kapferer refers to as "the strongest manifestation of evil," is not in some respects unlike the Sinhalese founding hero Vijaya and Pitiye who have both unruly and destructive princely profiles. He also, like Vijaya, kills his father. They all leave their places of origin in India with soiled reputations, but exuding warrior violence, and arrive in Sri Lanka to follow somewhat different careers. Vijaya prepares the ground for the later entry of Buddhism; Pitiye enables the Sinhala Buddhist agrarian society to expand; Oddi Raja is domesticated as the healer in order to keep disease and destruction at bay. In the Suniyam myth, however, we see the most radical characterization of an intrusion from outside in its most destructive and violent form (shades of the demonic behavior of Magha of Kalinga and his soldier-devils), the conjugation of the fire of arson and the fire of lust. The invading disease which is born in violence must be expelled with violence by wielding fire and smoke in the exorcism rite. This is powerfully conveyed by Bruce Kapferer's exegesis in *A Celebration of Demons*.[30] The myths connected with the exorcism ritual are thus another distinctive complex with their own center of gravity, but not thematically removed from the preoccupations of medieval Sinhala society carried into modern times.[31]
This second excerpt from Kapferer beautifully illustrates my point:

> Deva Sanniya [is] a collective representation of the eighteen demons, whose appearance in the exorcism signs the restoration of the integrated order of the hierarchy. . . .
> Deva Sanniya . . . is a benign transformation of Kola Sanniya. In the myth of Kola Sanniya's origin, the demon is born the son of the king of Visalamahanuwara, the legendary city of the Lichchavis of Nepal. In dreadful revenge for his father's slaying of his mother, Kola Sanniya . . . assuming demonic form furiously destroys his father's city. His horror is only ended, as in the case of

30. Bloomington: Indiana University Press, 1983.
31. For myths of the origin and domestication of demons who heal by virtue of authority delegated by the Buddha, see, in addition to Kapferer, Paul Wirz, *Exorcism and the Art of Healing in Ceylon* (Leiden: Brill, 1954), and Gananath Obeyesekere, "The Ritual Drama of Sanni Demons: Collective Representations of Disease in Ceylon," *Comparative Studies in Society and History* 11, no. 2 (1969): 174–216.

Oddi Raja or Suniyam, through the intervention of the Buddha. In the Sanni Yakuma ritual Kola Sanniya is not only depicted as devouring and fragmenting evil at the base of hierarchy but also threatening from the outside in.[32]

In one sense, all these myths may share in a more general set of ideas found in many parts of the world, about the origins of power and its creative transformation. Frequently, myths on this theme state that power, of which kingship is the quintessential expression, originates and comes from outside the society; "it is typically founded on an act of barbarism—murder, incest or both." The original violence of the incoming hero is a negation of kinship and communal values: it is as if the stranger hero must first "reproduce an original disorder" in order to then become a creative force and put the new society in order.[33] Frequently the "stranger-king" takes power in another place by union with an indigenous woman: not only the Vijaya myth, but many Southeast Asian myths of first kingship as well as some Greek myths develop this theme in variant ways. Though this paradigm fits best the conquest origins of kingship and state, it obviously is suited to contemplate the phenomenon of how foreign influences, often power-laden, productive as well as dangerous, are transformed into creative energies, domesticated, and directed toward the constitution of legitimate sovereignty. In the extreme case, when a stranger-intruder turns totally destructive, he creates internal chaos and must be expelled or negated or periodically reviled. (It is clear that Magha of Kalinga, with his accumulated heap of evil reputation, represents this extreme.)

Point Counterpoint: The Nayakkars in the Kandyan Kingdom

The Nayakkar interlude provides a forum for searching and for nuanced explication of social, religious, and political forces at work in a volatile period of the island's history in the very twilight before its total conquest by the British, the only foreign power to have gained total dominance. The Portuguese and the Dutch had failed to subjugate the hill kingdom of Kandy.

The period of Nayakkar rule poses two tasks, mapping and inter-

---

32. Kapferer, *Legends of People, Myths of State: Violence, Intolerance, and Political Culture in Sri Lanka and Australia* (Washington, D. C.: Smithsonian Institution Press, 1988), pp. 89–90.

33. See Marshall Sahlins, "The Stranger-King; or Dumézil among the Fijians" in *Islands of History* (Chicago: University of Chicago Press, 1985), pp. 73–103.

weaving the various ideological strands in place and following the play of divisive and competitive interests among the immigrant and local leadership factions. It reflects the vital prominence of a Buddhist religious, cultural, and literary renaissance achieved during the rule of a dynasty of south Indian origins. The period on the one hand creatively incorporated south Indian influences and yet at the same time elicited anti-Tamil sentiments—especially through the critical and denunciatory voice of a section of prominent Buddhist monks, literati themselves, and guardians of orthodox traditions, associated with the Mahavihara fraternity in the past and the Malvatta fraternity in the Kandyan period.

Both the melting pot blendings and the segregationist separations of late medieval times have been thickly documented by a number of scholars.[34]

The period of rule by the Nayakkar dynasty was some seventy-five years, extending from 1739 to 1815, and consisting of the reign of four kings. Given the volatile politics of the medieval period, this in itself is a measure of its durability. But the connection between the Kandyan Sinhala ruling houses and the Nayakkars began earlier in the reign of King Rajasinghe II (1635–87). According to a much cited source, the *Mandaram Pura Puvata* (a text composed later in time, in the middle period of King Kirti Sir Rajasinghe's reign, 1747–82), Rajasinghe II began a series of marriage alliances with the Nayakkar rulers and warrior nobility established in south India in Madurai. He is alleged to have made two Nayakkar women his royal consorts. Rajasinghe's action was new only in regard to the source of the royal wives; for Sinhala royal houses have long and episodic histories of marriage connections with Indian royals and nobility rated as being of *ksatriya*

---

34. The best source on the Nayakkar period in English still remains L. S. Dewaraja, *The Kandyan Kingdom, 1707–1760.* Other valuable sources are Kitsiri Malalgoda, *Buddhism in Sinhalese Society, 1750–1900* (Berkeley: University of California Press, 1976); H. L. Seneviratne, *Rituals of the Kandyan State* (Cambridge: Cambridge University Press, 1978); and idem, "The Alien King: Nayakkars on the Throne of Kandy," *Ceylon Journal of Historical and Social Studies,* n.s., 6, no. 1 (1976):55–61; John Clifford Holt, *Buddha in the Crown,* is the latest assessment which I find congenial. I give a special place in the discussion to the dissenting submissions made by K. N. O. Dharmadasa, "The Sinhala-Buddhist Identity and the Nayakkar Dynasty in the Politics of the Kandyan Kingdom, 1739–1815," *Ceylon Journal of Historical and Social Studies,* n.s., 6, no. 1 (1976):1–23, and "The People of the Lion: Ethnic Identity, Ideology, and Historical Revisionism in Contemporary Sri Lanka," *Sri Lanka Journal of the Humanities,* 15 (1989):1–35.

status. Rajasinghe II's son, Vimaladharmasuriya II (1687–1707), and his son, Narendrasinghe (1707–39), in turn continued the alleged tradition of installing simultaneously two Nayakkar queens.

But then in 1739 Narendrasinghe died without male heirs of royal status. Harems consisting of multiple wives and concubines ranging from chief queen(s) and lesser wives to concubines were a widespread practice among South Asian and Southeast Asian royalty. Their numerous royal children, graduated according to eligibility to succeed and according to the rank and status of their mothers, produced perennial problems manifest as succession disputes, palace rebellions, attempted usurpations. Although Narendrasinghe had no male royal heir by his Nayakkar consorts, he had a son, Unambuve, by a Sinhalese woman (presumably a concubine), who was, however, passed over as ineligible. The throne went to a brother, Sri Vijaya, of a Nayakkar queen presumably because he was of *ksatriya* status. His identity was wholly Nayakkar.

In matters of royal succession and counting ancestry, let me remind the reader, that the Sinhalese mode of counting ethnic or national identity was patrilineal. Whatever the mother's identity, it was the father's affiliation that the child inherited, even if that child's mother was non-Sinhala. Thus in the matter of succession disputes and accession to the throne we must constantly keep in mind that, as in the case of the royal marriages beginning with Rajasinghe II, two succeeding Sinhala kings had Nayakkar mothers, and the impact of these mixed marriages in the incorporation and absorption of Nayakkar customs and practices must be kept in view. While we assign Sinhala identity as officially or conventionally recognized on a patrilineal basis, the Nayakkars are credited with a matrilineal descent and succession whereby descent is counted through females, and the office passes from a man to his sister's son, who both belong to the same lineage.

Now begins an important discontinuity in the royal house, because the full-blown Nayakkar king on the Kandyan throne, Sri Vijaya Rajasinghe, took an exclusively Nayakkar consort as his queen; and it is this queen's brother who became his heir in the person of King Kirti Sri Rajasinghe (1747–82), whose rule poses for us fascinating issues to weigh in regard to the interpretation of his achievements and the reaction of his Sinhala subjects to his conduct, both public and private. He was succeeded by Rajadhi Rajasinghe (1782–98), and the Nayakkar dynasty, with no further royal alliance with Sinhala queens, concluded with the reign of Sri Wickrama Rajasinghe, who was dethroned in 1815 by the British, with assistance from a certain number of Kandyan Sinhala chiefs, principally Ahelapola. Although it is clear that the king did engage in some excessive acts and caused some disaffection among the people, the extent of popular participation in and desire for Sri Wikrama Rajasinghe's deposition is uncertain: For example, Kingsley de Silva points out that both Pilima Talauve (in 1810–11) and Ahelapola (in 1814) failed in their attempts to raise a rebellion against the king and that the latter's rule "was singularly and significantly free of any such demonstration of the people's dissatisfaction."[35] The king did toward the end commit severe punitive acts against some of the chiefs and their families in response to their "conspiracy," but de Silva asserts that the turmoil in 1814–15 can "by no stretch of the imagination be described as a civil war" (*History*, p. 23).

Malalgoda gives an elegant analysis of the factional politics that brought about the fall of the last king: the presence of British power on the coast, and their meddling and interventions, and the slide into despotism in the last years when a previously factionalized Kandyan aristocracy coalesced to combine with the British. Thus, the rival *adigars* (chief ministers), Ahelapola and Molligoda, eventually joined hands in the final episode which took their kingdom away from them for good, but ethnic sentiments against the "Tamils" form no significant part of Malalgoda's account (*Buddhism*).

It would seem, especially in the light of some recent submission by K. N. O. Dharmadasa (whose views on the Nayakkars will be described shortly), that there is some space for dispute, ambivalence, and reevaluation.

Most Sri Lankan historians have at least been impressed with the two Nayakkar kings preceding the last. "The Nayakkar dynasty, especially under Kirti Sri Rajasingha and Rajadi Rajasinha, had identified with the Kandyan national interest and blended the Nayakkar personality into the Kandyan background with consummate skill. Its policy of transforming itself into an indigenous dynasty whose claims to that status were accepted by the people had proved so successful that a restoration of a Sinhalese dynasty was not a viable policy" (de Silva, *History*, p. 222).

With respect to this assertion L. S. Dewaraja's documentation is in-

35. Kingsley de Silva says that "the fall of the last Sinhalese kingdom was a case of political suicide, and the king and the chiefs share the blame in this essay in self-destruction" (*A History of Sri Lanka* [London: C. Hurst & Co., 1981], p. 226). See de Silva's reading of the last phase of the Kandyan Kingdom, chap. 7.

formative for understanding the larger context of palace politics. The Kandyan Kingdom being landbound and the maritime areas being controlled by the Dutch (the British replaced the Dutch after 1796), it was politic for the Kandyan polity to have overseas diplomatic and commercial contact with south Indian polities equally ranged against the colonial menace.

Perhaps even more of a strategic calculation from the viewpoint of internal politics was that the Sinhalese royalty intentionally formed a marriage alliance with the Nayakkars in order to secure its alleged *ksatriya* status (which was proclaimed as a requisite to ascend the throne), and thereby exclude from claims to kingship rivals among the Sinhalese aristocracy. This move, however, while it could stave off the claims of local challengers, also kept the incoming Nayakkar royal kinsmen separated as a stratum, with little reach into the provincial administration of the local chiefs, who in turn could and did object when Nayakkar nobles were put in charge of royal stores or given royal villages as office tenures (as happened in the reign of Narendrasinghe). These structural tensions and contradictions are relevant in deciphering the vexed question of the Sinhala public mood at large.

Malalgoda's assessment of the Nayakkar epoch is relevant for us, especially as regards its impact on the condition of Buddhism as both *sasana* and *sangha*. Malalgoda has pointed out the initiative of the monk, Valvita Saranamkara, in launching a reformist movement within the *sangha,* while the *sasana* was at a low ebb.

King Narendrasinghe (after whose reign the first Nayakkar king would be installed) became a patron of Saranamkara and backed his mendicant fraternity (the Silvat Samagama). "According to *Mandaram Pura Puvata,* the king also entrusted the education of his heir—who, being of south Indian origin, was a stranger to Sinhalese laws and customs—to Saranamkara" (Malalgoda, p. 60). It was this pupil and heir who, as Sri Vijaya Rajasinghe (regnal years, 1739–47), sponsored a delegation to Siam to reestablish *upasampada* ordination of monks. His successor and brother-in-law Kirti Sri Rajasinghe in turn sponsored that historic mission to Siam, which, returning in 1753, established the Malvatta and Asgiriya Vihares as the centers of the orthodox Siyam Nikaya. Malalgoda recalls Ananda Coomaraswamy's comment: "There is hardly a vihara of any importance in the Kandy district which was not restored by him, or newly built" (ibid., p. 6). It is also relevant to note here that it was under this king's patronage that the Buddha's tooth relic became the centerpiece in the annual *per-*

ahera, previously staged to honor exclusively the kingdom's four guardian deities (see Seneviratne, *Rituals*).

But Malalgoda at the same time alludes to the famous plot to assassinate Kirti Sri Rajasinghe and to replace him with a Siamese substitute. The king's personal act of applying ash to his forehead (a mark of Saivite practice) was cited as the ostensible reason for mounting the conspiracy. Malalgoda suggests that "the more important causes . . . lay deeper than this in the chronic factionalism within the Kandyan court which acquired a new dimension with the accession of the Nayakkars to the throne" (*Buddhism*, p. 65). But there was a fly in the ointment. Two of the most prominent monks, the *sangharaja*, the celebrated Saranamkara, and a *mahanayake* by the name of Tibbotuvave Buddharakhita of the Malvatta chapter, together with a chief, the second *adigar* Samanakodi, were actively implicated in the plot against the king, who had been vilified as "a Tamil heretic" and, worse still, as "a villianous, wicked, and heretical eunuch of a king." The king successfully dealt with the plot, and generously with the monks, thus meriting Malalgoda's approval: "His reputation as the greatest patron of Buddhism during the Kandyan period was thus preserved completely intact" (*ibid.*, p. 66).

The plot thickens, and it is time for Dharmadasa to enter the arena. Against the run of these historically and sociologically oriented accounts we now must consider the documentation and arguments from the point of view of Sinhalese literary expertise.[36] I have previously reported the difference in views between Gunawardena and Dharmadasa on dating the beginnings of the Sinhala Buddhist identity. Dharmadasa also wants to modify, even reverse, the extant views on the degree of unpopularity of the Nayakkar regime. His second response is directly related to Gunawardena's disagreement with Dharmadasa's earlier essay on Sinhala attitudes to the Nayakkar dynasty.[37]

Dharmadasa oscillates between making a weak claim and a strong claim. His weak claim that "there was a long-standing *strand* [emphasis added] of anti-Nayakkar feeling in Kandyan court circles" in my view may be tenable (it would have been better if he had said "in some Kandyan court circles"). But his claim is stronger and in need of

36. K. N. O. Dharmadasa is professor of Sinhalese literature at Peradeniya University, Sri Lanka.

37. This earlier essay is Dharmadasa's "Sinhala-Buddhist Identity." Gunawardena's skepticism is voiced in his "People of the Lion" and I shall refer to it in due course.

a tighter specification when he urges, contra Gunawardena, that the evidence of "ethnic invective" (his words) in the texts he cites is "an expression of a deep-rooted ethnic animosity" against the Tamils. Dharmadasa submits that he has identified signs of what could be identified as "a Sinhala-Buddhist ideology" that generated "the plots and conspiracies against the Nayakkar rulers during the last phase of the Kandyan Kingdom." Aside from references to some Dutch sources of peripheral value and secondary sources of relevance, Dharmadasa relies *primarily* (but not exclusively) on four Sinhalese sources to establish anti-Nayakkar (and anti-Tamil) sentiments: (1) *The Mandaram Pura Puvata* (hereafter MP), written during Kirti Sri Rajasinghe's reign in the latter part of the eighteenth century, which is a standard source also cited by others (e.g., Dewaraja and Malalgoda). It is a historical poem compiled in three stages by different authors, the first part during the reign of Rajasinghe II (1635–87), the second during the reign of Vimaladharmasuriya II (1687–1707), and the third during the reign of Kirti Sri Rajasinghe (1747–82). *Immediately after* the last Nayakkar king, Sri Wickrema Rajasinghe, was deposed, sources (2) and (3), the *Kirala Sandesaya* and the *Vadiga Hatana,* were written by two monks, Kitalagama Devamitta and Kavisundera Mudali, respectively, who, besides being members of "the literary elite," were ardent supporters of the first *adigar* Ahelapola's rebellion and claim to the throne. The last source (4) is *Sasanavatirna Varanava,* composed in the mid-nineteenth century, some decades after the deposition of the last king, also by a monk. (Dharmadasa also cites as a possible precedent for the authors, the *Pujavaliya,* belonging to the thirteenth century.)

Dharmadasa uses the first source, MP, to establish that during the reign of Narendrasinghe, the last Sinhalese king before the Nayakkar takeover, there was a serious rebellion when the king in 1732 appointed a "Vadiga Tamil" to be chief of the king's stores; the foreigner and his retinue were killed. The king put down the rebellion with massive severity with the help of the Dutch. It seems also that the local aristocracy objected to the king's "Vadiga kinsmen" because of their Hindu (Saivite) affiliation. Dharmadasa cites this forceful statement by Dewaraja: "never again, not even when a Nayakkar sat on the throne, do we hear of an administrative appointment being given to a Nayakkar, at least not in the higher ranks of the services." (Dharmadasa might have explicitly seen in this exclusion and sealing off a good argument for why the populace at large could not have been oppressed thereafter by Nayakkar court circles and could not have had any direct experience of their alleged oppression.)

Dharmadasa, this time relying on secondary sources, brings to our attention further disaffection at the time when at Narendrasinghe's death a faction led by Leuke, an ex-monk, Pali scholar, and teacher of Saranamkara, championed the claim of Unambuve, the king's son by a Sinhala woman. But we find that soon afterward the new king made a reconciliation with Leuke, who then played an important role in the revival of Buddhism under Nayakkar sponsorship. We may also note that hereafter every effort to put a Sinhalese candidate on the throne was a failure, a commentary at least on the factional divisiveness among the Kandyan aristocrats.

We come next to the crucial conspiracy of 1760 formed to assassinate Kirti Sri Rajasinghe. The monk Saranamkara, who spearheaded the Buddhist revival with royal help and who is reported to have supported Narendrasinghe's choice of his Nayakkar successor, now as the head of the *sangha,* became a key plotter against the king's life together with Tibbotuvave Buddharakhita, the former's able pupil and deputy. Tibbotuvave was also the head of the Malvatta chapter. It is important for us to bear in mind that these two leading monks wrote many scholarly texts in Pali and Sinhala and may be considered as exemplars of the clerical literary elite.

Dharmadasa has recourse to the mid-nineteenth-century text *Sasanavatirna Varanava* (SV), and secondarily another nineteenth-century text, the *Rajavaliya,* to document his case of deep resentments expressed against Tamils in the motivations of the conspirators.[38] (Both sources are retrospective accounts.) The SV contains the famous castigation of Kirti Sri as the "heretical Tamil" and reports that Saranamkara and other monks tried to persuade the king to renounce the practice of daubing his forehead with ash (the stereotyped mark of the Saivite, which is also, as we have noted before, a literary trope transmitted from text to text).

Although modern scholars such as Dewaraja, Malalgoda, de Silva, Gunawardena have tended to minimize the reach, beyond the monk conspirators, of the 1760 conspiracy against the Kandyan Kingdom's most illustrious monarch, I think that we can agree with Dharmadasa to this extent at least: that there is evidence of anti-Nayakkar feeling

---

38. He also cites another account attributed to De la Nerolle, who was a palace official, who later settled in Dutch territory.

among *some* of the highly placed monks especially of the Malvatte chapter and *some* of the Kandyan chiefly circles. However, we also have to construe the significance of the king's restoration of the chief clerical plotters: Saranamkara to his former prestigious position as *sangharaja* and Tibbotuvave to the headship of the Malvatta chapter. Indeed Tibbotuvave, entrusted after his reinstatement by the king with the task of updating the official history, the *Mahavamsa,* wrote this glowing panegyric about Kirti Sri in which no hint of anti-Buddhist heresy or subversion of Buddhism is perceptible:

> Dowered with faith and many virtues, devoted to the Buddha, his doctrines and his order . . . shining over the island with faith in the Enlightened one, living according to the good doctrine of the Sage, dowered with the ten powers, ever giving alms and performing other meritorious works . . . he ever acted in this way for the welfare of all men. (*Culavamsa,* part 2, 98:66–68)

Dharmadasa disarmingly comments that "politics being such" Tibbotuvave glorifies the king in the most laudatory terms." Surely then, "politics being such," the same suspicion and skepticism should attach to the rhetoric of the assassination plot! The volte-face demonstrated by the two eminent monks illustrates the ambiguities of events, the mercurial play of interests and strategy, and the switches between disaffection and support that inform a vast number of the political episodes reported in the *Mahavamsa* and *Culavamsa* as official history.

Dharmadasa uses two texts *written* immediately after 1815, when the last king of Kandy was deposed, to provide evidence of the most explicitly anti-Nayakkar sentiments ("Sinhala-Buddhist Identity," p. 3). The texts are the *Kirala Sandesaya* and the *Vadiga Hatana,* written by two monks, Kitalagama Devamitta of the Malvatta fraternity and Valigala Kavisundera Mudali.

It is noteworthy that Dharmadasa refers to these authors as "propagandist poets" and to their texts as expressing "anti-Tamil invective," and states that "no pain is spared to condemn and vilify the *demalu* who were 'destroying' the land of the Sinhalese." He also remarks that "while being primarily motivated by personal animosity towards Sri Vikrama [the texts] had a racialist aspect as well—being directed against the Nayakkars in general" (ibid.). Thus while recognizing their bias, Dharmadasa, nevertheless, appears to want to argue that the invective goes beyond a personal attack on Sri Vikrama to being "a deep-rooted ethnic animosity" against the cumulative influence of the *demalu* (Tamils) as a group.

We may begin the deconstruction of these texts by noting that both texts are written in the style of poetic literary genres traditionally used in praise of royalty and that both works tendentiously have Ahelapola, the first adigar, as their hero and present him in heroic terms patently exaggerated and unrealistic when tested against the prosaic reality:[39] Ahelapola, "the pinnacle of his law, having radiated his powerful valour throughout the world," like King Dutthagamani in order to destroy "the uncouth Tamils mobilized a countless army," and even did better than the archetypal hero by capturing the Tamil ruler in seven days whereas Dutthagamani took several years.[40]

Second, running parallel to this exaggerated glorification of Ahelapola, the sun who "destroyed the Tamil fireflies," is an equally exaggerated but inverse representation of the Nayakkar "Tamils." To report only fragments of this invective: besides swearing at Sri Vikrama himself as the "heretical eunuch, . . . most villainous . . . Tamil rogue," who in the manner of Angulimala (the notorious killer whom Buddha domesticated and converted) committed murder, appropriated wealth, and tried to destroy the "serene and pure *sasana* of the Buddha," there are more generalized insults cast upon the Tamils in general as "crooked, wicked, ugly, . . . scoundrels" ruining the Buddhist religion, having taken "weird guises resembling demons and devils," and so on.

Now it should be obvious to any reader that these images of devils and demons setting the country on fire draw on well-known precedents to be found in the *Mahavamsa* and *Culavamsa* and in a number of subsequent texts. Their original applications were to the Cola invaders and the depredations of Magha of Kalinga. These original denunciations were generated in the context of *actual* south Indian invasions and acts of destruction. But the same invective can hardly apply to the Nayakkars, who came not as invaders but in peaceful migration through dynastic marriage and ruled by invitation, so to say. Thus we are faced on the one hand with a "rhetorical vilification" which is part

---

39. As Kingsley de Silva presents the details (*History*, pp. 228–29), the British governor prepared his campaign to invade Kandy with Ahelapola's assistance. It was the British army that marched into Kandy unopposed (because Molligoda, the second adigar refrained from resisting) and captured the king. Also note that in 1814, when Ahelapola raised the flag of rebellion, there was no public support for him.

40. See Dharmadasa, "The Sinhala-Buddhist Identity" for more unnerving details.

of a textual legacy and tradition transmitted through monk-scribes and authors and on the other hand with literary creations of the early nineteenth century that are patently ill-fitted to the historical situations they claim to represent. Dharmadasa himself remarks that it is difficult to extrapolate "from the individual acts of oppression by Sri Vikrama to the 'tyranny' of the Nayakkar dynasty as a whole" and that whatever the misdeeds of the Nayakkars, and despite the "anti-Nayakkar propaganda," no massive demonstration of popular feeling in fact occurred. Moreover, he remarks, "Although the Nayakkars came to be conveniently categorized as *demala* ('Tamil') by the Kandyans, no evidence is forthcoming to suggest that there was an identification of interests between them and the traditional *demala* population of Sri Lanka" (ibid., pp. 20–22).

Therefore, a haunting problem remains. What does one make of, and how does one understand, the deep anti-Tamil resentment, which Dharmadasa has documented, that is conveyed by certain members of a monkish literary elite? What are the springs of their sentiments and the purpose of their acts? Are they merely duplicating by the constant reiteration of commentary, and embroidering and re-presenting literary tropes and formulaic missiles embedded in a string of *vamsa* literary texts—the *Mahavamsa, Culavamsa, Pujavaliya, Dhatuvamsa, Thupavamsa,* etc.—which they will have read as part of their pedagogical training? Are they using these formulas for rhetorical purposes to define and manipulate a current political situation? And are they, in addition, conveying an emotionally felt and internalized resentment against historicized enemies who allegedly "destroyed" their classical civilization and/or who as Saivites (or Hindus) endanger the purity of the Buddhist religion of which the *sangha* are the guardians and watchdogs? If there is such a continuous antagonism to a felt south Indian presence and menace, then how do these agents square those attitudes with the other knowledge they have that there are so many south Indian peoples and their religious cults and practices which have been successfully incorporated within the Buddhist cosmology without endangering the higher truths that the Buddha preached? Finally, and this too is an open-ended question, is there a perennial imperative that energizes and motivates certain kinds of scholar-monks, composers of *vamsa* and *sandesa* literary works, eloquent preachers in a vocation that has always emphasized the *dhamma* as word and doctrine, whose ambitions to achieve in terms of learning, creative endeavor, and religio-political position and power are such that their activism is frequently frustrated by the political regimes in place, which they find inadequate in providing those conditions that will allow them to fulfill their careers and at the same time make the island the ideal Dhammadvipa and Sinhaladvipa?

My own search in the foregoing pages has brought me to a conclusion, which both Gunawardena and Dharmadasa in their best moments themselves arrive at in separate but nearly concordant summation. Dharmadasa writes in particular of the monks Kitalagama and Valigala (and I think his point is capable of extension to other cases) that their

> ideological stances have to be understood in the context of the *gurukul* (lineage of teachers) tradition. These writers were not only influenced by their teachers . . . but were also affected by the ideological themes found in the literary and scholarly tradition coming down from antiquity in the *vamsa* literature. . . . The fact that there was such a strand of opinion in Kandyan society did not mean that everybody subscribed to it. It appears to have been confined to a small section of the literati. Among the bulk of the population on the other hand the Nayakkar kings were "the divine lords who had come down in the lineage of Mahasammata" through Vijaya and the other rulers of Lanka. Hence the potency of the Nayakkar connection when several pretenders appeared obtaining wide support during the post-1815 period [that is, in the first decades of British rule].[41]

Gunawardena similarly concludes that his survey "highlights the role that the literati, the group which occupies the misty regions on the boundaries of class divisions, played in identity formation in ancient as well as modern times. In selecting and reformulating myths and in giving them literary form, the literati played a significant role in the development of Sinhala identity in ancient society."[42]

On this issue of the motivations and orientations of monk-writers through the centuries as producers of the chronicles, Kapferer attributes to these literati a deep ontological commitment to the Buddhist cosmology which implies that the alien must be domesticated, subordinated, and then incorporated into its hierarchical scheme; the

41. Dharmadasa, "The People of the Lion," pp. 47–48.
42. Gunawardena, "The People of the Lion," p. 98.

corollary is that anything that challenges this scheme is necessarily seen as evil, demonic, outside, and threatening to the very core of Sinhalese Buddhist identity and existence. The association of Tamils with the latter evaluation derives from this ontology. Kapferer, therefore, sees that

> continuities from one chronicle to the next [elaborations or transformations in texts though they take place do not change this thesis] are not merely continuities born of the fact that the texts deal with broadly the same legendary occurrences. Their continuity is a continuity of logical scheme. . . . That many of the chronicles were written by monks undoubtedly accounts for the recurrent theme of the relation of power, the kingship, and the state to Buddhism. The ideological distortions are also produced in the ontological commitments of monks who are proponents of a cosmological attitude that has deep implications for their orientation in the world. In so far as the chronicles are important references in the political discourse of modern Sri Lanka, the ideological distortions of the past become the foundation of the ideological distortions of the present. (*Legends,* p. 82)

Kapferer may well be right, at least in part, for some but not all the clerical literati. My documentation of the ideological work of certain modern monks (and their lay associates) has also shown that they have taken on new tasks, such as the self-conscious articulation of the role of monk as political activist and marshalling and reinterpretation of canonical doctrine and fusing such trends with Marxist, socialist, democratic conceptions to promote and justify a democratic, righteous, and welfare-oriented Buddhist state. Undoubtedly, as I have argued in the previous chapter, the submissions of many Buddhist monk-ideologues, while creative, are in some respects framed within certain constricting parameters of Sinhala Buddhist hegemony which derive from the past. But there are also thoughtful monks who see germinal ideas embodied in the Buddhist *suttas* composed before the *Mahavamsa,* and in the postcanonical traditions relating to Asoka, that they can invoke and elaborate together with ideas derived from the modern context to meet the challenge of solving the ethnic crisis and creating a pluralist universe. In this sense, I would want as a Sri Lankan and an anthropologist to be committed not overly to the deterministic and near-primordialist straitjacket of a single past but to the promising presence of many pasts, multiple precedents, and an open-ended future negotiated and created by historic agents who are alive to the possibilities of voluntaristic action.

A Dialogue with Bruce Kapferer

Having introduced him just now on the issue of chronicles and their authors, I want to engage in greater detail with Kapferer's challenging and powerful submission, which I referred to at the beginning of this essay. My dialogue is meant to pay tribute to his contribution, *Legends of People, Myths of State*, and to articulate some concerns that need to be clarified.[43]

Kapferer's book is constructed around three postulates in its treatment of Sri Lanka. (It is relevant to note that it is a sequel to the turmoil of the 1983 riots and their aftermath.) The first is that in the Sinhala mytho-historical chronicles, like the *Mahavamsa*, written in A.D. 600, is found a hierarchical cosmology. Heroes like Dutthagamani, the rebellious Sinhalese prince, start their careers from the periphery, and progressively defeat the enemy (the Tamils) and reach the center where they are celebrated as unifiers of the kingdom and as exemplary kings. In this schema, the Tamils, as the enemy, are subordinated within the hierarchy, or successfully expelled as invaders.

The second is that the same hierarchical cosmology is present in the contemporary exorcism and sorcery rites that Kapferer studied and described in his *Celebration of Demons*. The demonic agent that attacks a Sinhala victim is successfully domesticated, subordinated, degraded, and expelled, and the ritual enacts this violence against the demonic that threatens the unity and coherence of the cosmological order.

Kapferer thus asserts that the Sinhala aggression and violence against the Tamil minority is partly "understandable" in the sense of being generated from this deep structure.[44]

The third, and this is his foundational postulate, is that behind the cosmological schemes, mythic stories, and modern ideology lies an ontology as a deep logical structure which actively structures and in-

43. It is important to note that Kapferer's study compares Sri Lanka and Australia, and I am concerned here only with his characterization of the former.

44. For example, "In Sri Lanka the Sinhalese Buddhist logic of hierarchy yields some insight into the violent destruction of Tamils in rioting by Sinhalese, of the violence of Buddhist monks, and of the ideological weight behind various public pronouncements of politicians" (ibid., pp. 17–18).

terprets reality and is embedded in a wide array of cultural practices.[45]

The question might be raised whether Kapferer's thesis as it stands is ahistorical: it makes a leap from a cosmology inferred from a sixth-century mytho-historical text composed in Pali by monks of the Mahavihara fraternity to another cosmology he infers from present-day demon rituals.[46] Does a possible homology between the two cosmologies mean a continuity in historical consciousness from the sixth to the twentieth century?

Kapferer has a brief (less than a page) reference to the connections and changes in successive texts—between the *Mahavamsa* (sixth century), the *Pujavaliya* (thirteenth century), and the *Rajavaliya* (at the time of Dutch taking control of the maritime regions)—in their conception of Elara, the Tamil king defeated by Dutthagamani. The changing conception takes place after Magha's destructive invasion and subsequent social and political dislocation. The worsening of Elara's stature from being "righteous" to "unrighteous" is in a manner consistent within the terms of the ontology, which transforms Elara into the "fragmented subordination" of demonic status. Except for this there is no demonstration of continuous transmission of an ontology-cosmology-ideology over time or of what validity it had for historical actors over time to the present day.

But would it be possible to demonstrate Kapferer's thesis by recourse to literary and other evidence? To some significant but incomplete degree, scholars like Gunawardena and Dharmadasa, discussed earlier, have examined the literary and inscriptional evidence on the formation and continuity of Sinhala Buddhist identity. It is an open question whether this scholarship plus other materials on myths and rituals and folklore can be used to sustain Kapferer's thesis of an ingrained ontological Sinhala Buddhist nationalist generative structure. On this score my own view is that Kapferer's cosmological conception while

45. Such a thesis is implied in this sample quotation: "Attention to the ontological dimensions of ideology and to the embeddedness of ontology in a wide array of cultural practices may also extend an understanding of the power of ideological rhetoric. . . . Ontology as I use the word is beneath the level of conscious reflection, is prereflective. Ideology, in contrast, is overt in the reflected world, active as assertion about, and interpretation of, reality. Ontology is neither subjective nor objective but both. Ideology forms with the logic of ontology and realizing some of its potential is simultaneously part of the historical world toward which human beings move" (ibid., p. 84).

46. This question has been raised by Jonathan Spencer, "Writing Within: Anthropology, Nationalism, and Culture in Sri Lanka," *Current Anthropology* 31, no. 3 (1990): 269. Spencer is not alone in raising this issue.

insightful and apt is, as now sketched, restrictive if taken as the only dominant basis structuring ideology and cultural practices. I think, first, there are, as my previous documentation establishes, more coexisting grids and frames, and more various discourses and practices of the premodern (that is pre-British) Sinhalese society than he has presented. They have to be differentiated and then dialectically related. Second, there has been a distinct transformative shift in the discourse of Sinhalese Buddhist nationalism in the last hundred years, which is related to the play of new currents of thought, the social changes wrought by a unitary and autocratic British colonial regime, and the new space, opportunities, and modes of influencing and mobilizing public opinion in postindependence Sri Lanka dedicated to the project of "nation-state"–making hitched to the juggernaut of mass participatory politics. This modern Sinhala Buddhist nationalism, while it carries or activates a legacy from the past, is a change to a new nationalist and nation-state–making complex. Kapferer, as we shall see shortly, recognizes and skillfully depicts it, while at the same time leaving some knotty issues in his wake.

One of the obstacles for me is Kapferer's use of the concept "state" in his comparison of the Sri Lankan polity and nationalism of the past and present with Australian nationalism and state. The concept of "state" as a political construct took shape in modern European history to connote a political community organized under a distinct government invested with the monopoly of force and accepted by the people qua citizens as owing conformity. The state was conceived as legitimately administering a bounded territory. When the concept of nation also matured to signify and give body to a collectivity of individuals homogeneously united as a community, the twin concepts of nation and state fused to produce the nation-state. "The gaze and emblem of the nation's 'felt freedom' [was] the sovereign state."[47]

47. As Benedict Anderson in *Imagined Communities, Reflections on the Origin and Spread of Nationalism* (London: Verso Editions and NLB, 1983), pp. 13–16, has pointed out, "nationalism" and "nations" as special "imagined communities" were furthered, among other developments, by communication media, especially "print capitalism," and crystallized as a "spontaneous distillation of a complex 'crossing' of discrete historical forces" toward the end of the eighteenth century. The nation (and I might add the "nation-state") is imagined as bounded and limited, beyond which lie other nations; it is imagined as sovereign because the "concept was born in an age in which Enlightenment and Revolution were destroying the legitimacy of the divinely-ordained, hierarchical dynastic realm"; it is imagined as a community and a fraternity regardless of actual inequality and exploitation.

Note that Louis Dumont, whose concept of hierarchy has influenced Kapferer, has

To my mind none of the pre-British polities in Sri Lanka, the classical Anuradhapura and Polonnaruva kingdoms nor the subsequent polities smaller in scale, comprised unitary states of the kind specified above. I have developed the concept of "galactic polities" of South and Southeast Asia to describe polities, focused on kings and lesser kings and chiefs, which are center-oriented formations with shifting and blurred boundaries (rather than bounded exclusive spaces).[48] The polities modelled on mandala-type patterning had central royal domains surrounded by satellite principalities and provinces replicating the center on a smaller scale and at the margins had even more autonomous tributary principalities. The effective political arena extends beyond any single "kingdom"; it is multicentric, with rival "kingdoms" jostling each other, changing their margins, expanding and contracting, according to the fortunes of wars, skirmishes, raids, and diplomacy. They were pulsating galactic polities. Internally, within each major or minor principality, there were checks and balances, such as duplication within administrative "departments," interlocking and contesting factional formations of patrons and clients, and devolutionary processes of power parcelization. Mobilization for warfare or monumental projects and other "king's work" was possible on a short-term and rotational but not a sustained basis.

The information on the Kandyan kingdom, for example, is adequate to construct this kind of model of the galactic polity. Its contours are perceptible in other polities and earlier times as well. The following is a skeletal blueprint of the Kandyan kingdom, say in the late eighteenth and early nineteenth centuries, that illustrates the checks and balances and devolutionary arrangements in place.[49]

The central royal domain immediately surrounding the capital city of Kandy was made up of some nine small districts (*rata*) under the charge of officials called *rate mahatvaru*. Surrounding the central domain was an arrangement of 12 provinces (*disa*) of varying size: there

firmly asserted that a state exercising territorial sovereignty over all within its territories is a distinctly modern conception. See Dumont, "Are Cultures Living Beings? German Ideology in Interaction," *Man*, n.s., 21 (1986): 591–92.

48. The concept of galactic polity was first developed by me in *World Conqueror and World Renouncer: A Study of Religion and Polity in Thailand against a Historical Background* (Cambridge: Cambridge University Press, 1976). "The Galactic Polity in Southeast Asia," in my *Culture, Thought, and Social Action* (Cambridge, Mass.: Harvard University Press, 1985), is a distilled statement.

49. The basic features are contained in these works: Sir John D'Oyly, *A Sketch of the Kandyan Kingdom (Ceylon)* (Colombo: H. Ross Cottle, 1929); A. M. Hocart, *The Temple of the Tooth in Kandy.* Memoirs of the Archaeological Survey of Ceylon, vol. 4

was an inner circle of smaller provinces, and an outer circle of larger and remoter provinces. These provinces were governed by *disvara*, belonging to the chiefly *radala* stratum, who had their own seats and retinues. The king's authority waned as the provinces stretched farther away from the capital, and recurrent rebellions mounted from the interior, especially from those provinces on the border of the maritime regions under European control, exemplified this tendency. There was a diminishing replication of the central domain in the satellite units. The kingdom as a whole was divided into the northern and southern halves, each placed in the charge of one of two, first and second, *adigars*. The dualistic structuring of offices and departments was prominent: for example, the two most prominent palace officials were also paired off as the *maha diyavadana nilame* (in charge of the royal bath and grooming the king's hair) and the *haluvadana nilame* (in charge of the king's wardrobe and his dressing); the order of monks (*sangha*) was divided into two parallel chapters, Malvatta and Asgirya, with their heads and lesser clerical officers, and this symmetrical structuring was carried through all the levels of the monastic system. The functionaries of the Temple of the Tooth Relic were divided into the "outer" (general administration) and "inner" (the ritual work) groups. The administrative involution was profuse in the form of "redundant" officials entrusted with minute tasks. Perhaps, the most critical feature of the devolutionary process was the parceling out of agricultural and forest lands and the manpower settled on them (finely graded by caste and tenurial rights) in terms of monastic (*viharagam*) and temple (*devalegam*) endowments, estates attached to offices held by the nobility (*nindagam*) and the royal estates (*gabadagam*). The specification of duties and work owed the king (*rajakariya*) according to caste and tenurial status and attachment to type of overlord, and the procedures and mechanisms for mobilization of labor for this work were involved.

All these features allowed for and produced social and political processes that were flexible, accommodative, and inclusionary as well as competitive, factional, and fragmenting. They elaborated the division of labor, and provided niches for immigrant groups, or stranger groups of different "ethnic" origins and different "religions," and assigned special functions such as serving as mercenaries, conducting overland

(London: Luzac & Co., 1931); Ralph Pieris, *Sinhalese Social Organization: The Kandyan Period;* and H. L. Seneviratne, *Rituals of the Kandyan State.*

trade, or making luxury artifacts.[50] They, too, provide the space and opportunity for mounting rebellions and insurrections against the center and for rival chiefs to compete for power.

What I want to underscore here is that such political formations were flexible, incorporationist, and inclusive, in more ways than have been captured by Kapferer. The mandala pattern of devolution and replication could and did solicit and tolerate, positively place and mutually benefit from the presence of and engagement with satellite principalities, specialized minorities and sectarian or heterodox communities, waves of immigrants, and groups of war captives all given niches and incorporated within the larger cosmological and politico-economic framework. Indeed it was this galactic blueprint that positively enabled the Sinhalization and Buddhicization of south Indian peoples and gods to continue uncoerced.

Kapferer's conception of hierarchy and inclusion, which in many ways accords with and enriches my views on the galactic polity, however, fits ill with his notion of a nationalist Sinhala Buddhist state of earlier times, which is given the bounded, fusing, and enabling, even *reified* presence that is more appropriately associated with the modern nation-state.[51]

---

50. For example, Sir John D'Oyly, *A Sketch of the Kandyan Kingdom*, reports that a section of the Madige or Carriage Bullock Department was composed of "Moormen," and another of "the fisher caste." The former were involved in "the conveyance of grain" and the latter with delivering salt and fish to the royal stores.

The following example illustrates social variety conjoined with spatial contiguity. Demala (Tamil) Pattu, also called Hatpattuwe Rata, was that part of the Puttalam region that came under the jurisdiction of the Kandyan Kingdom in the early nineteenth century. D'Oyly's listing includes villages granted to those of "the Moor Religion" and to "Malabar people," some of whom had recently landed. "Wanniyar" officials of Moor identity; "Panikki (Barbers) of Moor religion"; "Kammal Minissu, who are of Malabar extraction but now Singalese"; "Wanni" officials of the "Mukara" caste who marry among themselves but "not with the Singalese"—these are some of the categories, aside from lands and offices assigned to Sinhala persons, that made up the rich mosaic of peoples residing in their niches in this border district of the Kandyan Kingdom.

51. This is the impression that I gather from this statement: "Broadly, I consider that in Sinhalese Buddhist nationalist cosmology the nation and the state compose a unity. In cosmological conception the state protectively encloses the nation of Sinhalese Buddhists, whose integrity as persons is dependent on this encompassment. The state in such a conception encloses other peoples or nations who are not Sinhalese Buddhists. But critical here is that these peoples are maintained in hierarchical subordination to Sinhalese Buddhists. . . . The failure in the power of the Sinhalese Buddhist state to maintain hierarchy in the whole order it circumscribes threatens the integrity of persons. Thus the fragmentation of the state is also the fragmentation of the nation and is also the fragmentation of the person" (Kapferer, *Legends*, p. 7).

Now it is true that Kapferer does mention that in precolonial times "The nation is encompassed by the state symbolized in the kingship. These in turn are encompassed by the Buddhist religion or the Triple Gem. In this unity of the whole is the integrity of the parts." He and I meet in holding the view that the Theravada Buddhist polities were predicated on a special relationship between the *sangha* (the community of monks) and the kingship which provides the institutional support for and protection of the *sangha* and the Buddha *sasana*. He and I agree on the ideological links between cosmos and polity in earlier times, and how this orientation affects modern politics. But I prefer my "galactic polity" to his bounded "state" with its bonding of nation with state, because the former allows more easily for movements and processes of different kinds from the blurred and changing peripheries to the center (or multiple centers).

It is this lack of fit between a rigid notion of bounded state and the flexible processes of hierarchical incorporation or expulsion that impels Kapferer to explain problems that would not arise if one accepted the picture of movements of diverse kinds and trajectories from the blurred periphery to the center, which do not have to be located as starting outside or inside the state and whose location in this precise sense is not the crucial issue for their subsequent fate.[52] They do become issues, however, when as in the late twentieth century the Sri Lankan "nation-state" with its centralized power is problematically impelled by calculations of majoritarian arithmetic to be conflated with Sinhala Buddhist nationalism in an exclusivist manner. It is primarily in the late nineteenth and especially in the twentieth centuries, that historical charters were reactivated, cathected and reinterpreted, and fused with entirely new streams of influences—colonial, Western, Christian, global—to construe the objectives and immanence of Sinhala Buddhist nationalism and to make it the experience and aspirations of the masses and public at large.

The cosmological structure Kapferer attributes to the Sinhalese consciousness requires that the Tamils (equated in the contemporary ethnic conflict with the demonic because they threaten the unity, integ-

---

52. For example, consider this statement: "I have said that the myths of evil, disorder, and fragmentation come from outside the state. This may seem to be contradicted by the fact that the agents of evil have close kinship with the agents of order. It can be argued, therefore, that evil comes from within the state, an analytic position that would not greatly affect my discussion. I suggest, however, that when evil manifests its power, the logic of the myths indicates that this power is external and in opposition to the state. In other words, what may have been inside moves to the outside and achieves its negating contradiction accordingly" (*Legends*, pp. 67–68).

rity, and hierarchy of the Sinhala Buddhist polity) be actually subordinated and inferiorized and incorporated within the hierarchy of Sinhala dominance. But this requirement is clearly *inefficacious* as a cure to the current ethnic conflict (while the exorcism ritual is thought by officiants, patients, and audience to be ritually and performatively *efficacious* in its treatment of the demonic illness), because it is precisely this attitude that the Tamils, who are insiders and not "alien," are resisting as discriminatory and antithetical to the norms of democracy. In other words, the homology that Kapferer sees between the Sinhalese treatment of the demonic in their exorcism rites and the Sinhalese treatment of Tamils as the demonic in the present-day polity is not a felicitous or a realistic parallel for the Sinhalese themselves. Many Sinhalese, before and now, have accepted that the Tamils in the north and east of the island have long been domiciled, with a separate polity in the north existing in its own right since the thirteenth century and that the label of "alien" or "foreign" invaders is not applicable to them. The civil war in Sri Lanka is precisely about the terms of incorporation of Sinhalese, Tamils, Muslims (and other minorities) in a polity that all can accept as "just" and democratic. And it is patently clear—and Kapferer is *not* asserting otherwise—that the pattern of treatment of an ailment presented by Sinhalese exorcism rites is *not* the pattern that can cure the current ethnic conflict. Hence his deep sense of the tragedy engulfing Sri Lanka and his adjuration that a solution to the current strife, "self-evident," from his analysis, lies in "the removal of ethnic identity and hierarchy as dominant state-sanctified principles of political and social order" (Kapferer, *Legends,* p. 114).

The Modern Nationalist Ideology

Under the heading "Ethnic Nationalism and New Meaning," Kapferer makes an interpretive move that accords with what I (and others) have argued—that Sinhala Buddhist nationalism has taken on new meanings in our present time: "Statements to the effect that the meanings of the past continue into the present are likely to be ideological in that they are born of current realities; that is, they are arguments about the past or interpretations of it which are motivated from within the structural conditions and processes of the historical present" (ibid., p. 90). Kapferer agrees with Gunawardena's thesis in "People of the Lion," which we have examined before, that Dutthagamani's political aggregation cut across "ethnic applications of modern meaning" and has no bearing on "modern ethnic nationalism" of both Sinhalese and Tamils of today. "Modern nationalist ideol-

ogy," states Kapferer, "that fuels and supports the present tragic
situation of interethnic hostility and warfare was formed in the colonial and postcolonial situations of the emergence of the modern
nation-state" (ibid., pp. 90–91). The contribution of colonial rule to
the drawing of ethnic boundaries, the colonially introduced system of
ethnic representation in the political process that preceded and led to
independence, the formation of political parties on considerations of
ethnic interests, the competition within dominant class fractions for
political control by seeking mass support by means of exacerbating
historically created structural faults, the close relation between the in-
flation of nationalism and the expansion of bureaucratic state power,
the propensity for "Sinhalese nationalism, like all nationalism" to
"fetishize culture" and to reify it as an object in itself, the advent of
print capitalism that enables the making of folk knowledge into common knowledge, and folk history into popular history; the structural
and institutional processes of the present that make "false history,"
from the point of view of critical scholars, objectively true for those
participating in those processes—these are many of the contemporary developments that Kapferer in a dazzling flurry runs through
in his very acceptable delineation of present-day Sinhala Buddhist
nationalism.

But an area of darkness remains for me. Is this profile of the new
ethnic nationalism a shift from the hierarchical cosmology and
bounded state of the past into a homogenizing nation-state of mass participation in politics of the present, or is it some kind of dynamic coexistent with, paralleling, or superimposed on the past?

Is Kapferer having it both ways, and if so has he made his position
comprehensible when he says, first, that the Sinhalese culture that is
asserted in current nationalism to be Buddhist is "a unity in hierarchy,
wherein state, society, and person are placed in cosmically determined
relations of incorporation and differentiation and are ordered and
made whole accordingly," and, second, that it gives "particular value
to the kinds of ontology of state and person I have discussed with reference to the chronicles" (ibid., pp. 98–99)? Continuity and change are
not clarified by this seeming conflation of the past and present.

As I have previously said, I find it difficult to attribute to earlier
times a strong sense of "the state," let alone a strong sense of the fusion
of "state and person." Moreover, I also find it difficult to accept that
present-day Sinhalese nationalism is for many people at large wedded
to a particular ontology-based "ideology of the state" or that most con-

temporary Sinhalese "recognize their personal integrity and the quality of their social relations and experience as being dependent on the order of the state." It is against the power of the Sri Lankan "state" (which in practice is realized in terms of the control of the public media and the use of force available to the government in power, its agencies and security forces) that the JVP insurrections and counterviolence of Sinhala, mostly Buddhist youth (and many young monks), was mounted in 1971, and which erupted again to be cruelly and implacably eliminated in the late eighties. At present, while the war against the Tamil insurgents is being waged by the government's forces and is being quite successfully countered by them, no doubt at a terrible price inflicted on the Tamil civilians, there are, despite the frequent impositions of curfew and martial law, lively antigovernment counterstatements and resistances being made by many members of the Sinhalese "lower social orders" in the form of posters, popular theater, and back-stage "transcripts" and other forms of "weapons of the weak." It is almost inevitable that the "state" as a constructed entity is usually "appropriated" by those in power. And if the conception of "nation-state" is a feature of "official nationalism" promoted by the agents who control the "state," the other current conceptions of "Buddhist socialism," or even "Buddhist-administered state," are powerful, if utopian, critiques of "unrighteous" societies which generate divisive inequalities and recreate the law of the fishes among the Sinhalese majority people themselves. (The political platforms of other extant secular political parties and associations also constitute a criticism of that party in power which has temporarily appropriated the state.)

There is one final remark to be made about the heavily centralized and unitary character of the present Sri Lankan state, which is a legacy of the British raj, further enlarged in postindependence times, and which in no way was a feature of the precolonial polities. Wilson and Manor have documented different aspects of this thesis effectively.[53] Wilson indicates that the British colonial state at its very inception, especially after the early rebellions which it feared were spawned by the Kandyan chiefs, constructed a repressive regime which while giv-

53. A. Jeyaratnam Wilson, *The Break-up of Sri Lanka: The Sinhalese-Tamil Conflict* (Honolulu: University of Hawaii Press, 1988); James Manor, "The Failure of Political Integration in Sri Lanka (Ceylon)," *Journal of Commonwealth and Comparative Politics* 17, no. 1 (1979): 21–44.

ing administrative discretion to British officers gave no space for regional autonomy for the local people. The political considerations favoring administrative centralization were further augmented when the capital city of Colombo developed into the country's only primary mercantile center. It was only after this structure was in place that features of representative government and parliamentary democracy were gradually grafted.

At independence, the apparatus of a heavily centralized regime was transferred to the local political elite, and successive waves of politicians in power, primarily Sinhalese in origin and representing the heavily Sinhalese majority, and an administrative service, imbued with "paternalistic" and hierarchical values of dispensing law and order, progress and enlightenment, to the ordinary man-in-the-street public at large, has found it handy for fostering the kind of official nationalism and majoritarian policies that have in large part, but not exclusively, led to the present crisis. At any rate, the inheritance and continuation of a centralized and Colombo-centered state unresponsive and inimical to the notion of devolution of power to regions and provinces cannot be traced back to the customs and practices of precolonial times.

Manor has argued that in Sri Lanka the same fundamental weakness in the political system is primarily responsible for the alternation of parties in power and for the inability to implement solutions to the ethnic problem. This weakness is "the failure of political integration," which he attributes in turn to "the failure of the national political elite both to endow local government institutions in small towns and villages with substantive powers and to link them effectively into the political system beyond the locality" (Manor, pp. 21–22). The gap between the elite and the mass and the desire of the former to control power at the center, from the Donoughmore era through independence to the present, have prevented the development of strong intermediary local government organizations between local and national levels, and the effective participation of the rural masses in particular from participating "routinely and substantively in the political system" (ibid., p. 36). This situation has further ramifications. One is that the traditional reluctance of the ruling politicians to decentralize power (and their reliance on administrative officers attached to departments under the control of ministers) has made any serious solution of the Sinhala-Tamil ethnic conflict through devolution of power very difficult to achieve. Another is that because the political parties have by and large "failed to build reliable, systematic integrating structures between themselves and the local level," the national political elections generate "a cycle of soaring expectations and bitter disappointment" as ruling parties change position and fail to deliver on their promises (ibid., pp. 37–38). It is no accident that in Sri Lanka national elections have frequently served as occasions for manifesting as well as generating ethnic and insurrectionary violence.

Appendix: Testing Some Charges in *The Betrayal of Buddhism*

Grants-in-Aid Schools

With regard to the charge that the colonial government's policy favored the Christian missions' grant-aided schools, and placed obstacles to the founding of Buddhist (and Hindu) schools, it clearly seems that by and large the authors of *The Betrayal of Buddhism* were correct in their allegations.

The grant-in-aid scheme proposal by the Morgan Committee of 1865 recommended quite liberal grants to private schools for providing education in secular subjects while at the same time placing no restriction on the teaching of religion. The Christian missionary bodies were naturally enthusiastic because they were the principal beneficiaries, and there was a rush of applications from them for grants. In 1869, the year when the new grant-in-aid scheme was implemented, 21 schools earned grants. In 1870 there were 223 (with 10,000 pupils); in 1872, 462 schools (with 25,440 pupils); and in 1876, 697 schools (with 45,440 pupils). The schools in question were both English and vernacular schools, with the former type being the more highly regarded.

The so-called distance rules did in fact work in favor of the Protestant mission schools to the disadvantage of Roman Catholic schools, which began later, and the greatest disadvantage of Buddhist schools, which began to be established later still, especially after the founding of the Buddhist Theosophical Society in 1881 soon after Olcott's arrival.

In November 1874 was passed the three-mile rule which stated that "No grant will be made to any school established after the date of this circular, within a distance of three miles from existing Government or Aided-school of the same class, save in exceptional circumstances." The government's explanation for this rule was the avoidance of unnecessary competition between different religious bodies to extend their schools.

This rule heavily favored the Protestant missionary schools which were already established. The first to voice a protest against this rule were the Roman Catholics; the local religious groups, whether Buddhist, Hindu, or Muslim, were not yet organized to do so. The Catholics claimed that the Protestant missionaries had stolen a march on them and had in numerous instances planted their schools in the vicinity of Catholic villages—and the three-mile rule virtually compelled Catholic children in this situation to attend Protestant schools.

While it seemed that in due course the Roman Catholics were allowed to institute their own schools when they could demonstrate the presence of a sufficient number of Catholics to warrant a school, these exceptional considerations were not readily granted to "Buddhists and heathens."

In 1880 the three-mile rule was replaced by a two-mile rule which stated that no application for aid to a boys' school will be entertained "when there already exists a flourishing boys' school of the same class within two miles of the proposed site, unless the average daily attendance for six months prior to the date of the application exceeds 60."

"The practical effect of this rule," remarked W. Blair, inspector of schools, "in the majority of small towns and large villages in which there are mission schools, the people are virtually compelled to send their children to mission school or none."[1] However, the amendment, also specified that no application to run schools will be allowed "when there already exists a school of the same class within a quarter mile of the site of the proposed new school." This quarter-mile restriction was seen as a hindrance to the founding of schools by Buddhist sponsors in those settlements and towns with heavy concentrations of Buddhists which could therefore provide the necessary number of students to make the schools viable.

So in 1892 a further amendment allowed for exceptions "in towns with special claims," but this was interpreted illiberally, and, in fact, because the rule was applied with retrospective effect, it was claimed by Buddhist objectors that many schools which had been opened long before the new clause was introduced were now forced to close down. The retrospective interpretation also applied to schools that had already filed their applications and were awaiting recognition.

Both the two-mile and quarter-mile rules in due course generated a

1. Cited in J. E. Jayasuriya, *Educational Policies and Progress during the British Rule in Ceylon, 1796–1948* (Colombo: Associated Educational Publishers, n.d.), p. 263.

mounting and increasingly organized campaign of protests from the Buddhists. For example, the Sinhalese newspaper *Sarasavi* and the English journal *The Buddhist* articulated these objections. Olcott fumed in *The Buddhist* (7 October 1892) that the quarter-mile rule was "one of those inequities, those violations of British policy, which can only be perpetrated with comparative safety in a distant colony. Once exposed in the London papers, an inquiry is sure to be made in Parliament, and redress to follow after exposure." Olcott was sure that Her Majesty's ministers knew perfectly well that "the surest way to breed discontent and rebellion is to wantonly act against the religious feelings of "the Asiatic races of the Empire."

T. B. Panabokke, the Kandyan representative to the legislative council submitted in November 1892 a protest against the quarter-mile rule signed by 2,135 Buddhists. The main thrust was that this (and the two-mile rule) were placing difficulties in the way of efforts by Buddhists to start their own schools, that the rules being imposed with retrospective effect meant that "three schools at Katugastota, Kurunegala, and Madapata have already been declined to be registered because of the Quarter Mile Clause, and that the schools at Weragampita, Nugegoda, Karagampitiya, Hatton, etc. established before the introduction of the Clause will also come under its operation" (cited in Jayasuriya, pp. 266–68).

Panabokke's memorial also contained this argument and complaint: "That as the greater portion of revenue is raised by Government from the taxes paid by the Buddhist, it is manifestly unfair that moneys so raised should be expended on about 1,000 schools of other denominations whereas less than thirty Buddhist schools have hitherto been registered even granting that this is largely due to their own ignorant neglect of prescribed Department rules" (ibid., p. 268).

At first the government refused to provide any relief—even against the retrospective application of the quarter-mile rule. But matters changed after Olcott's return to Ceylon in May 1894. At a convention of Buddhist School managers held in July, Olcott was appointed the representative of the Buddhists "to lay before the Secretary of State for the Colonies the grievances of the Buddhists in regard to the quarter mile rule and to secure adoption of the principle of local option." The memorial to the secretary of state for the colonies was accordingly composed—and he in due course gave qualified relief in that while ruling against the retrospective application of the rule, he refused to reverse it with regard to new schools.

Inspired by Olcott's urging, several educational societies formed by the Buddhists began to found schools and to seek grants, but they were eligible only after satisfying certain conditions which impeded their speedy growth, for example, that the headmaster of a grant-in-aid school must be a certified teacher and that the average daily attendance had to exceed 60 for a minimum period of one year before a school could apply to be recognized as a grant-in-aid school. It cannot be said that in the 1890s the Department of Public Instruction was sympathetic to new schools being opened by Buddhists, Hindus, and Muslims.

The most important activity of the Buddhist Theosophical Society was the establishment of Buddhist schools for which purpose it started an education fund; the society also initiated a publication fund and began printing Buddhist texts for schools and also other publications. Dharmapala was the first manager of these two funds, and a third called the defense fund.

Between 1886 and 1900 the BTS founded an increasing number of schools. In 1886 was founded the English high school in Colombo, which in 1895 changed its name to Ananda College and prospered under the leadership of A. E. Bultjens. In 1887 was founded Dharmaraja College in Kandy, and in 1892 Mahinda College in Galle. These three schools situated in the three principal cities of the island were, and still remain today, the jewels of the Buddhist educational enterprise.

The increasing educational success of the BTS may be judged by these figures: in 1880 it had sponsored four schools with 246 pupils; in 1885 the schools had multiplied to 8, in 1890 to 18, in 1885 to 54, and in 1900 to 142 schools with a total of 18,700 pupils.[2]

Buddhist Temporalities

With regard to the charge that the colonial government imposed restrictions on the funds and property of the Buddhist *viharas* which they did not impose on the Christian missions, the situation seems to have been somewhat misrepresented. Whether or not the British raj's disassociation from the administration of temple lands in the early 1850s caused subsequent problems, the fact is that by the 1870s not only members of the colonial government (as for example, Governor Gregory) but also many well-known Buddhist representatives of the local elite were much concerned with the way in which both head monks and lay managers of both *vihara* and *devale* proper-

2. I am indebted to Sarath Amunugama for this information.

ties were managing the lands and handling the rents and monies they received as income. It was because of problems of mismanagement of lands, misappropriation of monies, and poor maintenance of temples that a special commission was convened and a report written to offer solutions.[3] It is therefore difficult to attribute the serious deficiencies of management on the part of the monk-incumbents of temple and Buddhist lay managers to the "restrictive" and "confining" policies of the colonial authorities.[4]

In any case, in 1889 an ordinance was passed for the appointment of trustees in whom were vested all property belonging to a *vihara* together with rents and profits accruing from it. These trustees were to be elected by district committees, which in turn were composed of one member from each subdistrict elected by the resident monk and male Buddhist householders. A commissioner was appointed to oversee and assist these committees. But we should note that this ordinance covered only certain *viharas*. There were left untouched *viharas* whose properties were managed by its monk-incumbents, who could transmit this property to their monk successors through two forms of pupillage: from incumbent to his eldest pupil (*sisyanusisya paramparava*) and from incumbent to his relative who is ordained and designated (*sivuru paramparava*). This appendix does not refer to the administration of property belonging to the Dalada Maligawa in Kandy (under the care of the Diyawadana Nilame) and the *devales* (under the care of the Basnayaka Nilame);[5] the officers in question were elected by defined electoral committees.

Successive amendments to the ordinance of 1889 were made in 1905, and revisions made in 1931 when a public trustee was appointed to control the incumbents and trustees of *vihara* and *devale* properties, who had to submit yearly statements of income and expenditure to the public trustee for auditing.[6]

3. See *Report of Commissioners Appointed to Inquire into the Administration of the Buddhist Temporalities*, Sessional Paper of the Legislative Council, 1876–77, No. 17, 7–52.

4. For a discussion of issues relating to Buddhist temporalities, see John D. Rogers, "Religious Belief, Economic Interest, and Social Policy: Temple Endowments in Sri Lanka during the Governorship of William Gregory, 1872–77," *Modern Asian Studies* 21, no. 2 (1987): 349–69.

5. For details, see H. W. Tambiah, "Buddhist Ecclesiastical Law," *Journal of the Ceylon Branch of the Royal Asiatic Society*, n.s., 8, part 1 (1963): 71–107.

6. See H. W. Tambiah, *Sinhalese Laws and Customs* (Colombo: Lake House, 1968), chap. 14.

References

Ali, Ameer. "The 1915 Racial Riots in Ceylon (Sri Lanka): A Reappraisal of Its Causes." *South Asia,* n.s., 4, no. 2 (1981): 1–20.

Alles, A. C. *Insurgency—1971.* Colombo: Colombo Apothecaries' Co., 1976.

Amunugama, Sarath. "Anagarika Dharmapala (1864–1933) and the Transformation of Sinhala Buddhist Organization in a Colonial Setting." *Social Science Information* 24, no. 4 (1985): 697–730.

————. "Buddhaputra and Bhumiputra? Dilemmas of Modern Sinhala Buddhist Monks in Relation to Ethnic and Political Conflict." *Religion* 21 (1991): 115–39.

Anderson, Benedict. *Imagined Communities: Reflection on the Origin and Spread of Nationalism.* London: Verso Editions and NLB, 1983.

Ariyasena Maha Thera, Venerable Pundit Kamburupitiye. *An Introduction to Buddhist Philosophy of the State.* Colombo: Lake House Printers, 1986.

Balasooriya, Somaratna; André Bareau; et al., eds. *Buddhist Studies in Honour of Walpola Rahula.* London: Gordon Fraser, 1980.

Bastian, Sunil. "Education and Social Conflict in Sri Lanka." Unpublished essay.

————. "University Admission and the National Question." *Ethnicity and Social Change in Sri Lanka.* Social Scientists' Association. Colombo: Navamaga Printers, 1985.

Bechert, Heinz. "The Beginnings of Buddhist Historiography: *Mahavamsa* and Political Thinking." *Religion and Legitimation of Power in Sri Lanka,* edited by Bardwell Smith. Chambersburg, Pa.: Anima Books, 1987.

————. "Buddhism in the Modern States of South East Asia." *South East Asia in the Modern World,* edited by B. Grossman. Wiesbaden, 1972.

Bond, George. *The Buddhist Revival in Sri Lanka: The Religious Tradition, Reinterpretation and Response.* Columbia: University of South Carolina Press, 1988.

Culavamsa. Translated by Wilhelm Geiger. Colombo: Ceylon Government Information Department, 1953.

De Silva, C. R. "The Impact of Nationalism on Education: The Schools Takeover (1961) and the University Admissions Crisis, 1970–1975." *Collec-*

tive Identities, Nationalisms, and Protest in Modern Sri Lanka. Edited by Michael Roberts. Colombo: Marga Institute, 1979.

De Silva, K. M. *A History of Sri Lanka.* London: C. Hurst & Co., 1981.

————. *Managing Ethnic Tensions in Multi-Ethnic Societies: Sri Lanka, 1880–1985.* Lanham, Md.: University Press of America, 1986.

Dewaraja, L. S. *The Kandyan Kingdom, 1707–1760.* Colombo: Lake House Publishers, 1971.

Dharmadasa, K. N. O. "The People of the Lion: Ethnic Identity, Ideology, and Historical Revisionism in Contemporary Sri Lanka." *Sri Lanka Journal of the Humanities* 15 (1989): 1–35.

————. "The Sinhala-Buddhist Identity and the Nayakkar Dynasty in the Politics of the Kandyan Kingdom, 1739–1815." *Ceylon Journal of Historical and Social Studies,* n.s., 6, no. 1 (January–June 1976): 1–23.

D'Oyly, Sir John. *A Sketch of the Kandyan Kingdom (Ceylon).* Colombo: H. Ross Cottle, 1929.

Dumont, Louis. *Homo Hierarchicus: The Caste System and Its Implications.* Translated by Mark Sainsbury. London: Weidenfeld & Nicolson, 1970.

Dumont, Louis. "Are Cultures Living Beings? German Ideology in Interaction." *Man,* n.s., 21 (1986): 587–604.

Gnanasiha Thera, Henpitagedera. "Why Do We Need a Buddhist Administered Country?" Unpublished translation by Steven Kemper of *Apata Bauddha Palana Kramayak Avashy Ayi?* Ratnapura, Sri Lanka: Samupakara Mudranalaye, 1982.

Godakumbura, C. E. *Sinhalese Literature.* Colombo: Colombo Apothecaries' Co., 1955.

Gombrich, Richard, and Gananath Obeyesekere. *Buddhism Transformed: Religious Change in Sri Lanka.* Princeton: Princeton University Press, 1988.

Gooneratne, Yasmine. *Relative Merits: A Personal Memoir of the Bandaranaike Family of Sri Lanka.* London: C. Hurst & Co., 1986.

Gunasingha, Newton. "The Symbolic Role of the Sangha." *Lanka Guardian,* October 15 1986, pp. 9–10.

Gunawardena, R. A. L. H. "The People of the Lion: Sinhala Consciousness in History and Historiography." *Ethnicity and Social Change in Sri Lanka.* Social Scientists' Association. Colombo: Navamaga Printers, 1985.

Guruge, Ananda, ed. *Return to Righteousness: A Collection of Speeches, Essays, and Letters of the Anagarika Dharmapala.* Colombo: Government Press, 1965.

Hocart, A. M. *The Temple of the Tooth in Kandy.* Memoirs of the Archaeological Survey of Ceylon, vol. 4. London: Luzac & Co., 1931.

Holt, John Clifford. *Buddha in the Crown: Avalokitesvara in the Buddhist Traditions of Sri Lanka.* New York: Oxford University Press, 1991.

Hulugalle, H. A. J. *The Life and Times of D. R. Wijewardena.* Colombo: Lake House, 1960.

Jayasuriya, J. E. *Educational Policies and Progress during the British Rule in Ceylon, 1796–1948.* Colombo: Associated Educational Publishers, n.d.

Jayatilake, K. N. "The Principles of International Law in Buddhist Doctrine." *Academy of International Law* 11 (1977).

Jayawardena, Visakha Kumari. "Bhikkus in Revolt." *Lanka Guardian,* May 15, June 15, July 1, and July 15, 1979.

―――. *Ethnic and Class Conflicts in Sri Lanka.* Colombo: Navagama Printers, 1986.

―――. "Ethnic Consciousness in Sri Lanka: Continuity and Change." *Sri Lanka, The Ethnic Conflict: Myths, Realities, and Perspectives.* Committee for Rational Development. New Delhi: Navrang, 1984.

―――. *The Rise of the Labor Movement in Ceylon.* Durham, N.C.: Duke University Press, 1972.

Jayawickrama, N. A., and W. G. Weeraratne. *World Fellowship of Buddhists and Its Founder President G. P. Malalasekera.* Colombo: World Fellowship of Buddhists, 1982.

Juergensmeyer, Mark. "What the Bhikkhu Said: Reflections on the Rise of Militant Religious Nationalism." *Religion* 20 (1990): 53–75.

Kannangara, A. P. "The Riots of 1915 in Sri Lanka: A Study in the Roots of Communal Violence." *Past and Present,* no. 102 (1983):130–65.

Kantowsky, Detlef. *Sarvodaya: The Other Development.* Delhi: Vikas, 1980.

Kapferer, Bruce. *A Celebration of Demons.* Bloomington: Indiana University Press, 1983.

―――. *Legends of People, Myths of State: Violence, Intolerance, and Political Culture in Sri Lanka and Australia.* Washington, D.C.: Smithsonian Institution Press, 1988.

―――. "Nationalist Ideology and Comparative Anthropology." Unpublished essay.

Kearney, Robert. "The 1915 Riots in Ceylon: A Symposium." *Journal of Asian Studies* 24, no. 2 (1970):219–66.

―――. *Communalism and Language in the Politics of Ceylon.* Durham, N.C.: Duke University Press, 1967.

Kemper, Steven. *The Presence of the Past: Chronicles, Politics, and Culture in Sinhala Nationalism.* Forthcoming.

Ludowyk, E. F. C. "Thinking of Rahula." *Buddhist Studies in Honour of Walpola Rahula,* edited by Somaratna Balasooriya, André Bareau, et al. London: Gordon Fraser, 1980.

Mahavamsa, or The Great Chronicle of Ceylon. Colombo: Ceylon Government Information Department, 1950.

Malalgoda, Kitsiri. *Buddhism in Sinhalese Society, 1750–1900: A Study of Religious Revival and Change.* Berkeley: University of California Press, 1976.

Mallawarachchi, Udaya. "Walpola Rahula: A Brief Biographical Sketch." *Buddhist Studies in Honour of Walpola Rahula,* edited by Somaratra Balasooriya, André Bareau, et al. London: Gordon Fraser, 1980.

Manor, James. *The Expedient Utopian: Bandaranaike and Ceylon.* Cambridge: Cambridge University Press, 1989.

Manor, James. "The Failure of Political Integration in Sri Lanka (Ceylon)." *Journal of Commonwealth and Comparative Politics* 17, no. 1. (1979): 21–46.

Mydans, Seth. *New York Times,* July 29, 1987.

Nissan, Elizabeth. "The Sacred City of Anuradhapura: Aspects of Sinhalese Buddhism and Nationhood." Ph.D. diss., London School of Economics and Political Science, August 1985.

Obeyesekere, Gananath. *The Cult of the Goddess Pattini.* Chicago: University of Chicago Press, 1984.

———. *A Meditation on Conscience.* Social Scientists' Association of Sri Lanka, Occasional Papers. Colombo: Navamaga, 1988.

———. "The Ritual Drama of Sanni Demons: Collective Representations of Disease in Ceylon." *Comparative Studies in Society and History* 11, no. 2 (1969): 174–216.

Paranavitana, S. *History of Ceylon,* vol. 1. Colombo: University of Ceylon Press Board, 1960.

Peebles, Patrick. "Colonization and Ethnic Conflict in the Dry Zone of Sri Lanka." *Journal of Asian Studies* 49, no. 1 (1990):30–55.

Phadnis, Urmila. *Religion and Politics in Sri Lanka.* London: C. Hurst & Co., 1976.

Pieris, Ralph. *Sinhalese Social Organization: The Kandyan Period.* Colombo: University of Ceylon Press Board, 1956.

Rahula, Walpola. *The Heritage of the Bhikkhu: A Short History of the Bhikkhu in the Educational, Cultural, Social, and Political Life.* New York: Grove Press, 1974.

———. *History of Buddhism in Ceylon.* Colombo: Gunasena, 1956.

———. *What the Buddha Taught.* Bedford: Gordon Fraser, 1959.

Ramanathan, P. *Riots and Martial Law in Ceylon, 1915.* London: St. Martin's Press, 1915.

Report of Commissioners Appointed to Inquire into the Administration of the Buddhist Temporalities. Sessional Paper of the Legislative Council, 1876–77, no. 17. Colombo: Government Press, 1876.

Rogers, John D. "Religious Belief, Economic Interest, and Social Policy: Temple Endowments in Sri Lanka during the Governorship of William Gregory, 1872–77." *Modern Asian Studies* 21, no. 2 (1987): 349–69.

Russell, Jane. *Communal Politics under the Donoughmore Constitution.* Colombo: Tisara Press, 1982.

Ryan, Bryce. *Caste in Modern Ceylon.* New Brunswick: Rutgers University Press, 1953.

Sahlins, Marshall. "The Stranger-King; or Dumézil among the Fijians." *Islands of History.* Chicago: University of Chicago Press, 1985.

Schalk, Peter. "'Unity' and 'Sovereignty': Key Concepts of a Militant Buddhist Organization in the Present Conflict in Sri Lanka." *Temenos* 24 (1988): 55–82.

Seneviratne, H. L. "The Alien King: Nayakkars on the Throne of Kandy." *Ceylon Journal of Historical and Social Studies,* n.s., 6, no. 1 (1976): 55–61.

———. *Rituals of the Kandyan State.* Cambridge: Cambridge University Press, 1978.

Seneviratne, H. L., and Swarna Wickremaratne. "Bodhipuja: Collective Representations of Sri Lanka Youth." *American Ethnologist* 7, no. 4 (1980): 734–43.

Shastri, Amita. "The Material Basis for Separatism: The Tamil Eelam Movement in Sri Lanka." *Journal of Asian Studies* 49, no. 1 (1990): 56–77.

Spencer, Jonathan, ed. *Sri Lanka: History and the Roots of Conflict.* London: Routledge, 1990.

———. "Writing Within: Anthropology, Nationalism, and Culture in Sri Lanka." *Current Anthropology* 31, no. 3 (1990): 294–310.

Strong, John. *The Legend of King Asoka: A Study and Translation of the Asokavadana.* Princeton: Princeton University Press, 1983.

Tambiah, H. W. "Buddhist Ecclesiastical Law." *Journal of the Ceylon Branch of the Royal Asiatic Society,* n.s., 8, part 1 (1963): 71–107.

———. *Sinhalese Laws and Customs.* Colombo: Lake House, 1968.

Tambiah, Stanley J. *The Buddhist Conception of Universal King and Its Manifestations in South and Southeast Asia.* Kuala Lumpur: University of Malaya, 1987.

———. "Ethnic Fratricide in Sri Lanka: An Update." In *Ethnicities and Nations,* edited by Remo Guidieri, Francesco Pellizzi, and Stanley J. Tambiah. Austin: University of Texas Press, 1988.

———. *Sri Lanka: Ethnic Fratricide and the Dismantling of Democracy.* Chicago: University of Chicago Press, 1986.

———. *World Conqueror and World Renouncer.* Cambridge: Cambridge University Press, 1976.

Tennekoon, N. Serena. "Rituals of Development: The Accelerated Mahavali Development Program of Sri Lanka." *American Ethnologist* 15, no. 2 (1988): 294–310.

Vittachi, Tarzie. *Emergency '58: The Story of the Ceylon Race Riots.* London: Andre Deutsch, 1958.

Wijewardena (Vijayawardhana), D. C. *Dharma-Vijaya, or The Revolt in the Temple.* Colombo: Sinha Publications, 1953.

Wilson, A. Jeyaratnam. *The Break-up of Sri Lanka: The Sinhalese-Tamil Conflict.* Honolulu: University of Hawaii Press, 1988.

Wirz, Paul. *Exorcism and the Art of Healing in Ceylon.* Leiden: Brill, 1954.

Wriggins, W. Howard. *Dilemmas of a New Nation.* Princeton, N.J.: Princeton University Press, 1960.

Index

Stochastic Effects (Late Effects of Radiation)

Bioeffects that occur years after exposure to low doses of radiation (less than 0.25 Gy) are considered stochastic effects or late effects.

Stochastic effects are those for which the probability of the effect increases as the dose increases and for which there is no threshold dose. For stochastic effects, there is no risk-free dose.

Stochastic effects can occur at the local tissue level and can cause life-span shortening, radiation-induced malignancy, and hereditary effects.

Tissue Effects

These effects are non-malignancies that can appear in the skin, eyes, and chromosomes.

- "The skin develops a weathered, callused, and discolored appearance" (Bushong, 1997).
- Damage has been observed in the chromosomes of circulatory lymphocytes.
- Cataracts have also been observed in the eye as a late effect of radiation.

It is important to note that these effects are not significant in diagnostic radiology, except for skin damage from patients who may have lengthy interventional angiographic procedures.

Life-Span Shortening

There is no need for radiologists and technologists working in diagnostic radiology to be concerned about life-span effects.

Radiation-Induced Cancers

Cancer induction is the most significant stochastic effect of radiation. The evidence stems from radium dial painters, uranium miners, atomic bomb survivors, patients exposed to radiation in fluoroscopy, and for ankylosing spondylitis.

Additionally, cancer induction is associated with tissues and organs that are highly radiosensitive, such as the lymphoid tissue, bone marrow, the breast and gonads, and the gastrointestinal tract.

Radiation-induced cancers include:

- Leukemia. The incidence of leukemia is dependent on the dose (incidences increase with increased dose). Leukemia may appear 2 to 3 years after exposure.
- Lung cancer
- Breast cancer
- Thyroid cancer
- Bone cancer
- Liver cancer

Hereditary Effects

Hereditary effects are stochastic or late effects that occur in the offspring of the irradiated individual.

Irradiation of germ cells (spermatozoa or ova) can result in:

- Chromosomal mutations
- Gene mutations

Genetic effects of radiation have been studied extensively in animals, the results of which have been extrapolated to humans because the data for humans is limited. As Travis (1997) points out:

- Most mutations are harmful.
- Any dose of radiation, no matter how small, can cause genetic changes.
- There is a linear relationship between dose and the number of mutations, thus information after low doses can be extrapolated from high-dose data.
- Man is not more sensitive than mouse and may in fact be less sensitive.
- Mouse data can provide reasonable estimates of the risk of radiation-induced genetic effects in humans.

RADIATION EXPOSURE IN UTERO

The human embryo and fetus are highly sensitive to radiation, thus every effort must be made to protect them from unnecessary radiation exposure.

Travis points out that the effects of radiation on the embryo and fetus can be placed into three categories, which she refers to as the "classic triad of radiation embryologic syndromes" (1997). This triad includes lethal effects, congenital malformations, and growth disturbances.

- Lethal effects can occur before or after implantation of the fertilized ovum, as well as during intrauterine development. Death can occur before birth or at birth. In utero exposure during preimplantation will result in a high probability of prenatal (before birth) deaths since this is a highly radiosensitive period.
- Congenital malformations arise as a result of in-utero radiation exposure during major organogenesis. Effects include a high incidence of abnormalities and neonatal death (death at birth). Examples of abnormalities include skeletal and organ abnormalities, microcephaly (small head), and mental retardation.
- Growth disturbances can occur before birth or after birth.

Exposure at the fetal stage results in a reduced percentage of abnormalities or deaths. However, cancer and other malignancies may appear in later years (late effects or stochastic effects).

The following points are noteworthy, according to Bushong:

- "The first two weeks of pregnancy are the safest because the only response is resorption of the conceptus and therefore no pregnancy."
- "During the second to tenth week of pregnancy, the most likely response is a congenital abnormality."
- "During any stage of pregnancy, radiation can induce a malignancy that will appear during childhood."
- "The first trimester is more sensitive than the second, which is more sensitive than the third trimester" (1998).

Current Standards for Radiation Protection

Chapter at a glance

In Chapter 4, the bioeffects of radiation are described. In summary, there are two types of bioeffects:

- *Deterministic effects.* These are effects (nonstochastic) for which the severity of the effect increases as the dose increases, and for which there is a threshold dose; below this threshold, no effect occurs. Examples of such effects include skin reddening (erythema), epilation (loss of hair), cataracts, and impairment of fertility. These effects require high doses of radiation, greater than 0.5 Gy (50 rads), and are also referred to as early effects of radiation.

- *Stochastic effects.* These are effects for which the probability of occurrence increases with increasing dose and for which there is no threshold dose, meaning that there is no risk-free dose. With doses of less than 0.5 Gy (50 rad), cancer and genetic damage are a concern. Stochastic effects are also referred to as late effects, among which radiation-induced malignant disease (which may appear years after the exposure) is of a major concern in diagnostic radiology.

The purpose of this chapter is to outline the essential elements of the steps to prevent deterministic effects and minimize stochastic effects. In other words, this chapter examines the objectives of radiation protection and the two triads that serve as a framework for radiation protection.

These concepts are important to the technologist because patients receive exposures in radiology that are intended to provide some benefit, namely, to restore health. The objectives and two triads of radiation protection help us to optimize the examination so that the patient (and others involved in the examination) receive minimal radiation exposure without compromising image quality.

Radiation Protection Organizations

There are several radiation protection organizations responsible for providing guidelines and recommendations on radiation protection. While some of these address radiation risks, others are devoted to radiation protection based on the radiation risks data.

Important organizations include:

- The International Commission on Radiologic Protection (ICRP), founded in 1928, issued Publication 26 in 1977. Subsequently in 1990, the commission issued Publication 60, which provides updated recommendations to Publication 26. These two reports provide the basis for regulations and recommendations, not only in the United States and Canada but also in other countries as well.

- The International Commission on Radiological Units and Measurements (ICRU), established in 1925, deals primarily with radiation quantities and units and measurement techniques. This commission ensures uniform reporting of data and information on radiation risks and protection.

- The United Nations Scientific Committee on the Effects of Atomic Radiation (UNSCEAR) is a committee that issues reports concerning the risks associated with radiation.

- The Biological Effects of Ionizing Radiation Committee (BEIR) also deals with radiation risks. In 1990, BEIR issued Report V, which provides updated information on radiation risks. This report states that the risks of radiation are three to four times greater than they (BEIR) had previously estimated. It was this finding that led the ICRP to revise their radiation protection guidelines and recommendations in 1990.

- The National Council on Radiation Protection and Measurements (NCRP) is a United States organization that advises federal and state regulators on matters of radiation protection.

- The Food and Drug Administration (FDA) in the United States regulates the design and manufacture of x-ray equipment; the regulations are in *Title 21 of the Code of Federal Regulations (CFR)*.

- In Canada, the organization responsible for radiation protection in diagnostic radiology is the Radiation Protection Bureau, Health Canada (RPB-HC). For diagnostic radiology, recommendations are stated in *Safety Code-20A: X-Ray Equipment in Medical Diagnosis—Part A: Recommended Safety Procedures for Installation and Use.*

OBJECTIVES OF RADIATION PROTECTION

The objectives of a radiation protection are twofold:

- To prevent the occurrence of deterministic effects by ensuring that doses are kept below the threshold levels.

- To minimize the induction of stochastic effects by using a radiation-protection philosophy that ensures that radiologic examinations are optimized to produce the best image quality with the minimum radiation dose to the patient.

A radiation protection philosophy that forms the basis of current radiation protection criteria and standards can achieve these objectives.

RADIATION PROTECTION CRITERIA AND STANDARDS

Radiation protection criteria and standards are based on two triads (Figure 5-1):

- Radiation Protection Principles
- Radiation Protection Actions

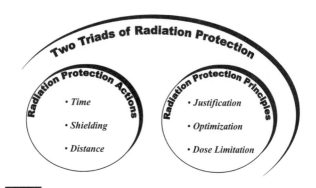

Figure 5-1 Two triads of radiation protection. *(Reproduced with permission from Seeram E. Dose in CT.* Radiologic Tech *July-August 1999; 70(6)534–556.)*

Radiation Protection Principles

The ICRP advocates the following three principles of radiation protection that are currently used by the NCRP and the RPB-HC to provide guidelines for the safe use of radiation when imaging patients:

- *Justification.* There should be a net benefit associated with exposure to ionizing radiation in light of the known risks of radiation. As pointed out by Wolbarst, "Justification provides an essential moral stance for the intelligent use of radiation" (1993).

- *Optimization-ALARA.* The principle of optimization ensures that doses are kept As Low As Reasonably Achievable (ALARA), with economic and social factors taken into account. The ICRP also uses the term optimization of radiation protection (ORP). ALARA and ORP are synonymous.

- *ALARA.* ALARA dictates that technologists optimize radiologic examinations by practicing the guidelines and recommendations for the safe and prudent use of radiation when imaging patients. Essentially, ALARA deals with the technical elements of radiation protection, which are intended to ensure optimal image quality using minimal radiation doses. These technical elements will be described later in another chapter. As Wolbarst points out, "Optimization of the use of radiation is thus viewed as a general societal cost-benefit issue" (1993).

■ *Dose limitation.* This principle addresses the legal limits on the radiation dose received per year or accumulated over a working lifetime for persons who are occupationally exposed and for others as well. There are no limits for patients. The ICRP and national radiation protection organizations such as the NCRP and RPB-HC have established these limits. Additionally, these limits are intended to minimize stochastic effects to acceptable levels and certainly to prevent deterministic effects since they are well below threshold doses.

Radiation Protection Actions

These actions are the second triad of radiation protection and include time, shielding, and distance.

■ *Time.* Because the exposure dose is directly proportional to the time of exposure, keeping the time as short as possible will reduce the dose to the individual exposed.

■ *Shielding.* This aspect involves the use of materials such as concrete or lead between the source of the radiation exposure and the individual exposed. Lead is used in aprons and in the walls of x-ray rooms. The lead will attenuate the radiation, thus reducing the intensity of the beam. Lead aprons are worn by radiation workers in fluoroscopy, for example, and are also used for gonadal shielding.

■ *Distance.* Distance is governed by the inverse square law stated as:

$$I \, \alpha \, \frac{1}{d^2}$$

where I is the radiation intensity and d is the distance between the individual exposed and the source of radiation. The law states that the radiation intensity (dose) is inversely proportional to the square of the distance. Therefore the dose decreases as the distance increases. If the distance from the radiation source is doubled, then the dose decreases by a factor of four. This law has applications in mobile and operating room radiography and in fluoroscopy. Because the patient is the main source of scatter, the technologists performing mobile radiography and fluoroscopy should stand as far away as possible from the patient when exposing the patient to the radiation beam.

For mobile radiography units, the NCRP recommends that the length of the exposure cord be at least two meters in length. In Canada, RPB-HC recommends a length of three meters. These lengths allow the technologist to stand between 2 and 3 meters from the patient during mobile work.

RECOMMENDED DOSE LIMITS

As stated earlier in this chapter, dose limitation is an important element in radiation protection. Dose limitation is based on the fact that radiation can cause biologic harm. That is, radiation can produce stochastic effects and deterministic effects. The following aspects regarding dose limitation are significant. Dose limits have been set:

- To minimize the risks of stochastic effects
- Using the linear dose-response model without a threshold
- For occupational and non-occupational exposures
- By the ICRP and the NCRP (United States) and the RPB (Health Canada) and are expressed as effective dose (E)

Dose Limits for Occupational Exposure

Occupational exposures are incurred by virtue of work. The dose limits for occupational exposure have been set for uniform whole-body exposure and individual organs, excluding exposures from medical procedures and from natural background.

Technologists wear TLD dosimeters to measure their occupational exposures. Although the TLD does not measure the effective dose (E), "for regulatory compliance it is considered to be E" (Bushong, 1998).

- The ICRP recommended dose limit for occupation exposure is 20 mSv per year averaged over defined periods of 5 years.
- The ICRP recommended dose limits for the lens of the eye, skin, and hands and feet, are 150 mSv/year, 500 mSv/year, and 500 mSv/year, respectively.

- The dose limits recommended by the NCRP (1993) for occupational exposures are 50 mSv per year; while it is 10 mSv × age of the individual for a cumulative dose limit.
- The NCRP (1993) recommended annual dose limits for the lens of the eye; skin, hands, and feet are 150 mSv and 500 mSv, respectively.
- The NCRP recommended annual dose limits for students (under the age of 18) in training is 1 mSv; while it is 15 mSv and 50 mSv per year for the lens of the eye; skin, hands, and feet, respectively. Students above the age of 18 are subject to the same limits for occupational exposure.
- The RPB (Health Canada) recommended annual dose limits for occupational exposures are the same as the ICRP limits.

Dose Limits for Pregnant Workers

With regard to pregnant workers who are in the occupational exposure category, the fetus is "normally considered to be a member of the public" (Huda, 1995). Pregnant workers wear TLD dosimeters under the apron to monitor dose limits to the embryo-fetus. Bushong notes that:

- "Once pregnancy is known, the recommended dose limit for the embryo-fetus takes precedence over the dose limit for the pregnant radiation worker" (1998).
- The NCRPs recommended dose limits for the fetus is:
  - ❏ 0.5 mSv per month
  - ❏ 5.0 mSv for the 9-month period
- The ICRPs recommended dose limit for the fetus (9 months) is 1 mSv.

Dose Limits for Members of the Public

Members of the public are individuals who accompany patients having x-ray examinations and are waiting in a room in close proximity to an x-ray room. In general, recommended dose limits for these individuals are about $1/10$ that of occupationally exposed individuals.

- For persons who receive continuous or frequent exposures, the NCRP annual limit is 1 mSv; for persons who receive infrequent exposures, the limit is 5 mSv.

■ The NCRP annual dose limits for the lens of the eye; skin, hands, and feet (for members of the public) are 15 mSv and 50 mSv, respectively.

In this respect, radiology facilities must be shielded (i.e., the walls of x-ray rooms should be lined with lead to ensure that the dose limits to the public are not exceeded).

Dose Factors in Radiography

Chapter at a glance

There are numerous factors affecting the dose to the patient in radiography. To optimize image quality using exposures as low as reasonably achievable (ALARA), it is mandatory that technologists have a firm understanding of how these factors influence patient dose.

The purpose of this chapter is to review the major factors contributing to patient dose in radiography and to outline the components of a radiographic imaging system that determine the overall quality of the examination. We will begin with the latter.

MAJOR COMPONENTS OF A RADIOGRAPHIC IMAGING SYSTEM

The major components of a radiographic imaging system are illustrated in Figure 6-1. These include:

- *X-ray generator.* This electrical unit provides the power to the x-ray tube. It allows the technologist to select and control x-ray production in terms of both the quality and the quantity of the radiation beam emanating from the x-ray tube. The generator can be single-phase, three-

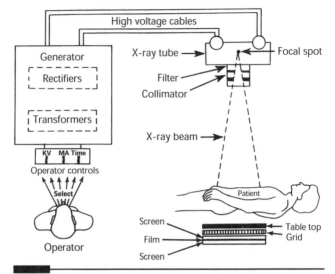

Figure 6-1 The major components of a radiographic imaging system. *(Reproduced with permission from Sprawls P. Principles of radiography for technologists. Gaithersburg, MD: Aspen Publishers, 1990.)*

phase, and high-frequency, depending on the various types of examinations in the radiology department. The high-frequency generator represents state-of-the-art equipment for imaging systems, whether for radiography, fluoroscopy, angiography, or computed tomography.

■ *Operator controls.* These controls are numerous and varied. However, the most significant is the exposure factor controls, which allow the technologist to select the kilovoltage (kVp), the milliamperage (mA), and the exposure time (seconds) appropriate to the nature of the examination. The kVp controls the quality or penetrating power of the radiation beam; the mAs controls the quantity of photons in the beam. Other controls that can be selected include the use of grids (Bucky selection) and automatic exposure control (AEC).

■ *X-ray tube.* The x-ray tube produces x-rays to meet the requirements of the examination. The type of x-ray tube determines the x-ray beam characteristics, which can play a role in determining the dose to the patients, as well as the image quality for the examination. The focal-spot size, for example, affects the detail of the image; however, it can also affect the dose from penumbral effects. The x-ray tube itself is not a controlling factor of dose, thus it will not be discussed further in this chapter.

■ *Filters.* These thin metal plates, usually made of aluminum, are inserted in the x-ray beam to remove low-energy photons from the beam. These photons do not play a role in image formation but increase patient dose because they do not have enough energy to penetrate the patient. For radiation protection of the patient, filters must be included in any x-ray imaging system.

■ *Collimator.* A collimator is a device for restricting or limiting the primary beam to the area of interest being imaged. Other beam restricting devices include cones, cylinders, and aperture diaphragms. Automatic beam collimation is referred to as primary beam limitation (PBL). Currently all collimators are equipped with this feature. Collimation determines the size of the radiation beam striking the patient.

■ *X-ray beam.* The quality and quantity of the x-ray beam are under the direct control of the technologist. Quality and quantity affect dose and image quality. Several factors affect beam quality and quantity (Chapter 2), and they are described later in this chapter.

■ *Patient.* The patient can be considered a major component of an imaging system in terms of dose considerations. More importantly, both the patient thickness and the density affect the dose in an examination.

■ *Table top.* Although not a major factor affecting dose to the patient, table tops made of high-attenuating materials will increase the dose to the patient.

■ *Grids.* These antiscatter devices are used to improve radiographic image contrast by absorbing scattered radiation from the patient, thus preventing scatter from reaching the film. The essential characteristics of grids that determine their efficiency at removing scattered radiation are the grid ratio, grid frequency (number of lines [lead strips] per inch or per centimeter), and several others. However, the major characteristic affecting dose is the grid ratio (a ratio of the height of the grid strips to the thickness of the interspace material between them). The ratio common to fixed radiographic systems is 12:1. Grids can be stationary or moving. Stationary grids are used in portable radiography; moving grids are essential devices in radiographic tables.

- **Film-screen combination.** This aspect refers to the image receptor. The important characteristics of the image receptor are the sensitivity or speed of the screens used in cassettes and the materials making up the front of the cassette. Radiographic screens can be fast (high-speed) and require little radiation to form the image, or they can be slow (low-speed), in which case they require more radiation to create acceptable images. The choice of the film-screen combination depends on the nature and type of examination.

- **Film processor.** One important component of a radiographic imaging system not shown in Figure 6-1 is the film processor. Proper processing is essential to optimize image quality and reduce dose to patients by eliminating the need to repeat the examination as a result of poor processing.

Factors Affecting Dose in Radiography

The major factors affecting dose in radiography include beam energy and filtration, exposure technique factors, beam collimation, the size of the x-ray field, the size of the patient, source-to-image receptor distance, grids, image receptor speed or sensitivity, and film processing conditions. Each of these will now be examined briefly.

Beam Energy and Filtration

The energy of the x-ray beam is often expressed as the beam quality or the penetrating power of the beam. Beam energy is dependent on at least three factors.

- *Peak kilovoltage or kVp.* Peak kilovoltage or kVp is the voltage applied between the cathode and anode, which affects the energy of the photons striking the patient. High kVp results in higher energy photons and a more penetrating beam; low-kVp techniques produce low-energy photons and a less penetrating beam. The dose to the patient is less for high-kVp techniques compared with low-kVp techniques since more photons are transmitted through the patient. In addition, at low kVp, photoelectric absorption predominates and the patient absorbs more photons, thus the dose increases.

- *X-ray generator.* The generator determines the voltage waveform across the x-ray tube. An important characteristic that describes the way in which the voltage is supplied to the tube is the ripple. When the value of the ripple is low, the efficiency of the generator is greater. Among the three types of generators mentioned earlier—single-phase, three-phase, and high-frequency—the high-frequency has the lowest ripple, which is less than 3%, compared with 100%, 13%, and 4% for single-phase full wave, three-phase six-pulse, and three-phase twelve-pulse generators, respectively.

  This factor means that a high-frequency generator can deliver greater x-ray quality and quantity compared with single- and three-phase generators. Additionally, higher kVp values (lower mAs) can be used to decrease the dose to the patient.

- *Filtration.* Filtration is intended to protect the patient by removing the low-energy photons in the x-ray beam. Filters are added to the x-ray tube (added filtration), which reduce the quantity of photons and increase the mean energy (quality) of the beam. The beam becomes harder (loss of low-energy photons) or more penetrating. Filtration reduces patient skin dose.

In radiography, aluminum is used as an added filter, the thickness of which depends on the kilovoltage used. The NCRP recommends that for most general radiographic examinations, the total filtration in the beam should be at least a 2.5 aluminum equivalent.

Exposure Technique Factors

Exposure technique factors include kVp, mA, and time of the exposure. These factors are under the direct control of the technologist who determines the appropriate set of factors, depending on the type of examination. These factors control the quality and quantity of radiation reaching the patient, thus they affect the dose in several ways.

- As noted earlier, kVp determines the penetration of the beam and controls the beam quality. High-kVp techniques decrease the dose to the patient, since more radiation penetrates the patient with less absorption.
- The mA determines the quantity of photons falling on the patient. The radiation dose is directly proportional to the mA. If the mA is doubled, then the dose is increased by a factor of two.
- The exposure time is directly proportional to the dose. If the time is doubled, then the dose is increased by a factor of two.
- Automatic exposure control (AEC) is designed to reduce exposures to patients since repeat exposures are minimized.

Beam Collimation

Collimation is a radiation protection mechanism included in the ALARA philosophy.

- Collimation reduces the dose to the patient by restricting the size of the radiation beam to the area of clinical interest. This protects the patient from unnecessary exposure.
- Collimation improves radiographic quality because the amount of scattered radiation reaching the film and the total mass of the patient irradiated is decreased.

Patient Size

The technologist has no control over the size of the patient, however:

- As the thickness and the density (mass per unit volume) increase, the dose to the patient increases, because more radiation is required to produce the image.
- Technologists should always use technique charts that provide proper exposure factors for various examinations and patient sizes.

Source-to-Image Receptor Distance

The source-to-image receptor distance (SID) or the source-to-skin distance are major factors that affect patient dose. Most radiology examinations are given at 101 cm (40 in) because:

- At a short SID, the dose to the patient increases, the radiation beam is more divergent at the patient's surface, and the concentration of photons (surface exposure) increases.
- A long SID produces a less divergent beam at the patient's surface and reduces patient dose, since the concentration of photons (or surface exposure) decreases.

Radiographic Antiscatter Grids

A grid improves radiographic contrast by absorbing scattered radiation from the patient thus preventing it from reaching the film. Whenever a grid is used in an examination, the dose to the patient increases compared with nongrid examinations. Among the performance characteristics of a grid, the grid ratio affects the dose to the patient.

- As the grid ratio increases, the dose to the patient increases.
- High-ratio grids should be used with high-kVp techniques.
- When high-ratio grids are used with high-kVp techniques, the dose to the patient decreases, because more radiation is transmitted through the patient and not absorbed by the patient. The entrance dose for a 12:1 grid at 90 kVp is 395 mrad, while the entrance dose is 290 mrad at 110 kVp (Bushong, 1997).
- Moving grids that have the same characteristics as stationary grids requiring approximately 15% more exposure. Therefore moving grids increase the dose to the patient (Bushong, 1997).

Image Receptor Speed or Sensitivity

The image receptor is the film-screen combination used to produce images of the patient. The speed refers to the amount of radiation used to produce the image (i.e., sensitivity refers to the overall efficiency of the image receptor). Image receptor speeds are expressed as numbers with 100 assigned to par-speed calcium tungstate screens. Speeds can be 200, 400, 800, and even as high as 1000.

Calcium tungstate has been replaced by rare-earth phosphors, which are significantly more efficient in absorbing x-rays (absorption efficiency) and converting them to light (conversion efficiency) than calcium tungstate screens.

- The dose to the patient (including gonadal dose) is inversely proportional to the sensitivity of the image receptor.
- This factor means that increasing the speed by a factor of two (i.e., going from a 200-speed system to a 400-speed system) will reduce the dose by one half.
- Depending on the phosphors being used and their conversion efficiencies, rare-earth image receptors can reduce exposures by 50% or more, compared with calcium tungstate screens.
- Image receptors with carbon fiber fronts will reduce the dose by 6% to 12% compared with cassettes having aluminum fronts.

Film Processing Conditions

When a film is exposed, it must be processed. Film processing should be performed according to the manufacturer's recommendations. Processing parameters, such as processing solution temperatures, replenishment rates, and film transport rates, must be within optimal values to produce good image quality.

- Poorly processed films lead to repeat examinations, thus directly affecting the patient dose.
- Repeat examinations in this respect can double patient dose (ICRP, 1993).

CHAPTER 7

Dose Factors in Fluoroscopy

Chapter at a glance

Fluoroscopy is an x-ray imaging technique that allows the radiologist to observe real-time images on a television screen to study the dynamics or motion of organ systems, particularly circulation and hollow internal anatomy. Fluoroscopy can provide diagnosis and guidance in interventional x-ray studies.

There are several reasons why the dose in fluoroscopy is important to radiology workers:

- Several recent reports indicate that patient doses in fluoroscopy are extremely high compared with most radiology procedures, and that some patients have experienced radiation-induced injuries such as skin burns (Parry et al., 1999).

- Occupational exposures are highest in fluoroscopy (Bushong, 1997).

■ The technologist is an integral part of the fluoroscopic examination and is present in the room to deal with the patient and to assist the radiologist during the fluoroscopic portion of the examination.

The purpose of this chapter is to provide a description of the major components of a fluoroscopic system and to highlight the significant factors affecting patient dose in fluoroscopy.

MAJOR COMPONENTS OF A FLUOROSCOPIC IMAGING SYSTEM

The basic fluoroscopic imaging system for use in routine gastrointestinal tract examinations is shown in Figure 7-1. These systems, however, are rapidly being replaced by digital fluoroscopic imaging systems (Figure 7-2). The major components in the imaging chain are:

■ *X-ray tube and generator.* The x-ray generator provides the power to the x-ray tube for the production of x-rays.

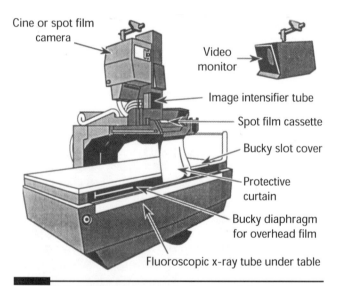

Figure 7-1 Major components of a fluoroscopic imaging system used for routine gastrointestinal tract examinations. (See text for further explanation.) *(Reproduced with permission from Bushong S. Radiologic science for technologists. 6th ed. St. Louis: Mosby, 2001.)*

In fluoroscopy, the kVp is high and the mA is low, since the x-ray tube is energized continuously. Naturally, other factors affect the choice of exposure aspects in fluoroscopy. For under-table fluoroscopy, the x-ray tube is located below the table; for overhead or over-table fluoroscopy, the x-ray tube is positioned over the table and is used for both fluoroscopy and radiography (films taken after the fluoroscopic portion of the examination). These films are generally referred to as "overhead films".

■ *Image intensifier tube.* The purpose of the image intensifier tube in the fluoroscopic imaging chain is to increase the brightness of the fluoroscopic image using extremely low mA values applied to the x-ray tube. Radiation transmitted through the patient falls on an input screen (cesium iodide phosphor) that converts x-ray photons to light. The light photons, in turn, are converted to electrons by a photocathode in the tube. These electrons are subsequently accelerated across the tube to strike an output screen that is approximately $1/10$ the diameter of the input screen (zinc cadmium sulfide phosphor). The image at the output screen is increased in brightness from the acceleration of the electrons and the minification at the output screen. This image cannot be observed directly, thus it must be sent to a monitor for display and viewing.

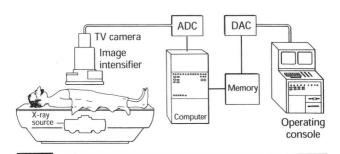

Figure 7-2 Major components of a digital fluoroscopic imaging system. (See text for further explanation.) *(Reproduced with permission from Bushong S. Radiologic science for technologists. 6th ed. St. Louis: Mosby, 2001.)*

To aid in visualization and diagnosis, image intensifiers can also magnify the image viewed on the television monitor. Magnification plays a significant role in the dose to the patient.

- **Image distributor.** This component of the imaging chain distributes the light from the output screen of the image intensifier tube. Approximately 90% of the light reaches the film recording camera (cine or spot-film camera); 10% is directed to the television camera.

- **Television camera or charge-coupled device.** The image at the output screen is picked up using a television camera tube or a solid-state device called a charge-coupled device (CCD) and is transmitted via a coaxial cable to the television monitor.

- **Television monitor.** The television monitor receives a video signal from the television camera tube or CCD and creates the image on the output screen of the image intensifier tube. The television monitor is the picture tube or cathode ray tube that displays the image for viewing by the radiologist.

- **Spot-film recording devices.** These devices include cassette-loaded spot films and films recorded by photo-spot cameras. Cassette-loaded spot films are considered large-format films (8 × 10 or 10 × 12); photo-spot film sizes range from 70 to 105 mm.

When using cassette-loaded spot films, the technologist assists the radiologist by loading and unloading these films from the spot-film device. This process tends to delay the completion of the examination. The large-format films offer better image quality and are exposed using radiographic factors.

The use of the photo-spot camera decreases the examination time since there is no interruption of the procedure to load and unload the spot-film device. The image quality, however, is not as good as cassette-loaded spot films. Photo-spot camera films are exposed using fluoroscopic exposure factors.

FACTORS AFFECTING DOSE IN FLUOROSCOPY

The major factors affecting the dose to the patient in fluoroscopy include:

- Beam energy or filtration
- Tube current
- Beam-on time
- Automatic dose-rate control
- Collimation
- Source-to-skin distance
- Patient-to-image intensifier distance
- Patient size
- Antiscatter grids
- Image magnification
- Last image hold
- Image recording method
- Pulsed fluoroscopy

Beam Energy

Beam energy refers to the penetrating power of the x-ray photons in the x-ray beam emanating from the x-ray tube. Kilovoltage (kVp), filtration, and the type of x-ray generator used to provide power to the x-ray tube affect the beam energy.

- When the kVp is high, the penetration of the x-ray beam is greater, and more photons are transmitted through the patient (less absorption), lowering the dose to the patient.
- Higher kVp beams, however, result in a loss of image contrast.
- Fluoroscopic imaging systems are provided with filters for the purpose of protecting the patient.
- Filters reduce the dose to the patient by absorbing the low-energy photons from the x-ray beam that are absorbed by the patient's skin surface and fail to reach the film.

- The removal of these photons increases the mean energy of the beam, thus increasing the penetrating power of the beam. The result is a smaller dose to the patient, since more photons are transmitted to the image receptor.

- High-frequency generators produce more photons with higher energies compared with single-phase and three-phase x-ray generators. Higher beam energies allow patients to receive a smaller dose.

Tube Current

The *tube current* is the mA. In fluoroscopy, the mA is low because the fluoroscopic exposure time can range from minutes to hours. Additionally, since high kVp values are generally used, the mA is reduced substantially.

- Fluoroscopic mA range from 1 to 3 mA.

- Lower kVp, however, will increase the mA(s), thus increasing the dose to the patient.

Beam-On Time

The *beam-on time* refers to the length of time that the x-ray tube is energized to produce x-rays for real-time image display.

- Continuous exposures increase beam-on time, thus increasing patient dose. The dose is directly proportional to the exposure time. If the beam-on time is doubled, the dose is increased by a factor of two.

- Short, intermittent exposures reduce patient dose, which is referred to as intermittent fluoroscopy (short-bursts of beam-on time).

Automatic Dose-Rate Control

Automatic dose-rate control (ADC) is also referred to as automatic brightness control (ABC) and is a technique that maintains the image brightness on the television monitor when the anatomic part thickness changes.

- When a nonuniform object such as a wedge (or from the patient's neck to abdomen) is being examined by fluoroscopy, the image brightness will change as the x-ray tube moves from the thick part to the thin part and from bright to extremely bright, respectively.

■ The x-ray beam intensity (therefore the dose) increases as the tube moves from the thick part to the thin part. Without ADC the dose to the thin part increases.

■ With ADC the exposure technique factors change automatically to maintain the same brightness of the image as the tube moves from the thicker to the thinner anatomic part.

Collimation

As stated in Chapter 6, *collimation* is intended to protect the patient from unnecessary radiation by limiting or restricting the beam to the clinical area of interest.

■ Fluoroscopy collimators ensure that the clinical area of interest receive minimal radiation by shaping the beam to cover only the desired region under study.

■ The smallest possible field size is recommended to ensure low doses to the patient.

■ Collimation also ensures good quality images by reducing the amount of scattered radiation reaching the image receptor (image intensifier input screen).

Source-to-Skin Distance

The source-to-skin distance (SSD) in fluoroscopy can affect the dose to the patient. The SSD can be described by three fluoroscopic beam geometrics (Figure 7–3, A–C).

■ The patient dose is reduced when the image intensifier tube is close to the patient and the x-ray tube is farther away from the patient (see Figure 7-3, C). This arrangement represents the best geometry of the three.

■ Two poor geometries are shown (see Figure 7-3, A and B). The x-ray tube is too close to the patient (see Figure 7-3, A), thus the dose is greater compared with the position shown in Figure 7-3, C.

■ Although the x-ray tube is farther away from the patient (see Figure 7-3, B), the image intensifier tube is too far away from the patient. This results in a greater dose to the patient compared with that shown in Figure 7-3, C.

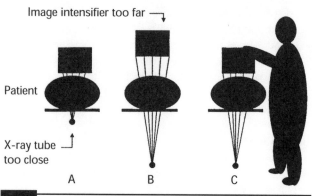

Figure 7-3 Three fluoroscopic beam geometries that describe the source-to-skin distance affecting dose to the patient. (See text for further explanation.) *(Reproduced with permission from Brateman L. Radiation safety consideration for diagnostic radiology personnel.* Radiographics *1999;19: 1037-1055.)*

Patient-to-Image Intensifier Distance

The distance between the patient and the image intensifier tube is another factor affecting the dose to the patient in fluoroscopy.

- When the distance between the patient and image intensifier is reduced, the dose to the patient will be lower compared with other scenarios.
- The scenario shown in Figure 7-3, C, is considered as the best practice in fluoroscopy.

Patient Size

This factor is not under the control of the fluoroscopist.

- Thicker patients will require more radiation to produce optimal image brightness, detail, and contrast compared with thinner patients.
- The kVp and mA must be increased to image thicker patients, resulting in a higher patient dose.

Antiscatter Grids

A grid is used in fluoroscopy to improve image contrast by preventing scattered radiation from reaching the input screen of the image intensifier tube.

- Grids introduced into the radiation beam during the examination will increase the patient dose by a factor of two or more. Therefore not using a grid can reduce the dose by a factor of two or more.
- Increasing the distance between the patient and the image intensifier tube by a reasonable quantity, can reduce the scattered radiation by using the air-gap technique (radiation scattered at extremely oblique angles will fall out of the gap and will not reach the image intensifier tube).

Image Magnification

The image in fluoroscopy can be magnified to facilitate diagnosis. *Image magnification* can be achieved by geometric and electronic means. The former involves increasing the distance between the patient and the image intensifier tube; the latter involves collimating the beam automatically to fall only on a small central portion of the image intensifier input screen.

- Geometric magnification increases the patient dose in fluoroscopy, as described earlier.
- Electronic magnification results in an increase in mA to maintain the brightness level on the television monitor, thus increasing the dose to the patient.
- The dose increase is approximately equal to the ratio of the sizes of the input screen used for the normal mode and for the magnification mode.
- A dual-mode (25/17 cm) image intensifier tube will deliver 2.2 times ($25^2 \div 17^2$) more dose to the patient when operating in the 17 cm mode, or the magnification mode (Bushong, 1997).

Last Image Hold

Last image hold is a technique used to describe images that can be stored digitally and displayed on the television continuously without the need for continuous fluoroscopy. Usually the last image is displayed on the monitor electronically for a period. Last-image-hold techniques can reduce patient dose by 50% to 80% (Bushberg, 1994).

Image Recording Methods

Several methods are used to record the fluoroscopic image, referred to as spot-filming methods. These methods include the use of cassette-loaded spot films, films taken with photo-spot cameras, and cine films. Since recording is no longer used in routine fluoroscopy, it is not described in this text.

- As the film size is increased, the image quality and the patient dose are increased.
- The cassette-loaded spot film (spot film) produces the best image quality compared with other recording methods, but results in the greatest dose to the patient. Remember that radiographic factors are used to record images on a cassette-loaded spot film.
- Photo-spot camera film can range from 70 mm to 105 mm. In general, the film size is directly proportional to the dose to the patient.
- The patient dose with 105 mm films is about one half of that obtained with spot films (Bushong, 1997). Fluoroscopic exposure technique factors (high-kVp and low-mA) are used to record images taken with a photo-spot camera, since the camera uses the light from the output screen of the image intensifier tube (shorter exposure times are also used).

Pulsed Fluoroscopy

Pulsed fluoroscopy is a technique during which the x-ray beam is pulsed (produced in short bursts) compared with being produced continuously.

- Pulsed fluoroscopy reduces the dose to the patient by as much as 90% (depending on the number of pulses per second) compared with non-pulsed units.
- In a study by Hernandez and Goodsitt, radiation exposures were reduced by 75% when the unit was operated at 7.5 pulses per second.
- Pulse fluoroscopy can reduce the scattered radiation exposures to personnel.

- Pulsed fluoroscopy can also be used as an effective means to reduce dose to children undergoing fluoroscopic examination.

SCATTERED RADIATION IN FLUOROSCOPY

Because occupational exposures are highest in fluoroscopy, it is essential to consider the nature of this exposure.

Technologists and radiologists are exposed to scattered radiation in fluoroscopy since they are in the room assisting the patient during the examination.

- The main source of scattered radiation is the patient, although the equipment can produce scattered radiation as well.
- When higher levels of primary beam exposures (also referred to as the high dose-rate mode or high-level control fluoroscopy) are used, more scattered radiation is produced.
- A higher level of scattered radiation reaches the fluoroscopist when the primary beam is off the patient's mid line, because there is less attenuation of the primary beam by the patient since it is closer to the operator.
- Figure 7-4, *A*, illustrates the distribution of scattered radiation when no protective curtain is hanging on the spot-film device. Note that the dose decreases as the distance from the patient increases. The distribution is reduced significantly when a protective curtain is used (Figure 7-4, *B*).
- To reduce occupational exposures in fluoroscopy, always wear lead aprons and try to stand back from the table during beam-on times.
- The radiation monitor must be worn at the level of the collar, outside the protective apron (in the United States) and under the apron at the waist level (in Canada) to record the dose from scattered radiation.

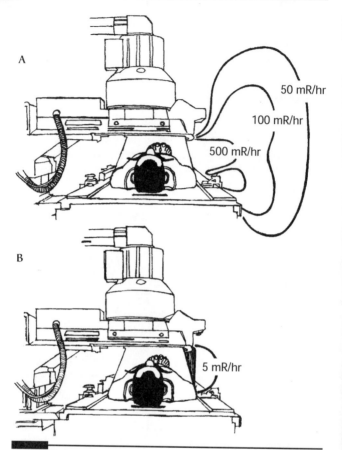

A

50 mR/hr

100 mR/hr

500 mR/hr

B

5 mR/hr

Figure 7-4 **A,** The distribution of scattered radiation from a fluoroscopic unit without a protective curtain hanging from the spot-film device, and **B,** with a protective curtain. *(Reproduced with permission from Bushong S. Radiation protection. New York: McGraw Hill, 1999.)*

CHAPTER 8

Dose Management Techniques

Chapter at a glance

The factors affecting dose in radiography and fluoroscopy are described in Chapters 6 and 7, respectively. This chapter outlines the techniques and methods for dose management.

Dose management examines various methods to reduce the dose to patients, personnel, and members of the public. Dose management is also guided by the two triads of radiation protection: time, shielding, and distance (radiation protection actions) and justification, optimization, and dose limitation (radiation protection principles) described in Chapter 5.

The purpose of this chapter is to summarize the major federal regulations for dose management in radiology, including the guidelines and recommendations for equipment specifications, procedures for minimizing the dose to patients and personnel, and shielding.

Why are these topics important to the technologist? They provide the technologist with the techniques that are mandatory to optimize the examination in an effort to reduce the dose to all individuals who may be exposed to radiation in the radiology department.

FEDERAL REGULATIONS FOR DOSE MANAGEMENT

Safety Reports for Guidelines and Responsibilities

The guidelines and recommendations for dose management are outlined in various reports. In this book, the regulations will be cited from the following radiation safety codes:

- Medical x-ray, electron beam, and gamma ray protection for energies up to 50 MeV: Equipment Design and Use, NCRP Report No. 102.
- Code of Federal Regulations (CFR) Title 21: Performance Standards for Ionizing Radiation Emitting Products, Washington, DC, US Department of Health and Human Services, Food and Drug Administration (FDA).

It is not within the scope of this text to address details of these reports. The student and instructor must refer to them for additional topics not covered here. Specifically, this chapter will focus on major recommendations for equipment specifications, procedures for minimizing dose to patients and personnel, and finally, shielding requirements for radiology.

Definition of Terms in Safety Reports

In the NCRP Report No. 102, the terms *shall* and *should* are used in the recommendations. The exact meanings are as follows:

- Shall and shall not are used to indicate that adherence to the recommendation is considered necessary to meet accepted standards of protection.
- Should and should not are used to indicate a prudent practice to which exceptions may be occasionally made in appropriate circumstances (NCRP, 1989, p. 2).

EQUIPMENT SPECIFICATIONS FOR RADIOGRAPHY

The regulations for equipment specifications are obviously intended for manufacturers of radiation emitting devices such as the x-ray machine. There are specifications particularly intended to protect both patients and operators when x-ray machines are producing radiation.

The specifications for radiographic equipment to be summarized here are those relating to the x-ray control panel, leakage radiation from the x-ray tube, filtration, collimation, source-to-image receptor distance, source-to-skin distance, and the exposure switch for fixed and mobile radiographic systems.

X-Ray Control Panel

The x-ray control panel features warning signs, markings, indicator lights, and various icons to indicate when the machine is being used and to ensure that exposures occur when the operator conducts the examination. The specifications are such that the control panel must:

- Bear visible signs indicating that only authorized and qualified personnel are permitted to operate the equipment.
- Show controls, meters, and lights indicating the operation of the various machine parameters, such as a visible light or audible tone when the exposure is made (when the beam is on).

Leakage Radiation from the X-Ray Tube

The x-ray tube housing must be lined with lead to reduce leakage radiation from the tube such that, at a distance of 1 meter from the x-ray tube, the leakage radiation must not exceed 26 μC/kg per hour (100 mr/hr).

Filtration

Remember that the purpose of filtration is to protect the patient by removing low-energy photons from the x-ray beam. The recommendations from the minimum total filtration (inherent and added) in the useful beam are:

- 2.5 mm aluminum equivalent when the tube is operating above 70 kVp.
- 1.5 mm aluminum equivalent when the tube is operating between 50 and 70 kVp.
- 0.5 mm aluminum equivalent when the tube is operating below 50 kVp.

Note that the thickness of the filter depends on the kVp and increases when the kVp increases.

Collimation and Beam Alignment

Collimation is intended to protect the patient by restricting the beam to the clinical area of interest. The recommendation for collimation and beam alignment is that the x-ray field and the light beam must be aligned to within 2% of the source-to-image receptor distance (SID) at the center of the image receptor.

Source-to-Image Receptor Distance

The SID is important in terms both of image quality and radiation dose. Examinations must be carried out at the correct SID (a chest x-ray should be performed at 180 cm [72 in]). The recommendation is as follows:

- An SID indicator (tape measure or laser measurement system) must be provided with all x-ray systems and it must be accurate to within 2% of the SID used.
- The source-to-film distance for tabletop work in radiography should not be less than 100 cm (40 in).

Source-to-Skin Distance

The source-to-skin distance (SSD) affects dose to the patient given that it determines the concentration of photons per unit area of the surface of the patient. The NCRP recommendation is that the SSD **shall not** be less than 30 cm (12 in) and **should not** be less than 38 cm (15 in).

Exposure Switch for Radiography

The purpose of the exposure switch is to allow the technologist to make an exposure for image formation. Recommendations for the exposure switch are as follows:

- For fixed radiographic equipment, the exposure switch must be on the control panel to ensure that the operator remains in the control booth during the exposure.
- The switch must be a "dead man" switch. That is, pressure must be applied to the switch for the exposure to occur.
- For mobile radiography units, the exposure switch shall be so arranged on a long cord to allow the operator to stand at least 2m (6 ft) from the patient and the unit.

EQUIPMENT SPECIFICATIONS FOR FLUOROSCOPY

The specifications for the fluoroscopic equipment are numerous and therefore only the major categories will be reviewed in this text. These specifications include filtration, collimation, source-to-skin distance, exposure switch, cumulative timer, protective curtain, table and Bucky-slot shielding, and accessory protective clothing.

Filtration

Filtration of the beam used in fluoroscopy is mandatory, and since high kVp beams are generally used in fluoroscopic examinations, the total filtration must be at least a 2.5 aluminum equivalent to protect the patient from low-energy photons.

Collimation

The NCRP recommendations for the collimator in fluoroscopy are:

- The collimator shall be coupled and centered to the image receptor and should be confined to the receptor at any source-to-image receptor distance.
- "For spot film radiography, the shutters shall automatically change to the required field size before each exposure" (*NCRP*, 1989, p. 15).

Source-to-Skin Distance

In fluoroscopy, the SSD **shall not** be less than 38 cm (15 in) for stationary fluoroscopic units and **shall not** be less than 30 cm (12 in) for mobile fluoroscopic units.

Exposure Switch

The exposure switch for fluoroscopy must be a dead-man type of switch. Both the foot switch and the switch on the spot-film device are the dead-man type of switch.

Cumulative Timer

This timer records the beam-on time during the examination.

- The timer shall provide the operator with an audible or visual signal when 5 minutes of beam-on time have elapsed.
- The signal should last at least 15 seconds at which time it must be reset to continue fluoroscopy.

Protective Curtain

A protective lead curtain is part of the fluoroscopic equipment that hangs from the spot-film device to reduce and prevent the scattered radiation from the patient from reaching the radiologist.

- The dimensions of the curtain should be not less than 45.7 cm × 45.7 cm (18 in × 18 in).
- The curtain should have at least 0.25 mm lead equivalent.

Bucky-Slot Shielding and Table

The Bucky slot is an opening on the table about 5 cm wide that allows the operator to move the Bucky tray to one end of the table when fluoroscopy is being conducted. The Bucky slot is shielded by a length of metal that covers the opening to prevent scattered radiation from reaching the operator at the gonadal level.

- Bucky-slot shielding should have a lead-equivalent thickness of at least 0.25 mm.

Similarly, the fluoroscopic table must also provide shielding to prevent scattered radiation from reaching personnel.

- The table should have a lead-equivalent thickness of 0.25 mm.

■ The table should have a lead-equivalent thickness of 0.25 mm to provide protection from scattered radiation.

Accessory Protective Clothing

These items include lead aprons, thyroid shields, and protective gloves worn by operators. Recommendations are as follows:

■ Protective aprons shall have at least a 0.5 mm lead equivalent.

■ Protective thyroid shields shall have at least a 0.5 mm lead equivalent.

■ Protective gloves shall have a lead-equivalent thickness of at least 0.25 mm.

PROCEDURES FOR MINIMIZING DOSE TO PATIENTS AND PERSONNEL

There are a number of practices and procedures to reduce the dose to the patients and personnel and to keep exposures according to the ALARA philosophy. Only the more common-place procedures will be reviewed. Technologists must refer to the safety codes for more detailed information.

Procedural Factors for Minimizing Dose to Patients in Radiography and Fluoroscopy

There are several factors under the direct control of the technologist that are intended to reduce the dose to the patient during the conduct of the examination. It is not within the scope of this book to discuss all of these factors. However, the following actions are significant and illustrative:

■ The radiologist should be consulted to ensure that the examination is warranted, especially in situations that are confusing.

■ Selection of correct film-screen combination (image receptor) should be appropriate to the examination, since the dose is inversely proportional to the sensitivity of the image receptor. Faster image receptor systems are now used to control the dose to the patient without compromising image quality.

■ Selection and use of the best possible exposure technique factors should keep the dose as low as reasonably achievable without compromising image quality. Generally, high-kVp techniques reduce the dose to the patient, as described in Chapter 6.

- The correct use of automatic exposure control can play a significant role in dose reduction, specifically with regard to repeat examinations.

- Repeat examinations should be kept to a minimum. Errors in positioning, exposure technique factors, collimation, and patient motion are major factors that affect repeat rates.

- Collimation to the size of the image receptor or smaller is the preferred action, and evidence of collimation on the film should be shown. Collimation alone can reduce the genetically significant dose (population gonadal dose) by 65%.

- The smallest film size should be chosen to match the diagnostic goal of the examination.

- The optimal source-to-image receptor distance appropriate to the anatomy being imaged should be used.

- Shielding should always be used to protect radiosensitive organs. Careful placement of the shield is mandatory to protect organs, while not compromising the goals of the examination.

During fluoroscopy, paying careful attention to the following factors can minimize the dose to the patient:

- The patient must understand the nature of the examination to avoid repeat exposures. Understanding the breathing instructions and being asked to assume various positions are examples.

- Fluoroscopy must be carried out by an appropriately trained individual, such as a radiologist.

- Although not under the direct control of the technologist, the fluoroscopy time should be kept as short as possible.

- The exposure rate in fluoroscopy must not exceed 2.6 mC/kilogram per minute (10 R per minute).

- Because the radiologist performs the examination, he or she should be certain that the beam is filtered and collimated, and that the fluoroscopic exposure technique is consistent with the clinical objectives of the examination.

Procedural Factors for Minimizing Dose to Personnel

To achieve the goal of reducing the dose to personnel, technologists must work within the ALARA philosophy. Examples of recommendations to ensure personnel dose reduction are:

- Only essential personnel must be present in an x-ray room during the exposure.
- Technologists must remain in the control booth during radiographic exposures and must wear protective aprons when the situation makes this impossible.
- Technologists must always pay attention to patients by observing them through the window in the control booth during the exposure.
- All room doors must be closed during the exposure to prevent scattered radiation from reaching personnel in close proximity to the room.
- Radiology personnel (including technologists) must refrain from holding patients during an examination. Immobilizing devices should be used or other nonradiology personnel. In this case, these individuals must be provided with protective clothing.
- Personnel dosimeters (TLDs, film badges) must always be worn during scheduled periods of work in the radiology department or when performing operating room and mobile radiographic examinations.

During fluoroscopic procedures:

- Aprons must always be worn during the fluoroscopic portion of the examination.
- Technologists should stand a few steps away from the patient during fluoroscopic exposures unless the situation warrants that someone assists the patient directly.

During mobile radiography:

- Technologists must stand the maximum distance allowed by the exposure cord (2m) from the x-ray machine and the patient.
- Protective aprons must always be worn, or the technologist can stand behind a portable shield if one is available.
- Direct the primary beam to the patient only, and be certain that no others will be exposed to the useful beam.

SHIELDING: DESIGN OF PROTECTIVE BARRIERS

Shielding is a radiation protection action and design criterion that is intended to protect patients, personnel, and members of the public. Shielding includes specific area shielding (protecting radiosensitive organs) and protective barriers (walls) positioned between the source of radiation and the individual. This type of shielding is specifically intended to protect personnel and members of the public from unnecessary radiation.

- Because x-ray rooms are in close proximity to other rooms that are occupied by personnel (lounges and offices) and by patients (waiting rooms and corridors), the walls of the x-ray room must be shielded.
- X-ray rooms are shielded with lead in most cases (concrete can also be used).
- The thickness of the lead depends on whether the wall is exposed by the primary beam (primary protective barriers) or to scattered radiation (secondary protective barrier).
- Lead may not be used for shielding secondary barriers since its four layers of thickness may be too thin (< 0.4 mm). Therefore lead acrylic gypsum brand of glass may be used ($^5/_8$ inch gypsum board with $^1/_2$ inch plate glass will offer adequate protection).
- The control booth is considered a secondary protective barrier and is subject to the same lead thickness criterion for secondary barriers (the primary beam must never be directed toward the control booth).

There are several factors that affect the thickness of protective barriers in radiology. These factors include the exposure rates for controlled and uncontrolled areas occupied by individuals, the distance between the radiation source and the barrier, workload, occupancy factor, use factor, and the kVp for examinations.

- A controlled area is an area in which an individual is occupationally exposed and includes radiology personnel and patients as well. Barriers for controlled areas must minimize the exposure rate to less than 26 µC/kilogram week (100 mR/wk).

- An uncontrolled area is one occupied by any individual. Barriers for uncontrolled areas must reduce the exposure rate to 0.5 µC/kilogram week (2 mR/week).
- Barriers for uncontrolled areas contain more lead than do barriers for controlled areas.
- The workload refers to the number of examinations performed per week, expressed as milliampere-minutes per week (mA−min/wk).
- The occupancy factor refers to the time that the area is occupied, expressed as a fraction of the work week. Levels of occupancy can be full (1), partial ($^1/_4$), and occasional ($^1/_{16}$) occupancy.
- The use factor is the fraction of time during which the primary beam is on and aimed at the barrier. Use factors are provided for levels of full use (1), partial use ($^1/_4$), and occasional use ($^1/_{16}$).
- The maximum and average kVp must also be known for calculating barrier thickness.

The barrier thickness can be determined by referring to precalculated shielding requirement tables or by performing a calculation using the data for the various factors previously identified.

QUALITY ASSURANCE: DOSE MANAGEMENT AND OPTIMIZATION

Quality Assurance (QA) includes quality administration and quality control (QC). Quality administration deals with the people and management of the entire QA program; QC deals with the technical aspects of machine performance.

The goals of QA and QC are to:
- Reduce the dose to the patient.
- Ensure optimal image quality to facilitate diagnostic interpretation.
- Reduce costs to the institution and the consumer.

QC ensures dose management and optimization through its three major steps of:
- Acceptance testing, during which new equipment is tested to ensure that manufacturer's specifications are met.

- Routine performance or carrying out QC tests on various parameters that affect patient dose and image quality. Specifically, equipment parameters are evaluated using a defined set of tools and procedures.
- Error correction, whereby the problems detected during routine performance testing are remedied to ensure proper functioning of the equipment.

Additionally, QC uses an important concept known as the tolerance limit or acceptance criterion.

- Tolerance limits can be assessed qualitatively (as a pass-fail) or quantitatively (as a ± value).
- If the QC test results fall within the tolerance limit, then the parameter under investigation is deemed acceptable and the equipment can be used to image the patient.
- If the test results fall outside the tolerance limits, the performance criterion has not been met and the equipment must be repaired to produce acceptable image quality.
- The NCRP tolerance limits for kVp accuracy, for example, are ±5% and less over a limited range (±2 kVp for 60 to 100 kVp).
- The NCRP tolerance limit for the light field and x-ray field alignment is ±3% of the SID.
- QC tests should be conducted on all the variables that affect image quality and dose, including collimation, filtration, focal spot size, kVp accuracy, mA linearity, and exposure timer accuracy, among others.

A QA-QC program is a management technique that ensures optimal image quality with reduced radiation dose to patients and personnel, through a performance evaluation of the factors affecting both image quality and radiation dose.

Pregnancy: Radiation Protection Considerations

Chapter at a glance

Being of childbearing age and being pregnant are two situations that warrant special radiation protection considerations, especially for in-utero exposure in diagnostic radiology.

This topic is of vital significance to the radiologic technologist for two reasons:

- There are known bioeffects of radiation exposure to the conceptus; that is, any product of conception (embryo or fetus).

- Many technologists are at the childbearing age and several others may be pregnant while working in the radiology department.

The purpose of this chapter is to summarize radiation protection considerations for pregnant patients and pregnant workers. Specifically, the effects of prenatal exposure will be listed and the factors affecting fetal dose in radiology, fetal dose estimation, and recommendations following in-utero exposure will be highlighted. Additionally, regulations for pregnant workers, including rights to privacy, dose limits, and maternity aprons and policies, will be outlined.

RATIONALE FOR RADIATION PROTECTION IN PREGNANCY

It is well known that radiation can cause injury to the conceptus. The effects of prenatal exposure to radiation as a function of gestational age are listed in Table 9-1. Data from animal experiments and survivors of the nuclear bombing of Hiroshima and Nagasaki (HN) suggest the following:

- Prenatal death results from exposure from 50 to 100 mGy (5 to 10 rad) received before embryonic implantation.
- Head size is small in the children of HN survivors.
- Most sensitive period for this effect is from 2 to 15 weeks after conception.
- Mental retardation is a concern at doses as low as 100 mGy (10 rad).
- Radiation-induced malignancy is also of great concern after in-utero exposure. "A fetus exposed in-utero to 1 rad [10 mGy] during the first trimester would be 35 times more likely to develop childhood cancer" (Parry, et al, 1999).

It is important to note that radiology procedures do not deliver doses such as these. If a pregnant patient must be imaged, then special precautions should be taken. These precautions will be listed later in this chapter.

FACTORS AFFECTING DOSE TO THE CONCEPTUS

The same factors that affect patient dose in radiography and fluoroscopy also affect dose to the conceptus. However, there are two factors that deserve special attention according to Parry, et al (1999).

- *Direct exposure.* For certain examinations such as the abdomen, pelvis, and lumbar spine, the fetus can be exposed directly to the primary beam. In this case, the dose to the fetus is extremely high, and lead shielding will not serve any useful purpose.
- *Indirect exposure.* For examinations such as the extremities and skull, the fetus will receive radiation scattered inside the womb. In this case, the dose to the fetus is less compared with direct exposure. A lead shield will not serve a useful purpose because the dose is from internal scattered radiation.

TABLE 9-1   Effects of Radiation Exposure on Prenatal Development as a Function of Gestational Age

GESTATIONAL AGE	DAYS AFTER CONCEPTION	FETAL DOSE rad	FETAL DOSE mGy	OBSERVED EFFECT
Preimplantation	0–14	5–10	50–100	Animal data suggest possibility of prenatal death
Major organogenesis	8–56	20–25	200–250	Animal and NBS data suggest that this is the most sensitive stage for growth retardation
	14–105			NBS data indicate small head size; those exposed before 8 wk do not display any intellectual deficit even with small head; most sensitive time for induction of childhood cancer
Rapid neuron development and migration	56–105	>10	>100	Small head size, seizures, decline in IQ points: 25 points/rad (1 Gy)
After organogenesis and rapid neuron development	105 to term	>10	>100	Associated with increased frequency of childhood cancer
		>50	>500	Severe mental retardation observed at 16–25 wk

NBS, Nuclear bombing survivor from Hiroshima or Nagasaki.

Reproduced with permission from Parry BA, Glaze SA, Archer BA. Typical patient radiation doses in diagnostic radiology. Radiographics 1999;19:1289–1302.

ESTIMATING THE DOSE TO THE CONCEPTUS

During situations in which the patient is concerned about the actual dose to her conceptus, the dose can be estimated and appropriate actions may be taken. These actions include at least two choices available to the patient:

- Continue the pregnancy to term.
- Terminate the pregnancy.

The fetal dose can be estimated and requires a physicist to perform the calculations. Several factors must be known to provide a reasonable estimation of the dose, such as the output intensity, half-value layer, location and number of views for radiography, and beam-on time for fluoroscopy, among others. Additionally, the fetal age at the time of the exposure, patient position, patient size (thickness), and fetal depths must also be known. The calculation procedure varies for direct and indirect exposures as follows:

- For direct exposures, the entrance exposure to the mother is first calculated and is subsequently used to obtain the dose of the fetus using additional data from published tables.
- For indirect exposures, the entrance exposure is calculated, "and then published scatter factors are applied to account for the location of the fetus relative to the location of the examination. The distance between the fetus and the area being imaged is a significant factor affecting the fetal dose for an indirect exposure" (Parry, et al., 1999).

Typical entrance exposures and fetal doses for several examinations are shown in Table 9-2. Some examinations deliver considerably low doses while others deliver high doses. However, Bushong points out that:

- "Fortunately, experience with such situations has shown that fetal doses have been consistently low. The fetal dose is usually in the 1- to 5-rad (10- to 50-mGy) range after a series of conventional x-ray examinations" (2001).

CONTINUING A PREGNANCY AFTER EXPOSURE: RECOMMENDATIONS

The notion of continuing or terminating a pregnancy is a matter between the patient and her physician and requires a benefit-risk analysis. Recommendations following in utero exposure are available in terms of continuing or terminating a pregnancy. For example,

- The NCRP in Report 54 recommends, "The risk [of abnormality] is considered to be negligible at 5 rad (50 mGy) or less when compared to other risks of pregnancy, and the risks of malformations is substantially increased above control levels only at doses above 15 rad (150 mGy). Therefore exposure of the fetus to radiation arising from diagnostic procedures would very rarely be cause by itself, for terminating a pregnancy" (*NCRP*, 1977).

- There are three instances when termination of the pregnancy may be considered:
  - ❏ At fetal doses of 50–150 mGy (5–15 rad) at a gestational age 2 to 8 weeks.
  - ❏ At fetal doses of 50–150 mGy (5–15 rad) at a gestational age of 8–15 weeks.
  - ❏ At fetal doses of over 150 mGy (over 15 rad) at a gestational age of 2 to 8 weeks (Wagner et al., 1997).

TABLE 9-2 **Entrance Exposure and Fetal Doses for Several Types of Radiologic Examinations Using a 200-Speed Image Receptor**

EXAMINATION	ENTRANCE SKIN EXPOSURE (mR)	FETAL DOSE (mrad)
Skull (lateral)	70	0
Cervical spine (AP)	110	0
Shoulder	90	0
Chest (PA)	10	0
Thoracic spine	180	1
Cholecystogram (PA)	150	1
Lumbosacral spine (AP)*	250	80
Abdomen or KUB (AP)*	220	70
Intravenous pyelogram (IVP)*	210	60
Hip*	220	50
Wrist or foot	5	0

*Gonadal shields should be used if possible.

(Reproduced with permission from Bushong S. Radiologic science for technologists. *St. Louis: Mosby, 2001.)*

DOSE REDUCTION TECHNIQUES FOR PREGNANT PATIENTS

The following techniques are intended to minimize the dose to a patient who is pregnant or potentially pregnant:

- Always check for pregnancy.
- Elective radiography (examinations that do not contribute to the diagnosis with respect to the patient's current health problems) must not be performed.
- Use signs and questionnaires to help the patient inform operators about her state of pregnancy.
- If a pregnant patient must be irradiated, then the technologist should perform the following:
  - ❑ Collimate the beam only to the clinical area of interest
  - ❑ Use high-kVp techniques
  - ❑ Ensure that the radiation beam has the appropriate filtration
  - ❑ Place gonadal shielding effectively so as not to compromise image quality
  - ❑ Execute all related departmental protocols regarding in-utero exposure such as:
    - ● Keeping the fluoroscopy time as short as possible
    - ● Reducing the number of images taken
    - ● Checking for the date of the last menstrual period

THE PREGNANT WORKER

There are specific radiation protection regulations and guidelines for pregnant workers in radiology. This section will consider rights to privacy, dose limits, protective clothing, and maternity policies.

Rights to Privacy

Regulations from the National Research Council (NRC) regarding a pregnancy "have found their way into state regulations for x-ray workers. Foremost in consideration is the right to privacy for the individual:

- "She is not required to make known that she is pregnant to her employer, even if it is obvious that she is" (Brateman, 1999).

■ Dose limits apply only after the worker voluntarily declares her pregnancy.

Dose Limits and Personnel Monitoring

There are special rules and dose limits for the conceptus once the pregnancy is declared.

■ For a pregnant worker, the equivalent dose limit to an embryo or fetus must not exceed 5 mSv (0.5 rem) over the entire gestational period, or an equivalent dose limit of 3.5 mSv (150 mrem) per month once the pregnancy is declared.

■ "Any dose must be received relatively uniformly over time, so that typical doses are not high in any one particular phase of gestational development" (Brateman, 1999).

■ The reading from an unshielded dosimeter (worn on the trunk of the individual) is used to determine the dose to the conceptus.

■ For pregnant workers who wear protective aprons, a dosimeter can be worn outside the apron, as well as one worn under the apron.

■ A dosimeter worn beneath the shielding can provide a reliable estimate of the dose to the conceptus.

Protective Aprons for Pregnant Workers

Specially designed protective lead aprons are commercially available for pregnant workers. The following points are important with respect to maternity aprons:

■ Wrap-around aprons are preferable to attenuate any radiation striking the back of the mother. When the dosimeter is in the front of the mother, an unshielded back would result in the radiation being attenuated by the embryo or fetus before it is detected by the dosimeter.

■ As noted by Brateman, "Aprons with additional protection may not be desirable for everyone because the extra weight may be burdensome" (1999).

■ A lead apron with a 0 to 5 mm lead-equivalent thickness will attenuate the radiation striking the apron by 90% at 75 kVp.

■ Lead aprons with a 1 mm lead equivalence are currently available.

Policies for Pregnant Workers

Employer policies for pregnant workers should be available and should focus on job expectations so as to eliminate any notion of special treatment that may subject pregnant workers to job discrimination.

- Policies should be intended to minimize the dose to the conceptus during normal periods of work.
- Policies should ensure, through education and counseling, that the pregnant worker perform her duties with a clear understanding of the risks of working while pregnant.

Three resources are currently available to help with education and counseling. The following materials focus on scientific facts and regulations:

- NCRP Report No. 116: Limitation of Exposure to Ionizing Radiation (1993). This report deals with risks and provides scientific guidance.
- US Nuclear Regulatory Commission. Instruction Concerning Prenatal Radiation Exposure. Draft Regulatory Guide (1994). This draft deals with risks and regulations.
- A paper by Wagner and Hayman (1982) entitled "Pregnancy and Women Radiologists", published in Radiology, a journal of the RSNA. This paper deals with an evaluation of different occupational situations in radiology.

References

Brateman L. Radiation safety consideration for diagnostic radiology personnel. *Radiographics* 1999;19:1037-1055.

Bushong S. *Radiation protection*. New York: McGraw Hill, 1999.

Bushong S. *Radiologic science for technologists*. 6th ed. Philadelphia: Mosby, 1997.

Dendy PP, Heaton B. *Physics of diagnostic radiology*. 2nd ed. Philadelphia: Institute of Physics Publishing, 1999.

Huda W, and Slone R. *Review of radiologic physics*. Baltimore: Williams & Wilkins, 1995.

McCollough CH. X-ray production. *Radiographics* 1997;18:967-984.

McKetty MH. X-ray attenuation. *Radiographics* 1998;18:151-163.

Parry BA, Glaze SA, Archer BR. Typical patient radiation doses in diagnostic radiology. *Radiographics* 1999;19:1289-1302.

Seeram E. *Radiation protection*. Philadelphia: Lippincott, 1997.

Seeram, E. Dose in CT. *Radiologic Technology*. 1999;70(6):534-556.

Sprawls P. *Principles of radiography for technologists*. Gaithersburg, MD: Aspen Publishers, 1990.

Index